Tastefully VEGAN

CREATIVE
VEGETARIAN COOKING

Challedon Publishing, Co.

Design and layout: Gerard and Kathryn McLane
Photography: Groomers Portrait Studio
Food Styling: Sylvia Mayer, Kathryn McLane
Printer: Mercury Press, Inc

First Edition
  First Printing - April, 1995
  Second Printing - December, 1997

Second Edition
  First Printing - May, 1998

Published by: Challedon Publishing Co., P.O. Box 940, Candler, NC 28715
         Fax: 828-665-1122 Email: challedon@aol.com

ISBN: 0-9664739-0-6

Tastefully VEGAN

CREATIVE
VEGETARIAN COOKING

Kathryn McLane, RN
Gerard McLane, DrPH, MPH

CONTENTS

Dedication

To our children, the joy of our lives;
Melissa , Stephen and Jonathan who happily and willingly became the
official taste testers for *Tastefully Vegan.*

Acknowledgments

The authors would like to express their heart-felt thanks and gratefully
acknowledge the contributions made by the following family and friends.

Bea Hadley, Kathryn's mother, for her inspiration to prepare delicious food
and for the many hours she unselfishly stood by Kathryn's side to help her
chop, cut, cook and clean up during the years of recipe development.

Carroll Hadley, Kathryn's dad, for his continual support and encouragement
to push forward with this project.

Sylvia Mayer, for sharing her exquisite artistic talent to help create the
scenes for the food photography.

Judy Jamison, for graciously donating her time to the many hours spent in
nutritional analysis.

Jo Dee Crandall, for assisting Kathryn in Cooking School at The Lifestyle
Center of America and for demonstrating a mutual joy in teaching vegan
vegetarian cooking.

Ricky and Vivian Seiler, caring neighbors who were always willing to help
out in a pinch whenever needed during the final months before publishing.

Friends in Guam and the Guam SDA Clinic, for sponsoring and supporting
our monthly vegetarian fiesta dinner demonstrations.

Staff and guests of The Lifestyle Center of America, who have tasted,
tested and enjoyed many of the recipes in this book.

1st Foreword

It is obvious that there is an upsurge in healthful living throughout our society. Americans are interested in improving the quality of their lives. They want to live longer and be healthier. Diet plays a major role in health. A significant number of the diseases that are killing Americans ----heart disease, stroke, cancer, diabetes, high blood pressure--- all have a relationship to diet. An improved diet means improved health.

You may be seeking a new lifestyle. The reason you have picked up this book is because you want to improve the quality of your health by improving your diet. Let me commend you for this intelligent step. As the speaker of It Is Written Television, my wife and I live an enormously hectic lifestyle.. We travel thousands of miles every year by plane. Yet we are extremely conscience of our diet. We are convinced that good nutrition, a vegetarian diet of fruits, nuts, grains and vegetables, gives us the nutrition and the energy necessary to function at optimum levels. We heartily endorse a vegetarian diet. We believe that the diet recommended in this book will reduce disease, increase longevity and dramatically improve the quality of life.

Dr. Gerard McLane and his wife, Kathryn, are health professionals. The diet they recommend is not some faddish, way-out, quack diet. It is solidly based in science and buttressed by formidable medical authorities. These recipes have been tested in the kitchen of the Lifestyle Center of America in Sulphur, Oklahoma. The food is not only healthy but it's also delicious. My wife and I have eaten in the dining room at the Lifestyle Center on numerous occasions. We have rarely eaten food that is as healthfully tasty as this. We heartily recommend the recipes in this book. As you put them into practice with your family, you will make a significant contribution to their long-term health and happiness.

Yours for better health,

Mark and Ernestine Finley
It Is Written Television

2nd Foreword

Perhaps nothing captures the essence of Kathryn McLane's cooking better than a particularly revealing experience. One of Kathryn's more outspoken cooking school students publicly declared that he had to eat his words. He was making good on a boisterous promise to do just that if Kathryn could duplicate the taste of one of his favorite recipes--without her using any of the "unhealthful" ingredients it called for. Needless to say, Kathryn had marvelously succeeded!

That incident provides a window into Kathryn McLane's unusual talent of making healthy foods taste good. This book is a testimony to that skill. As my patients have attended her classes at the Lifestyle Center of America, they find that Kathryn's recipes supply an abundance of options for those hard-to-find special dishes that still honor the highest principles of health. This book provides tangible evidence that individuals desiring better health can adopt the healthiest eating-style--a vegan diet--and yet not sacrifice taste. Having personally enjoyed many of Kathryn's recipes and seen the physical benefits that come to my patients from a diet that includes her creations, I can heartily endorse this book.

My enthusiasm for this edition is increased by Dr. Gerard McLane's contributions. Gerard is a much appreciated colleague who has used his editorial skills and health education expertise to make this book even more practical and "user friendly."

A promise of better health as well as good eating await you as you embark on your journey through **Tastefully Vegan.**

David D. DeRose, MD, MPH
Lifestyle Center of America

3rd Foreword

"Without continually exercising ingenuity, no one can excel in healthy cooking, but those whose hearts are open to impressions and suggestions from the Great Teacher, will also learn many things and will be able also to teach others; for He will give them skill and understanding."
Nineteenth Century Author

This is the first time that I have been asked to review and comment on a cookbook; but, of course, with my <u>vast</u> experience as an *eater* I am sure mine will be the LAST WORD on the subject.

This is no *ordinary* cookbook! I have seen and used many cookbooks when I was a bachelor and was well known for the many scrumptious delicacies that I would prepare on weekends after exams while I was in college in Montreal. That was gourmet cooking and I was a budding gourmet chef. Yet, never in my wildest imaginings would I , in those days, associate the words "gourmet" with "healthy"! Kathryn, this book surpasses your first edition and places you among the unique group of persons "wise in the kitchen".

This book is not a collection of healthy, esoteric recipes...the kind found in some health books which include recipes...far from it! What you have created is a truly GOURMET vegetarian cookbook that expands the envelope of meal preparation without the use of animal products. To this, you and Gerard have added the health principles that were used in the formulation of recipes and as the foundation for food preparation.

So now, no one needs be compelled to a life of tasteless, albeit nutritious, vegan meals on those special occasions which beg for more pleasure to the palate. There is, through this book, a tasty option in which otherwise healthy people can prepare exotic, mouth-watering vegan, gourmet meals without abandoning health practices. This is a cookbook-*plus* ... a masterfully crafted resource: ***Tastefully Vegan.***

Zeno Charles-Marcel, MD
Medical Director
Lifestyle Center of America

About the Authors

Kathryn's background as a nursing health professional and wife of a Preventive Care Specialist has opened for her opportunities she had never anticipated. Traveling to different countries of the world with her husband to conduct health seminars she began to see the need to help people learn how to cook great vegetarian food that was both healthful and delicious.

Each week, Kathryn teaches guests of the Lifestyle Center of America nearly eight hours of instruction in preparing tasteful and nutritious vegan vegetarian recipes which are low in fat and cholesterol free.

Cooking school participants experience hands-on cooking techniques in preparing a wide variety of recipes from exquisite vegetarian cuisine to quick and easy "on-the-go" meals. Her goal is to prepare and educate each guest before leaving with enough experience and knowledge of vegetarian cookery to ensure an easier transition when returning home. Kathryn believes confidence and a high level of comfort when preparing meals is the key to success in continuing this very important lifestyle change.

Kathryn began doing cooking schools in Singapore as a part of the health seminars offered at Youngberg Adventist Hospital. She and Gerard also conducted cooking demonstrations and health seminars in Thailand but their work in Guam became the cornerstone for the development of **Tastefully Vegan.**

He and Kathryn conducted a vegetarian fiesta once a month in the governor's mansion in Guam attended by over 100 participants. In the United States, they have conducted cooking schools and presented health seminars in several states for large church groups and hundreds of people at camp meetings. This cookbook has become a real hit with the guests who come to the Lifestyle Center of America

Dr. McLane has been a professional of preventive care since receiving his doctorate in 1977. He is a specialist in the therapeutic and motivational approaches to health risk management, disease prevention and lifestyle interventions and brings those skills to the Lifestyle Center of America where he serves as the Education/Program Director.

Dr. McLane earned both his Master's and Doctor of Public Health degrees from Loma Linda University School of Public Health in Loma Linda, CA.

He is a Fellow in the American Preventive Care Association, a Certified Nutrition Specialist, a Certified Health Education Specialist and Certified as a Preventive Care Provider with the American Board of Preventive Care.

Dr. McLane and his wife Kathryn worked at Hinsdale Hospital for 10 years prior to serving as medical missionaries in the Far Eastern Division from 1989 to 1994, with service in Singapore, Thailand, the Philippines, Indonesia, Guam, Chuuk and Palau.

While on Guam, Dr. McLane hosted "Health Talk Today," a twice-weekly program on public radio.

Kathryn McLane, RN
Gerard McLane, DrPH, MPH
The Preventive Care Group
2409 Ranch Road
Sulphur, OK 73086

For seminar information or questions about this book you may contact the authors at the address above or at the Email below.

Email: gdmclane@brightok.net
or
Email: TasteVegan@aol.com

You may also contact the publisher direct to order books at:

Challedon Publishing Co., P.O. Box 940, Candler, NC 28715 - 0940.
Fax: 828-665-1122 Email: challedon@aol.com

Introduction

Welcome to the adventure of **TASTEFULLY VEGAN,** a cookbook with a new approach to creative vegetarian cooking. You will find examples of beautifully planned vegetarian meals organized to help you easily plan and prepare delicious no-cholesterol meals in your home. This cookbook is divided into twelve sections each representing a different theme popular to vegetarians today who enjoy a wide variety of flavors.

Each menu theme offers an assortment of entrée, vegetable, bread, salad and dessert recipes to select. You can quickly plan an entire meal and save precious time. Specific meal themes are demonstrated which would be appropriate for any special occasion or celebration for each month of the year. For example, you might choose the "Sweetheart's Banquet" for Valentine's Day, "Stars and Stripes Sizzler" on the 4th of July, "Summertime Breeze" for those hot August days and of course the "Thanksgiving Tradition" and "Jingle Bells Buffet" for your holiday entertaining. There are over 330 recipes included to help you create your own favorite combination of delicious and "HEALTHY" meals any time of year.

The idea for this cookbook grew following a series of "Vegetarian Fiestas" conducted at the Governor's Mansion in the country of Guam. Each month, over 100 people attended and were offered a healthy full course meal. We wanted our guests to experience the joy of fine vegetarian cooking, one of life's simple pleasures!

This cookbook offers another unique bonus. It's VEGAN too! That means the recipes use no animal products including milk, cheese or eggs. We have also replaced the potentially "Bad Fats" for "Good Fats", given healthy substitutes for the harmful and irritating spices and created a variety of "guilt free" desserts for you to enjoy.

You may ask, "How can it still taste good?" There are few cookbooks that offer vegetarian recipes that are vegan, nutritious and delicious too. Our goal is to offer healthy recipes without sacrificing the pleasure of eating. This has been an interesting task to accomplish. The recipes found here have been tested and tasted by hundreds of people who now enjoy preparing them in their own homes. You will realize it is possible for healthy food to taste delicious with just a little extra work. Good health results from consistent good eating and good living habits. Be creative. Be smart. Provide the best for the ones you love and give them a gift that will last for a lifetime.

How to Use This Book

This book is primarily a cookbook with delicious vegan vegetarian recipes. The ADA position paper on vegetarianism on page 23 supports the viewpoint that you can be healthy eating a well planned vegan dietary. This book is not a book which discusses all of the nutritional concerns involved with eating a balanced vegan diet. There are abundant sources of information available for you to pursue this avenue of knowledge. We have presented some of the key pieces of information you may need to improve your eating habits which we have found to be useful to individuals while attending our seminars.

The Recipe Section
The recipe section in this book is divided into 12 chapters with specific recipe choices for each section to assist in menu planning.

The recipes will speak for themselves. Try them. Test them. We have found them to be tasteful and nutritious. You of course may also want to make changes. We invite you to be creative and have fun.

Nutritional Analysis
You will find an alphabetized recipe nutritional analysis chart. The Food Processor V6.11 from *esha* **Research** was utilized. The nutrient analyses are approximate values for calories, protein, carbohydrate, fiber, fat, Vitamins B12 and D, Calcium, iron, sodium and zinc; Cholesterol, which will always be 0 in vegan cooking was not included.

Use of Abbreviations
The following abbreviations are utilized to name ingredient amounts in recipes or to give directions:

T =	tablespoon		env =	envelope
tsp =	teaspoon		rec =	recipe
c =	cup		pkg =	package
oz =	ounce		sm =	small
qt =	quart		med =	medium
lb =	pound		lg =	large
F =	Fahrenheit		p =	page

Vegetarianism
The key to good health

What is a Vegetarian?

Vegetarians avoid the use of meat, fish, and poultry. Actually we prefer the term vegetarian to mean avoiding the use of all animal products as food. However, those that use some animal products such as milk, cheese and eggs, are called lacto-ovo vegetarians. In this complex world in which we live, Merriam Websters Collegiate Dictionary defines vegetarianism as the theory or practice of living on a diet made up of vegetables, fruits, grains, nuts, and sometimes eggs or dairy products. Also in Websters Dictionary herbivore is used as a second definition for vegetarianism. Herbivore is defined as a plant eating animal.

Vegan is a term used for a strict vegetarian. That is one who consumes no animal or dairy products. Some vegans will also avoid the use of animal products for clothing as well.

Whatever type of vegetarian you are now or wish to become you will find included in this book exciting and innovative recipes. Some are simple, some are complex. Choosing to eat vegetarian can be accomplished even in this fast food world we now live in.

The term "vegetarian" has been loosely used over the years to incorporate everything from those who eat solely a plant based diet to those who incorporate some foods of animal sources in their diets. There are three types of vegetarians who do not eat animal flesh.

1. **Vegan vegetarian**: Use no animal products of any type. Only foods of plant origin are included in the diet. Vegans are also considered to be strict vegetarians.

2. **Lacto vegetarian**: Are vegetarians who include dairy products such as milk, butter, cheese in their diets.

3. **Lacto-ovo vegetarian**: Are vegetarians who consume both dairy products and eggs.

12

Guidelines for a Balanced Vegetarian Diet

1. Eat a variety of whole grains, legumes (beans) vegetables and fruits. A vegetarian diet will be based on these foods.

2. Limit sweets, high fat foods, junk foods and highly processed foods. These foods add additional calories and are lacking in nutrients and fiber.

3. For lacto-ovo or lacto vegetarians, choose dairy products that are nonfat and limit egg yolks to 2 per week.

4. For vegans, supplement diet with a reliable B-12 source unless B-12 fortified foods are included in the diet. (some soymilks and soymeat analogs are fortified with B-12)

Reasons why people don't eat meat

1. Longer, healthier life. Vegetarians are at lower risk for heart disease, cancer, diabetes, high blood pressure and obesity. Only animal products contain cholesterol.

2. Environment. Meat production takes more resources, causing soil erosion, water depletion, pollution from pesticides and animal waste.

3. Economy. Raising grain and vegetables is cheaper than raising livestock, so it costs less to eat.

4. World hunger: The amount of grain needed to produce an 8 oz. steak could feed 40 people a cup of grain each.

5. Other reasons: Some protest the cruel treatment of animals mass-produced for their meat while others will not eat meat for religious reasons.

Debunking the Myths of Vegetarianism

Vegetarians eat chicken and fish: Total vegetarians will not eat any animal flesh.

Starch is fattening: Actually carbohydrates are low in fat. Dairy foods and meat however are high in fat. Fat has over twice the calories as carbohydrates.

Meat is the only good source of protein: Grains, vegetables and legumes can supply all the protein we need. The key is choosing variety and consuming enough calories to meet energy needs.

Vegetarians don't get enough vitamins and minerals: Well planned vegetarian diets supply all the nutritional requirements. The American Dietetic Association has confirmed this to be true.

Vegetarians have to carefully mix proteins in each meal: A mixture of proteins from plant sources will naturally complement each other over a day's time. It is not a major nutritional concern.

Vegetarian food is not good tasting: Not true! Vegetarian meals can be diverse, colorful, and delicious. Try these recipes and check with the multitude of chefs who create exciting dishes at many restaurants across the nation.

Tips for the transition to a Vegetarian Diet

1. Start by limiting your meat, poultry or fish intake to one meal a day, then once a week. You don't have to go cold turkey. Remember serving sizes are only 2 - 3 ounces.

2. Try to make one of your favorite meals vegetarian by replacing the meat with beans, tofu or a soybean analog (textured vegetable protein). A visit to the health food store might be a good place to start where you will find new products available. However, large supermarkets are now featuring many of these same products.

4. Begin increasing the fiber content in your meals. This should be done slowly if you were previously on a low fiber diet. Your body will adapt to the higher levels of fiber and your digestion will be improved.

5. Read labels to understand the list of ingredients. Things to look for are fat content, undesirable ingredients, and sodium content if you are on a sodium restriction. Other helpful information in a label includes total calories, sugar content and fiber content.

6. Clean out your cupboards, refrigerator and freezer to include only foods that are healthy. Purchase only the foods which will promote health and well-being. These foods can be served to family members and guests alike.

7. Many foreign cuisines offer interesting meatless dishes. Look for these types of restaurants when eating out. Also many family-type restaurants will make up a vegetable plate when requested to do so.

8. Avoid fast-food establishments as few offer meatless choices. However, salad bars, potato bars, and veggie burgers are becoming more popular.

9. Connect with others who can help you to become a vegetarian. The Vegetarian Resource Group is on the Internet at www.vrg.com to help you. Many books and magazines are also available on the subject. Get together with friends who also want to cook vegetarian and share ideas.

10. Visit your local health food stores. If they do not carry products you want they will usually order them for you.

11. Contact the manager of your favorite grocery store. If you inform them what specialty items you wish to purchase on a regular basis they will often order them for you.

12. Join up with a food cooperative. They carry most of the specialty foods needed. Often they will deliver right to your door.

The Vegan Diet Philosophy

Plain and Simple
vs
Variety-The Spice of Life

There are two approaches to eating a vegan diet. One would consist of a diet which is plain and simple filled with the foods nature has to offer in its most natural state. The other would be taking these same foods, giving them a new look and enhancing their flavors with the help of sweet herbs and spices, creative mixtures of ingredients and some specially prepared health foods. This would ultimately broaden the "variety" to which a tasteful vegan diet can offer.

The simple "quick and easy" method has it's place in today's fast pace world. But unfortunately, most rely on "convenience foods" or "prepared foods" to meet these demands which in most cases immediately raises a red flag when healthful eating is a priority. If one can be satisfied with a diet requiring only basic cooking skills and consisting only of raw nuts and seeds, raw or steamed vegetables, whole fruits and grains, then that individual must be well aware of the benefit reaped from a simple, wholesome and uncomplicated diet. I believe people should also be taught how to do the little extras that provide variety in the simple vegan diet while maintaining a healthy standard.   To accomplish a vegan diet with "variety" without compromising the recommended guidelines of daily fat, protein, fiber and sodium content requires without any question a commitment to some extra time spent in the kitchen. It cannot always compete with the ease, speed and simplicity of TV dinners or convenience foods, but surpasses all in quality and taste while consistently promoting health. Without question, a vegan diet is not and cannot be an effortless task. The truly dedicated believers of health promotion who also enjoy knowing how to do all the little "extras" welcome variety in the diet.   Preparation becomes a joy rather than a chore. As with all things in life, moderation should also be practiced in time spent for preparation. We believe our diets should consist of a realistic combination of the simple wholesome foods always available to us as well as the flavorful recipes we devote our time to in preparation. Our objective is to supply you with those recipes in *Tastefully Vegan* which will assist you in providing "variety" and "spice" to you life.

SETTING UP A VEGAN KITCHEN

"The Basics"

LEGUMES:
(Dry, canned or frozen)
Black beans
Black-eyed peas
Garbanzos (chick peas)
Kidney beans
Lentils, brown and red
Lima beans
Navy beans
Pinto beans
Red beans
Soy beans

GRAINS:
Barley, pearled
Barley, rolled
Brown rice, long grain
Brown rice, instant
Millet
Oats, rolled (old fashioned)
Oats, quick
Wheat, bulgar (cracked)
Wheat germ
Wheat, hard winter
Wheat, rolled

FROZEN FRUITS & JUICES:
Apple Juice Concentrate
Blackberries
Blueberries
Grape Juice Concentrates
(purple, white, white/peach)
Lemon Juice
Orange Juice Concentrate
Peaches
Pineapple Juice Concentrate
Raspberries
Strawberries

DRIED FRUITS:
Apples
Apricots
Currants
Dates
Figs
Mango
Papaya
Pineapple
Prunes
Raisins

RAW NUTS:
Almonds (sliced, slivered, whole)
Almond Butter
Cashews (pieces, halves, whole)
Peanuts
Peanut Butter
Pecans (chopped, halves)
Walnuts, English

RAW SEEDS:
Flax
Poppy
Pumpkin
Sesame, hulled or whole
Sesame Butter (Tahini)
Sunflower

17

"The Basics"
Continued

BAKING SUPPLIES:
Arrowroot
Baking powder, non-aluminum (Rumford)
Bran, oat
Bran, wheat
Brown sugar
Canola oil
Carob powder
Citric acid, crystals
Coconut, unsweetened grated (dry)
Coconut, unsweetened grated (frozen)
Coconut milk, "lite" canned unsweetened
Cooking sprays, no-stick
Coffee substitute (Roma)
Cornstarch
Flavoring, natural butter (non-dairy)
Flavoring, natural maple
Flavoring, natural vanilla
Flavoring, walnut
Flour, barley
Flour, garbanzo
Flour, rye
Flour, soy
Flour, unbleached white or all purpose
Flour, vital wheat gluten
Flour, whole wheat
Honey, liquid or spun
Maple syrup, pure
Molasses
Olive oil, extra virgin "cold pressed"
Powdered sugar
Sunflower oil
Tapioca, minute or pearled
Tofu, fresh (silken, soft, firm, extra-firm)
Tofu, aseptic box (soft, firm, extra-firm)
Yeast, active or rapid rise

HERBS - SPICES:
Allspice
Basil
Cardamom
Celery seed, ground
Cinnamon
Coriander
Cumin
Dillweed
Garlic powder
Garlic salt
Italian seasoning
Marjoram
Nutmeg
Nutritional yeast
Onion flakes
Onion powder
Onion salt
Oregano
Paprika
Parsley
Pumpkin pie spice
Rosemary
Sage
Salt
Savory
Thyme
Turmeric

SETTING UP A VEGAN KITCHEN

"Specialty Items"

Specific company name brands of specialty items are not "always" named in the recipes. The following list consists of those products which have been tested and used for the recipes in *Tastefully Vegan*. If the listed name brands are not available in your location, similar substitutions are recommended.

COOKING SPRAYS:
A. Pam
  1. Original
  2. Olive oil

MEAT SUBSTITUTES:
A. Companion
  1. Mock Chicken
  2. Mock Duck
B. Loma Linda
  1. Linketts
  2. Little Links
  3. Tender Bits
C. Natural Touch
  1. Vegan Burger Crumbles
  2. Vegan Sausage Crumbles
D. Worthington
  1. Chic-Ketts, frozen chicken
  2. Choplets, canned
  3. Granburger, dehydrated (TVP)
  4. Ground Meatless, burger
  5. Ground Meatless, sausage
  6. Vegetarian Burger, canned
E. Yves Veggie Cuisine
  1. Canadian Veggie Bacon
  2. Veggie Wieners, "low fat"
  3. Veggie Wieners, "fat free"
  4. Deli Slices
  5. Just Like Ground

SEASONINGS:
A. Bernard Jensons
  1. Vegetable seasoning
B. Bragg
  1. Liquid Aminos
C. Cook's
  1. Vanilla powder
D. Frontier
  1. Beef-Style Seasoning
  2. Chicken-Style Seasoning
  3. Pumpkin Pie Spice
  4. Vegetable Broth Seasoning
E. McCormick (or) Schilling
  1. Garlic & Herb "Salt-Free"
  2. Imitation Butter Flavored Salt
  3. Pizza Seasoning
F. McKay's
  1. Beef-style Seasoning, no MSG
  2. Chicken-Style Seasoning, (no MSG, no whey)
G. Modern Products, Inc.
  1. Spike, "Original" All Purpose
  2. Vege-Sal, All Purpose
H. Old El Paso
  1. Mild green chilies
I. Spicery Shoppe
  1. Natural Butter Flavoring
  2. Natural Maple Flavoring
  3. Natural Vanilla Flavoring

"Specialty Items"
continued

NATURAL SWEETENERS:
A. Lundberg
   1. Brown rice syrup
B. Date Sugar (any brand)
   1. Granulated dates
C. Fructose
   1. Fruit sugar
D. Fruitsouce
   1. Grain and fruit sweetener
E. Sucanat
   1. Dehydrated cane juice

BAKING AIDS:
A. Emes Kosher-Jel, plain
   1. Vegetable "gelatin"
B. ENER-G
   1. Baking Powder Substitute
   2. Baking Soda Substitute
   3. Egg Replacer
C. Instant Clear Jel
   1. Instant Food Thickener
D. Lighter Bake
   1. Fat and Egg Substitute
E. Wonderslim
   1. Fat and Egg Substitute

MILK ALTERNATIVES:
A. Almond Mylk, liquid
   1. Nut milk
B. Dari-Free, powdered
   1. Potato milk
C. Better Than Milk, plain *
   1. Tofu milk
D. Soyagen, powdered
   1. Soy milk
E. Solait "low fat", powdered
   1. Soy milk
F. Soy Supreme, powdered
   1. Soy milk
G. West Soy "Plus", liquid
   1. Soy milk

*Recipes is this book often call for Better Than Milk. The plain, "caseinate free" formula is the recommended choice for the recipes. The "light" formula resembles skim milk and is not as suitable for the recipes. The "European" formula has the richer flavor of whole milk due to the extra ingredients added containing sweeteners, fat and casein. Although this may be the preferred product for some individuals, this formula has not been tested with our recipes.

SELECTING COOKING OILS
Why Be Choosy?

As terms like "monounsaturated fats", "essential fatty acids" (EFA's), or "trans fatty acids" become more common in today's vocabulary, the concern of selecting the proper oil plays an important role in good health and fine cooking. More people today have begun to understand that "all" fats are not forbidden and that some actually support good health. Our bodies welcome "good fats" as a means of transporting the fat soluble vitamins (A, D, E and K) to key areas of the body, and as contributors of EFA's in regulating and maintaining cell growth, and even assist in the development of healthy bones, nerves, skin and cell membranes. While depending primarily on the "good fats" in wholesome foods to provide our bodies with the necessary tools of good health, it would be difficult and is unnecessary to exclude completely the use of cooking oils from our diets. Even the small allowance of "free oils" add tremendously to the flavors and textures of carefully planned meals.

Like all fats, oils differ in their molecular structure and are categorized by their degree of "saturation". This basically is defined as the arrangement of "carbon atoms" linked with hydrogen and oxygen. While all oils contain various ratios of saturated to unsaturated fats, they are classified by the type of fat that is most concentrated in its composition.

There are four main categories of interest:

1. Highly saturated oils, which impose definite heart health risks, are those oils that remain solid at room temperature. Coconut and palm oil fall into this category and are not recommended for use any time.

2. Monounsaturated oils, (oils containing only one double carbon bond) remain liquid at room temperature but cloud and thicken when chilled. Because of the molecular structure of monounsaturated fats, oils remain stable when exposed to higher temperatures. Olive, canola, almond, peanut and avocado oil are the most common oils available in this group. Monounsaturated oils also tend reduce total blood cholesterol including the "bad" low density lipoproteins (LDL) without affecting the "good" high density lipoproteins (HDL) levels.

3. Polyunsaturated oils, (oils containing two double carbon bonds) remain liquid even when chilled. Examples include corn, safflower, soybean and sunflower oils. These oils lower total cholesterol and LDL but unfortunately also lower HDL. Also, polyunsaturated oils are unstable when exposed to

higher heat and are highly susceptible to attack by "free radicals" or un-bonded oxygen molecules. Polyunsaturated oils can also be hydrogenated to improve their shelf life and use in packaged or processed foods producing a harmful by-product called "trans fatty acids" which can promote cancer and heart disease. However, some polyunsaturated oil is necessary to obtain EFA's. Therefore these oils are recommended for use in limited amounts in foods such as salad dressings, sauces, dips and spreads which are not exposed to high heat.

4. Super-unsaturated oils, (oils containing 3 double carbon bonds) remain liquid no matter how cold and contain EFA's including omega-3. Flaxseed oil is the most common oil in this group and is often used as a dietary supplement. Because it is extremely unstable in heat, it should never be used in cooking over 210° F.

In summary, when cooking with oils, choose the monounsaturated oil group most frequently, polyunsaturated oils occasionally and saturated oils rarely. Your best quality oils will be found in health food stores or gourmet shops. Looking on the label for the words "Cold Pressed" is advisable to assure prevention of any over-exposure to heat during processing. However, wherever you purchase cooking oil, it is important to keep it fresh and good tasting as long as possible. To prevent oil from becoming rancid, store oils in the refrigerator and take them out just long enough to use them. All oils are sensitive to heat, light, and exposure to oxygen. Expose all oils to as little heat as is feasible. This means we would not recommend the use of deep fat frying or frying over high heat. Use oils sparingly and only when necessary to enhance the delightful flavors of "Tastefully" prepared "Vegan" meals.

Position of the American Dietetic Association: Vegetarian Diets (1997)

This paper (pages 23 - 36) is reproduced in full and with the permission of the American Dietetic Association, (ADA). This position paper by the ADA has been published in The Journal of the American Dietetic Association, November 1997, Volume 97, Number 11.

Scientific data suggest positive relationships between a vegetarian diet and reduced risk for several chronic degenerative diseases and conditions, including obesity, coronary artery disease, hypertension, diabetes mellitus, and some types of cancer. Vegetarian diets, like all diets, need to be planned appropriately to be nutritionally adequate.

POSITION STATEMENT

It is the position of The American Dietetic Association (ADA) that appropriately planned vegetarian diets are healthful, are nutritionally adequate, and provide health benefits in the prevention and treatment of certain diseases.

Vegetarianism in Perspective

The eating patterns of vegetarians vary considerably. The lacto-ovo-vegetarian eating pattern is based on grains, vegetables, fruits, legumes, seeds, nuts, dairy products, and eggs, and excludes meat, fish, and fowl. The vegan, or total vegetarian, eating pattern is similar to the lacto-ovo-vegetarian pattern except for the additional exclusion of eggs, dairy, and other animal products. Even within these patterns, considerable variation may exist in the extent to which animal products are avoided. Therefore, individual assessment is required to accurately evaluate the nutritional quality of a vegetarian's dietary intake.

Studies indicate that vegetarians often have lower morbidity (1) and mortality (2) rates from several chronic degenerative diseases than do non-vegetarians. Although non-dietary factors, including physical activity and abstinence from smoking and alcohol, may play a role, diet is clearly a contributing factor.

In addition to the health advantages, other considerations that may lead a person to adopt a vegetarian diet pattern include concern for the environment, ecology, and world hunger issues.

Vegetarians also cite economic reasons, ethical considerations, and religious beliefs as their reasons for following this type of diet pattern. Consumer demand for vegetarian options has resulted in increasing numbers of food services that offer vegetarian options. Presently, most university food services offer vegetarian options.

Health Implications of Vegetarianism

Vegetarian diets low in fat or saturated fat have been used successfully as part of comprehensive health programs to reverse severe coronary artery disease (3,4). Vegetarian diets offer disease protection benefits because of their lower saturated fat, cholesterol, and animal protein content and often higher concentration of folate (which reduces serum homocysteine levels) (5), antioxidants such as vitamins C and E, carotenoids, and phytochemicals (6). Not only is mortality from coronary artery disease lower in vegetarians than in non-vegetarians (7), but vegetarian diets have also been successful in arresting coronary artery disease (8,9). Total serum cholesterol and low-density lipoprotein cholesterol levels are usually lower in vegetarians, but high-density lipoprotein cholesterol and triglyceride levels vary depending on the type of vegetarian diet followed (10).

Vegetarians tend to have a lower incidence of hypertension than non-vegetarians (11). This effect appears to be independent of both body weight and sodium intake. Type 2 diabetes mellitus is much less likely to be a cause of death in vegetarians than non-vegetarians, perhaps because of their higher intake of complex carbohydrates and lower body mass index (12).

Incidence of lung and colorectal cancer is lower in vegetarians than in non-vegetarians (2,13). Reduced colorectal cancer risk is associated with increased consumption of fiber, vegetables, and fruit (14,15). The environment of the colon differs notably in vegetarians compared with non-vegetarians in ways that could favorably affect colon cancer risk (16,17). Lower breast cancer rates have not been observed in Western vegetarians, but cross-cultural data indicate that breast cancer rates are lower in populations that consume plant-based diets (18). The lower estrogen levels in vegetarian women may be protective (19). A well-planned vegetarian diet may be useful in the prevention and treatment of renal disease. Studies using human being and animal models suggest that some plant proteins may increase survival rates and decrease proteinuria, glomerular filtration rate, renal blood flow, and histologic renal damage compared with a non-vegetarian diet (20,21).

Nutrition Considerations for Vegetarians

Plant sources of protein alone can provide adequate amounts of essential amino acids if a variety of plant foods are consumed and energy needs are met. Research suggests that complementary proteins do not need to be consumed at the same time and that consumption of various sources of amino acids over the course of the day should ensure adequate nitrogen retention and use in healthy persons (22). Although vegetarian diets are lower in total protein and a vegetarian's protein needs may be somewhat elevated because of the lower quality of some plant proteins, protein intake in both lacto-ovo-vegetarians and vegans appears to be adequate (16).

Plant foods contain only non-heme iron, which is more sensitive than heme iron to both inhibitors and enhancers of iron absorption. Although vegetarian diets are higher in total iron content than non-vegetarian diets, iron stores are lower in vegetarians because the iron from plant foods is more poorly absorbed (23). The clinical importance of this, if any, is unclear because iron deficiency anemia rates are similar in vegetarians and non-vegetarians (23). The higher vitamin C content of vegetarian diets may improve iron absorption.

Although plant foods can contain vitamin B-12 on their surface from soil residues, this is not a reliable source of B-12 for vegetarians. Much of the vitamin B-12 present in spirulina, sea vegetables, tempeh, and miso has been shown to be inactive B-12 analog rather than the active vitamin. Although dairy products and eggs contain vitamin B-12, research suggests that lacto-ovo-vegetarians have low blood levels of vitamin B-12. Supplementation or use of fortified foods is advised for vegetarians who avoid or limit animal foods (24).

Because vitamin B-12 requirements are small, and it is both stored and recycled in the body, symptoms of deficiency may be delayed for years. Absorption of vitamin B-12 becomes less efficient as the body ages, so supplements may be advised for all older vegetarians.

Lacto-ovo-vegetarians have calcium intakes that are comparable to or higher than those of non-vegetarians (25,26). Calcium intakes of vegans, however, are generally lower than those of both lacto-ovo-vegetarians and omnivores

(26). It should be noted that vegans may have lower calcium needs than non-vegetarians because diets that are low in total protein and more alkaline have been shown to have a calcium-sparing effect (27). Furthermore, when a person's diet is low in both protein and sodium and regular weight-bearing physical activity is engaged in, his or her calcium requirements may be lower than those of a sedentary person who eats a standard Western diet. These factors, and genetic influences, may help explain variations in bone health that are independent of calcium intake.

Because calcium requirements of vegans have not been established and inadequate calcium intakes are linked to risk for osteoporosis in all women, vegans should meet the calcium requirements established for their age group by the Institute of Medicine (28). Calcium is well absorbed from many plant foods, and vegan diets can provide adequate calcium if the diet regularly includes foods rich in calcium (29). In addition, many new vegetarian foods are calcium-fortified. Dietary supplements are advised for vegans only if they do not meet calcium requirements from food.

Vitamin D is poorly supplied in all diets unless vitamin D– fortified foods are consumed. Vegan diets may lack this nutrient because fortified cow's milk is its most common dietary source. However, vegan foods supplemented with vitamin D, such as soymilk and some cereals, are available.

Furthermore, findings indicate that sunlight exposure is a major factor affecting vitamin D status and that dietary intake is important only when sun exposure is inadequate (30). Sun exposure to hands, arms, and face for 5 to 15 minutes per day is believed to be adequate to provide sufficient amounts of vitamin D (31). People with dark skin or those who live at northern latitudes or in cloudy or smoggy areas may need increased exposure. Use of sunscreen interferes with vitamin D synthesis. If sun exposure is inadequate, vitamin D supplements are recommended for vegans. This is especially true for older persons who synthesize vitamin D less efficiently and who may have less sun exposure.

Studies show zinc intake to be lower or comparable in vegetarians compared with non-vegetarians (16). Most studies show that zinc levels in hair, serum, and saliva are in the normal range in vegetarians (32). Compensatory mechanisms may help vegetarians adapt to diets that may be low in zinc (33). However, because of the low bioavailability of zinc from plant foods and because the effects of marginal zinc status are poorly understood, vegetarians should strive to meet or exceed the Recommended Dietary Allowances for zinc.

Diets that do not include fish or eggs lack the long-chain n-3 fatty acid docosahexanoic acid (DHA). Vegetarians may have lower blood lipid levels of this fatty acid, although not all studies are in agreement with this finding (34,35). The essential fatty acid linolenic acid can be converted to DHA, although conversion rates appear to be inefficient and high intakes of linoleic acid interfere with conversion (36). The implications of low levels of DHA is not clear. However, it is recommended that vegetarians include good sources of linolenic acid in their diet.

Figure 1 below presents food sources of nutrients that are often of concern for vegetarians.

Iron (Milligrams per serving)

Breads, cereals, and grains

Whole wheat bread, 1 slice	0.9
White bread, 1 slice	0.7
Bran flakes, 1 c	11.0
Cream of wheat, 1/2 c cooked	5.5
Oatmeal, instant, 1 packet	6.3
Wheat germ, 2 Tbsp	1.2

Vegetables (1/2 c cooked)

Beet greens	1.4
Sea vegetables	18.1-42.0
Swiss chard	1.9
Tomato juice, 1 c	1.3
Turnip greens	1.5

Legumes (1/2 c cooked)

Baked beans, vegetarian	0.74
Black beans	1.8
Garbanzo beans	3.4
Kidney beans	1.5
Lentils	3.2
Lima beans	2.2
Navy beans	2.5

Soyfoods (1/2 c cooked)

Soybeans	4.4
Tempeh	1.8
Tofu	6.6
Soymilk, 1 c	1.8

Nuts/seeds (2 Tbsp)

Cashews	1.0
Pumpkin seeds	2.5
Tahini	1.2
Sunflower seeds	1.2

Other foods

Blackstrap molasses, 1 Tbsp	3.3

Zinc (Milligrams per serving)

Breads, grains, and cereals

Bran flakes, 1 c	5.0
Wheat germ, 2 Tbsp	2.3

Legumes (1/2 c cooked)

Adzuki beans	2.0
Chickpeas	1.3
Lima beans	1.0
Lentils	1.2

Dairy foods (for comparison)

Cow's milk, 1 c	1.0
Cheddar cheese, 1 oz	0.9

Soyfoods (1/2 c cooked)

Soybeans	1.0
Tempeh	1.5
Tofu	1.0
Textured vegetable protein	1.4

Vegetables (1/2 c cooked)

Corn	0.9
Peas	1.0
Sea vegetables	1.1-2.0
Yogurt, 1 c	1.8

Calcium (Milligrams per serving)

Legumes (1 c cooked)

Chickpeas	78
Great northern beans	121
Navy beans	128
Pinto beans	82
Black beans	103
Vegetarian baked beans	128

Soyfoods

Soybeans, 1 c cooked	175
Tofu, 1/2 c	120-350
Tempeh, 1/2 c	77
Textured vegetable protein, 1/2 c	85
Soymilk, 1 c	84
Soymilk, fortified, 1 c	250-300
Soynuts, 1/2 c	252

Nuts and seeds (2 Tbsp)

Almonds	50

Vegetables (1/2 c cooked)

Bok choy	79
Broccoli	89
Collard greens	178
Kale	90
Mustard greens	75
Turnip greens	125

Fruits

Dried figs, 5	258
Calcium-fortified orange juice, 1 c	300

Other Foods

Blackstrap molasses, 1 Tbsp	187
Cow's milk, 1 c	300
Yogurt, 1 c	275-400
Almond butter	86

Vitamin D (Micrograms per serving)

Fortified, ready-to-eat cereals, 3/4 c	1.0-2.5
Fortified soymilk or other non-dairy milk, 1 c	1.0-2.5

Vitamin B-12 (Micrograms per serving)

Ready-to-eat breakfast cereals, 3/4 c	1.5-6.0
Meat analogs (1 burger or 1 serving according to package)	2.0-7.0
Fortified soymilk or other non-dairy milks, 8 oz	0.2-5.0
Nutritional yeast (Red Star Vegetarian Support Formula, formerly T6635[a]), 1 Tbsp	4.0

Linolenic acid (Grams per serving)

Flax seed, 2 Tbsp	4.3
Walnuts, 1 oz	1.9
Walnut oil, 1 Tbsp	1.5
Canola oil, 1 Tbsp	1.6
Linseed oil, 1 Tbsp	7.6
Soybean oil, 1 Tbsp	0.9
Soybeans, 1/2 c cooked	0.5
Tofu, 1/2 c	0.4

FIG 1. *Food Sources of Nutrients*. Sources: Package information and data from: Pennington J. Bowe's and Church's; Food Values of Portions Commonly Used. 16th ed. Lippincott-Raven; 1994. Provisional Table on the Content of Omega-3 Fatty Acids and Other Fat Components in Selected Foods, 1988. Washington, DC: US Dept. of Agriculture: 1988: Publication No. HNIS/PT-103. Hytowitz DB, Matthews RH. Composition of Foods: Legumes and Legume Products. Washington, DC: US Dept. of Agriculture; 1986. Agriculture Handbook No. 8-16.

---

[a] Red Star Yeast and Products, a division of Universal Foods Corp, Milwaukee, WI

Vegetarianism Throughout the Life Cycle

Well-planned vegan and lacto-ovo-vegetarian diets are appropriate for all stages of the life cycle, including during pregnancy and lactation. Appropriately planned vegan and lacto-ovo-vegetarian diets satisfy nutrient needs of infants, children, and adolescents and promote normal growth (37). Dietary deficiencies are most likely to be observed in populations with very restrictive diets. All vegan children should have a reliable source of vitamin B-12 and, if sun exposure is limited, vitamin D supplements or fortified foods should be used. Foods rich in calcium, iron, and zinc should be emphasized. Frequent meals and snacks and the use of some refined foods and foods higher in fat can help vegetarian children meet energy needs. Guidelines for iron and vitamin D supplements and for the introduction of solid foods are the same for vegetarian and non-vegetarian infants. When it is time for protein-rich foods to be introduced, vegetarian infants can have pureed tofu, cottage cheese, and legumes (pureed and strained). Breast-fed vegan infants should receive a source of vitamin B-12 if the mother's diet is not supplemented and a source of vitamin D if sun exposure is inadequate.

Vegetarian diets are somewhat more common among adolescents with eating disorders than in the general adolescent population; therefore, dietetics professionals should be aware of young clients who greatly limit food choices and who exhibit symptoms of eating disorders (38). However, recent data suggest that adopting a vegetarian diet does not lead to eating disorders (39). With guidance in meal planning, vegetarian diets are appropriate and healthful choices for adolescents.

Vegetarian diets can also meet the needs of competitive athletes. Protein needs may be elevated because training increases amino acid metabolism, but vegetarian diets that meet energy needs and include good sources of protein (e.g., soyfoods, legumes) can provide adequate protein without use of special foods or supplements. For adolescent athletes, special attention should be given to meeting energy, protein, and iron needs. Amenorrhea may be more common among vegetarian than non-vegetarian athletes, although not all research supports this finding (40,41). Efforts to maintain normal menstrual cycles might include increasing energy and fat intake, reducing fiber, and reducing strenuous training.

Lacto-ovo-vegetarian and vegan diets can meet the nutrient and energy needs of pregnant women. Birth weights of infants born to well nourished vegetarian women have been shown to be similar to birth-weight norms and to birth weights of infants of non-vegetarians (42). Diets of pregnant and lactating vegans should be supplemented with 2.0 micrograms and 2.6

micrograms, respectively, of vitamin B-12 daily and, if sun exposure is limited, with 10 micrograms vitamin D daily (43,44).

Supplements of folate are advised for all pregnant women, although vegetarian women typically have higher intakes than non-vegetarians.

Meal Planning for Vegetarian Diets

A variety of menu-planning approaches can provide vegetarians with adequate nutrition. Figure 2 suggests one approach. In addition, the following guidelines can help vegetarians plan healthful diets.

- Choose a variety of foods, including whole grains, vegetables, fruits, legumes, nuts, seeds and, if desired, dairy products and eggs.

- Choose whole, unrefined foods often and minimize intake of highly sweetened, fatty, and heavily refined foods.

- Choose a variety of fruits and vegetables.

- If animal foods such as dairy products and eggs are used, choose lower-fat versions of these foods. Cheeses and other high-fat dairy foods and eggs should be limited in the diet because of their saturated fat content and because their frequent use displaces plant foods in some vegetarian diets.

- Vegans should include a regular source of vitamin B-12 in their diets along with a source of vitamin D if sun exposure is limited.

- Solely breast-fed infants should have supplements of iron after the age of 4 to 6 months and, if sun exposure is limited, a source of vitamin D. Breast-fed vegan infants should have vitamin B-12 supplements if the mother's diet is not fortified.

- Do not restrict dietary fat in children younger than 2 years. For older children, include some foods higher in unsaturated fats (e.g., nuts, seeds, nut and seed butters, avocado, and vegetable oils) to help meet nutrient and energy needs.

FIG 2. Food Guide Pyramid for Vegetarian Meal Planning

The text version of this Food Guide Pyramid follows:

Food Guide Pyramid for Vegetarian Meal Planning

FATS, OILS, AND SWEETS --(use sparingly)

candy, butter, margarine, salad dressing, cooking oil

MILK, YOGURT, AND CHEESE GROUP
(0-3 servings daily*)

milk or yogurt	1 cup
natural cheese	1½ oz

*Vegetarians who choose not to use milk, yogurt, or cheese need to select other food sources rich in calcium. For a list of calcium-rich foods, please see Figure 1.

DRY BEANS, NUTS, SEEDS, EGGS, AND MEAT SUBSTITUTES GROUP
(2-3 servings daily)

soy milk	1 cup
cooked dry beans/peas	1/2 cup
1 egg or 2 egg whites	
nuts or seeds	2 Tbsp
tofu or tempeh	1/4 cup
peanut butter	2 Tbsp

VEGETABLE GROUP
(3-5 servings daily)

cooked or chopped raw vegetables	1/2 cup
raw leafy vegetables	1 cup

FRUIT GROUP
(2-4 servings daily)

juice	3/4 cup
dried fruit	1/4 cup
chopped, raw fruit	1/2 cup
canned fruit	1/2 cup
1 medium-size piece of fruit, such as banana, apple, or orange	

BREAD, CEREAL, RICE, AND PASTA GROUP
(6-11 servings daily)

bread	1 slice	cooked cereal	1/2 cup
bagel	1/2	ready-to-eat	1 oz
cooked rice, pasta, or other grains	1/2 cup		

References

1. Knutsen SF. Lifestyle and the use of health services. Am J Clin Nutr. 1994;59(suppl):1171S-1175S.
2. Key TH, Thorogood M, Appleby PM, Burr ML. Dietary habits and mortality in 11,000 vegetarian and health conscious people: results of a 17-year follow up. BMJ. 1996;313:775-779.
3. Franklin TL, Kolasa KM, Griffin K, Mayo C, Badenhop DT. Adherence to very low fat diet by a group of cardiac rehabilitation patients in the rural southeastern United States. Arch Fam Med. 1995;4:551-554.
4. Gould KL, Ornish D, Scherwitz L, Brown S, Edens RP, Hess MJ, Mullani N, Bolomey L, Dobbs F, Armstrong WT, Merritt T, Ports T, Sparler S, Billings J. Changes in myocardial perusion abnormalities by positron emission tomography after long-term intense risk factor modification. JAMA. 1995;274:894-901.
5. Janelle KC, Barr SI. Nutrient intakes and eating behavior scores of vegetarian and non-vegetarian women. J Am Diet Assoc. 1995; 95:180-189.
6. Jacob RA, Burri BJ. Oxidative damage and defense. Am J Clin Nutr. 1996;63(suppl):985S-990S.
7. Thorogood M, Mann J, Appleby P, McPherson K. Risk of death from cancer and ischaemic heart disease in meat and non-meat eaters. BMJ. 1994;308:1667-1670.
8. Fraser GE, Lindsted KD, Beeson WL. Effect of risk factor values on lifetime risk of and age at first coronary event. The Adventist Health Study. Am J Epidemiol 1995;142:746-758.
9. Roberts WC. Preventing and arresting coronary atherosclerosis. Am Heart J. 1995;130:580-600.
10. Melby CL, Toohey ML, Cedrick J. Blood pressure and blood lipids among vegetarian, semi-vegetarian and non-vegetarian African Americans. Am J Clin Nutr. 1994;59:103-109.
11. Beilin LJ. Vegetarian and other complex diets, fats, fiber, and hypertension. Am J Clin Nutr. 1994;59(suppl):1130-1135.
12. Dwyer JT. Health aspects of vegetarian diets. Am J Clin Nutr. 1988;48(suppl):712-738.
13. Mills PK, Beeson WL, Phillips RL, Fraser GE. Cancer incidence among California Seventh-day Adventists, 1976-1982. Am J Clin Nutr. 1994;59(suppl):1136S-1142S.

14. Almendingen K, Trygg K, Vatn M. [Influence of the diet on cell proliferation in the large bowel and the rectum. Does a strict vegetarian diet reduce the risk of intestinal cancer?] Tidsskr Nor

Laegeforen. 1995;115(18):2252-2256.

15. Steinmetz KA, Potter JD. Vegetables, fruit and cancer. II. Mechanisms. Cancer Causes Control. 1991;1:427-442.

16. Messina MJ, Messina VL. The Dietitian's Guide to Vegetarian Diets: Issues and Applications. Gaithersburg, Md: Aspen Publishers; 1996.

17. Adlercreutz H, van der Wildt J, Kinzel J, Attalla H, Wahalla K, Makela T, Hase T, Fotsis T. Lignan and isoflavonoid conjugates in human urine. J Steroid Biochem Mol Biol. 1995;59:97-103.

18. Cancer Facts and Figures—1994. Atlanta, Ga: American Cancer Society; 1994.

19. Barbosa JC, Shultz TD, Filley SJ, Nieman DC. The relationship among adiposity, diet and hormone concentrations in vegetarian and non-vegetarian postmenopausal women. Am J Clin Nutr. 1990; 51:798-803.

20. Pagenkemper J. The impact of vegetarian diets on renal disease. Top Clin Nutr. 1995;10:22-26.

21. Barsotti G, Morelli E, Cupisti A, Meola M, Dani L, Giovannetti S. A low-nitrogen, low-phosphorus vegan diet for patients with chronic renal failure. Nephron. 1996;74:390-394.

22. Young VR, Pellett PL. Plant proteins in relation to human protein and amino acid nutrition. Am J Clin Nutr. 1994; 59 (suppl 5):1203S-1212S.

23. Craig WJ. Iron status of vegetarians. Am J Clin Nutr. 1994;59 (suppl):1233S-1237S.

24. Helman AD, Darnton-Hill I. Vitamin and iron status in new vegetarians. Am J Clin Nutr. 1987;45:785-789.

25. Slatter ML, Jacobs DR, Hilner JE Jr, Caan BJ, Van Horn L, Bragg C, Manolio TA, Kushi LH, Liu D. Meat consumption and its association with other diet and health factors in young adults: the CARDIA study. Am J Clin Nutr. 1992;56:699-704.

26. Tesar R, Notelovitz M, Shim E, Dauwell G, Brown J. Axial and peripheral bone density and nutrient intakes of postmenopausal vegetarian and omnivorous women. Am J Clin Nutr. 1992;56:699-704.

27. Remer T, Manz F. Estimation of the renal net acid excretion by adults consuming diets containing variable amounts of protein. Am J Clin Nutr. 1994; 59:1356-1361.

28. National Academy of Sciences, Institute of Medicine. Dietary Reference Intakes for Calcium, Phosphorus, Magnesium, Vitamin D and Flouride. Washington, DC: National Academy Press;1997.

29. Weaver CM, Plawecki KL. Dietary calcium: adequacy of a vegetarian diet. *Am J Clin Nutr.* 1994;59(suppl): 1238S-1241S.

30. Henderson JB, Dunnigan MG, McIntosh WB, Abdul-Motaal AA,

Gettinby G, Glekin BM. The importance of limited exposure to ultraviolet radiation and dietary factors in the aetiology of Asian rickets: a risk-factor model. *QJM.* 1987;63:413-425.

31. Holuck MF. Vitamin D and bone health. *J Nutr.* 1996; 126 (suppl): 1159S- 1164S.

32. Freeland-Graves JH, Bodzy PW, Epright MA. Zinc status of vegetarians. *J Am Diet Assoc.* 1980;77:655-661.

33. Lei S, Mingyan X, Miller LV, Tong L, Krebs NF, Hambidge KM. Zinc absorption and intestinal losses of endogenous zinc in young Chinese women with marginal zinc intakes. Am *J Clin Nutr.* 1996;63:348-353.

34. Sanders TAB, Roshanai F. Platelet phospholipid fatty acid composition and function in vegans compared with age-and sex-matched omnivore controls. Eur *J Clin Nutr.* 1992;46:823-831.

35. Conquer JA, Holub BJ. Dietary docosahexaenoic acid as a source of eicosapentaenoic acid in vegetarians and omnivores. *Lipids.* 1997; 32: 341-345.

36. Emken EA, Adlof RO, Gulley RM. Dietary linoleic acid influences desaturation and acylation of deuterium-labeled linoleic and linolenic acids in young adult males. *Biochim Biophys Acta.* 1994; 1213:277-288.

37. Sanders TAB, Reddy S. Vegetarian diets and children. Am *J Clin Nutr.* 1994;59(suppl): 1176S- 1181S.

38. O'Connor MA, Touyz SW, Dunn SM, Beaumont PJV. Vegetarianism in anorexia nervosa? A review of 116 consecutive cases. *Med J Aust.* 1987; 147:540-542.

39. Janelle KC, Barr SI. Nutrient intakes and eating behavior scores of vegetarian and nonvegetarian women. *J Am Diet Assoc.* 1995; 95:180-189.

40. Pedersen AB, Bartholomew MJ, Dolence LA, Aljadir LP, Netteburg KL, Lloyd T. Menstrual differences due to vegetarian and non-vegetarian diets. *Am J Clin Nutr.* 1991;54:520-525.

41. Slavin J, Lutter J, Cushman S. Amenorrhea in vegetarian athletes. *Lancet. 1984;* 1: 1474-1475.

42. O'Connell JM, Dibley MJ, Sierra J, Wallace B, Marks JS, Yip R. Growth of vegetarian children: the Farm Study. *Pediatrics.* 1989; 84: 475-481.

43. Food and Nutrition Board, Institute of Medicine. *Nutrition During Pregnancy.* Washington, DC: National Academy Press; 1991.

44. Food and Nutrition Board, Institute of Medicine. *Nutrition During Lactation.* Washington, DC: National Academy Press; 1991.

ADA Position adopted by the House of Delegates on October 18, 1987, and reaffirmed on September 12, 1992, and September 6, 1996. This position will be in effect until December 31, 2001. ADA authorizes republication of the position statement/support paper, in its entirety, provided full and proper credit is given. Requests to use portions of the position must be directed to ADA Headquarters at 800/877-1600, ext 4896, or hod@eatright.org.

Recognition is given to the following for their contributions:

Authors:
Virginia K. Messina, MPH, RD, and Kenneth I. Burke, PhD, RD

Reviewers:
Winston J. Craig, PhD, RD; Johanna Dwyer, DSc, RD; Suzanne Havala, MS, RD, FADA; D. Enette Larson, MS, RD; A. Reed Mangels, PhD, RD, FADA; Vegetarian Nutrition dietetic practice group (Lenore Hodges, PhD, RD; Cyndi Reeser, MPH, RD)

This position paper appeared in the Journal of the American Dietetic Association, November 1997, Volume 97, Number 11.

Proof Positive

Proof Positive: How to Reliably Combat Disease and Achieve Optimal Health through Nutrition and Lifestyle, written by Neil Nedley, MD and edited by David DeRose, MD, 1998

This book addresses the universal problem of personal health and disease, and is written for the general public as well as the health professional. It speaks to any person who wishes to attain (or maintain) good health and freedom from disease by natural means, minimizing the use of prescription drugs, food supplements, and diet fads. It contains specific medical advice to attain these goals. The prevention of a disease as well as the treatment, if it exists through lifestyle measures, are both addressed.

It is designed to be readable and easy to understand, with many color illustrations that clarify the subject at hand. Each of the 20 chapters covers a specific topic, and each "stands alone" which permits a free choice to begin at the topic of highest interest to the reader.

The book is based on the latest factual, reliable medical principles that have been used by Dr. Nedley for treating his patients for many years. Countless scientific studies conducted around the world, combined with the latest medical knowledge of the effects of lifestyle factors, form the basis for the information and advice given. Many specific diseases and ailments are addressed, in addition to stress, problems of addictions, common myths about nutrition, food supplements, substance abuse, and other health topics.

We highly recommend this book as a reference for beginning and maintaining positive lifestyle changes.

You may obtain a copy of this book by contacting the Gift Shop at the Lifestyle Center of America, RR 1, Box 4001, Sulphur, Oklahoma 73086 (580-993-2327) or direct from the publisher at 1-888-778-4445.

THE VEGETARIAN FOOD PYRAMID

A DAILY GUIDE TO FOOD CHOICES

VEGETABLE FATS AND OILS,
SWEETS, AND SALT
EAT SPARINGLY

LOW-FAT OR NON-FAT,
MILK, YOGURT, FRESH CHEESE,
AND FORTIFIED
ALTERNATIVE GROUP

2-3 SERVINGS

EAT MODERATELY

LEGUME, NUT, SEED, AND
MEAT ALTERNATIVE GROUP

2-3 SERVINGS

EAT MODERATELY

VEGETABLE GROUP

3-5 SERVINGS

**EAT
GENEROUSLY**

FRUIT GROUP

2-4 SERVINGS

EAT GENEROUSLY

WHOLE GRAIN
BREAD, CEREAL,
PASTA, AND RICE
GROUP

6-11
SERVINGS

**EAT
LIBERALLY**

HEALTH CONNECTIONS ◆ World St Paul Press Hagerstown, Maryland 21740-7390 USA ◆ Telephone (301) 791-7000 ◆ (800) 548-8700 ◆ Fax (301) 790-9733   Illustration by Merle Poirier

Build Your Own Pyramid
Eat a mixture of all food groups daily

Daily Servings	Serving Size	Kind of Food

Cereal, Pasta, Bread, Rice
6 - 11	1 slice	whole grain bread
	1	muffin, biscuit, tortilla
	3/4 c	dry cereal
	1/2 c	pasta, rice, cooked cereal
	1/2	bagel, hamburger bun, English muffin
	3 - 4	crackers

Vegetables
3 - 5	1 c raw	celery, tomato, cauliflower, corn, lettuce,
	or 3/4 c	carrots, broccoli, peas, zucchini,
	cooked	yellow squash, potato, cabbage,
	or 1/2 c	spinach, yams
	juice	greens--mustard, collard, beet, kale

Fruit
2 - 4	1	orange, tangerine, mango, pear
	1	papaya, apple, banana, peach
	2	apricots, nectarines, plums
	1 c	grapes
	3/4 c	juice
	1/2 c	strawberries, cantaloupe, grapefruit
	1/2 c	pineapple, cherries
	1/4 c	raisins or other dried fruit

Dry Beans, Nuts, Soy, Meat Substitutes
2 - 3	2 oz	soy or gluten meat substitute
	1/2 c cooked	tofu, beans--kidney, lima, soy, lentil
	1/2 c cooked	navy, mung, black, peas
	1/4 c	nuts, seeds
	2 T	nut butter

Soy Milk, Soy Cheese
2 - 3	1 c	soy or nut milk, fortified
	1½ - 2 oz	soy cheese
	1½ c	frozen fruit or soy ice cream

Fats, Oils, Sweets, Salt
Use	1 T	salad dressing, margarine, cooking oils
Sparingly		honey, molasses, candy, cake, cookies, jam, jelly,
		pickles, syrup, white or brown sugar
		fried foods

Note: Pay attention to the number of daily servings recommended as well as their serving size. Most people eat servings that are too large.

Food Guide Pyramid Summary

The food guide pyramid produced by the USDA in 1992 is a diet-planning tool sorting foods of similar origin and nutrient content into groups which then specifies that people should eat certain numbers of servings from each group to assure a proper amount of all the nutrients. It can be used by vegetarians and meat eaters alike. Vegetarians can substitute soy milk, soy cheese, and tofu for the dairy group. Vegetarians can also substitute tofu, gluten, and textured vegetable protein in the protein group. If you wish to purchase the lacto-ovo vegetarian food guide pyramid as shown on page 38 you can contact The Health Connection at 1-800-548-8700 or 1-301-790-9735. To purchase an Asian, Latin American, Mediterranean, or a Lacto-Ovo Vegetarian food guide pyramid you can also contact Oldways Preservation & Exchange Trust at 1-617-621-3000. There is no total vegetarian (vegan) food guide pyramid in print available at this time.

The food guide pyramid provides a moderate level of fat and sugar. It will not prevent disease but can slow down the progression of chronic diseases. To prevent and/or reverse disease you must adapt the food guide pyramid to select those foods found to be lower in fats and sugar, and higher in fiber and other nutrients.

The food guide pyramid will help you select more plant based foods. Raw nuts and seeds, whole grains, fruits, and vegetable foods are beneficial and protective foods. The foods of animal origin which contain high amounts of protein and saturated fats have been shown to be harmful especially when eaten in excessive amounts. The purpose of improving your nutrition habits is to help you select proper foods for adequate intake of carbohydrates, fiber, protein, fats, vitamins, minerals, anti-oxidants and trace elements from whole natural plant foods.

To begin, avoid fried foods and snacking between meals. Water between meals is recommended, 8 - 12 glasses per day.

Hi Protein Group: 2-3 servings per day. Extra servings are not recommended.

All legumes (dried beans) are recommended as a good protein source. Seeds, fresh and raw nuts, especially walnuts and almonds (1-2 oz. portions), in moderation are permitted.

Tofu is an excellent source of protein. Other meat substitutes include soy products found in dehydrated, frozen or canned form. Gluten (wheat protein) is available in canned and frozen form as well. It can also be made at home.

One serving equals 1/2 c cooked legumes, 1/4 c nuts and seeds, 2 T nut butter or 2 oz. of a meat substitute.

Fruit Group: 2 - 4 servings per day. Extra servings are allowed.

All fruits except coconut may be consumed freely. Fruit should be preferably fresh, unsweetened, frozen or canned in unsweetened fruit juice or packed in water.

One serving is a small to medium fruit, 1/2 cup cut mixed fruit or 1/4 c dried fruit

Grain Group: 6 - 11 servings per day. Extra servings are allowed.

All whole grains (rice, wheat, oats, barley, corn, rye, millet, etc.) are allowed. Whole grain breads and cereals are preferable with no added sugar. Oatmeal is one of the best cereals. Refined cereals and breads offer little or no fiber content. Natural sweeteners such as unsweetened apple sauce, bananas, raisins, peaches, etc. may be added. Brown rice is preferred to white rice. Experiment with some of the long grain wild rice and mix with your white rice to develop a flavor for brown rice. Avoid commercial pizza, lasagna and other high fat and high cheese dishes. Spaghetti with tomato sauce and other noodles are permitted. Whole grain pastas are available and provide additional nutrients.

One serving is 1 cup dry, 1/2 cup cooked or one slice of bread (1 oz.).

Vegetable Group: 3-5 servings per day. Extra servings are allowed.

All vegetables are allowed especially leafy dark greens and dark yellow varieties. Vegetables can be eaten raw or cooked. If cooked, cook only to be crispy-tender to maximize their flavor and nutrition.

One serving is 1 cup raw, 1/2 cup cooked vegetables or 1/4 cup juice.

Dairy Group: 2-3 servings per day. Extra servings are not recommended.

Soy and nut milks (we prefer both of these) may be used on cereals. Soy cheeses are available as a substitute for dairy cheeses. When using soy products, select fortified soymilk and soy cheese with added vitamin B12, calcium, and vitamin D.

The dairy group is abundant in calcium and B vitamins. However the calcium in milk is not readily absorbed. The dairy group is also typically high in fats and calories. As long as a low protein diet is eaten, abundant calcium can be found in vegetables, especially dark green leafy vegetables and broccoli. Additional calcium will also be found in beans, dried fruit, tofu, whole grain bread, cereal and rice.

One serving is 1 cup soy milk or 1-1/2 to 2 oz (1 slice) of soy cheese.

Extras, (Added Fats, Oils, and Sweets Group): Use sparingly, maximum 2 servings per day.

Use only plant based oils. Vegetable oils such as olive, canola, or soybean are preferable to corn, cottonseed, palm and coconut oil. They are best when consumed in the natural state as found in legumes, olives, nuts, and seeds. Hydrogenated fats such as margarine, regular peanut butter and fats found in prepared mixes are not recommended. Canola oil margarine may be used sparingly as a margarine. Make your own salad dressing or mayonnaise or use a light or fat free brand.

Some fats and sugars should be used in small amounts because of their high caloric density.

Note:

Eat vegetables, fruits, seeds and grains as close to their natural state as possible. These calories are beneficial unless they are adulterated with extra fats and sugars. Food processing, addition of food additives and extra storage used by the food industry can change the quality of the food we consume. For example, the potato is O.K. However when the potato appears as french fries you triple the calories. When the same potato is seen as potato chips you add five times the calories. We need to eat our food as close to the natural state as possible.

Be cautious when cooking. Follow these tips to reduce nutrient losses.

1. Avoid overcooking.
2. Use a minimum of water, steaming is preferable.
3. Cover the pan in which food is being cooked. Use as low a heat as is possible.
4. Save liquids from cooking and use in other dishes such as soups
5. Avoid cooking more than you need. Freeze any leftovers.
6. Avoid using wilted, overripe or bruised foods.

Replacing Nutrients

Vegetarians eating no animal products may need to be more aware of the recommeded daily allowances (RDA)[a] of some some nutrient sources.

- Vitamin B-12:   **Adults need 3 mcg/day**
  Source: fortified cereals, soy beverages, nutritional yeast   (Need intrinsic factor in intestine)

- Vitamin D: **Adults need 5 mcg/day**
  Source: fortified soy beverages and sunshine

- Calcium: **Adults need 800 mg/ day**
  Source: tofu processed with calcium, broccoli, seeds, nuts, kale, bok choy, legumes, greens, lime-processed tortillas, fortified soy beverages, grain products

- Iron: **Adults need 10-18 mg/day**
  Source: legumes, tofu, green leafy vegetables, dried fruit, whole grains, and iron-fortified cereals and whole wheat breads.

  (Absorption is improved by the vitamin C found in citrus fruits & juices, tomatoes, strawberries, broccoli, peppers, dark-green leafy vegetables, and potatoes with skins)

- Zinc: **Adults need 15 mg/day**
  Source: whole grains (especially the germ and bran), whole wheat bread, legumes, nuts, and tofu

- Protein: **Adults need 44 - 56 g/day**
  Source: tofu and other soy based products, legumes, seeds, nuts, grains, gluten, and vegetables

---

[a] The RDA estimated range for an average man and woman

The Bottom Line

Eat a wide **variety** of **unrefined** plant based foods in sufficient quantity to maintain ideal weight. Follow the daily food guide pyramid with the recommended servings to assure a good balance of all the nutrients. Each group in the pyramid provides a variety of plant based foods in which to make healthy food choices. Extra servings of grains, vegetables anf fruits are allowed to satisfy hunger. Extra servings for the remaining food groups ia discouraged.

ADA Recommendations for Vegetarians

Consult a registered dietitian or other qualified nutrition professional especially during periods of growth, breast-feeding, pregnancy, or recovery from illness

1. Minimize intake of less nutritious foods such as sweets and fatty foods
2. Choose whole or unrefined grain products instead of refined products
3. Choose a **variety** of nuts, seeds, legumes, grains, fruits, and vegetables, including good sources of vitamin C to improve iron absorption
4. For infants, children and teenagers, ensure adequate intakes of calories, vitamin D, calcium, iron, B12, protein, and zinc (Intakes of vitamin D, calcium, iron, protein, and zinc are usually adequate when a variety of foods and sufficient calories are consumed)
5. Usually, take iron and folate (folic acid) supplements during pregnancy
6. Use fortified food sources of vitamin B12
7. If sunlight is inadequate, take a vitamin D supplement during pregnancy or while breast-feeding

Plant Sources of Calcium

Vegetables, 1 c *	mg		mg
Collards	357	Broccoli Pieces	177
Turnip Greens	249	Okra	176
Kale	179	Mustard greens	104

Cooked Beans, 1 c			
Soybeans	131	Garbanzos	80
Navy	128	Black-eyed peas	106
Pinto	86	Lentils	37

Dried Fruits			
Figs, 3 large	78	Apricots, 1/2 c	50
Currants, 1/2 c	62	Raisins, 2 oz	36
Pitted Dates, 1/2 c	58	Prunes, 1/2 c	30

Others			
Fortified Soy Milk, 1 c	100-500	Tofu, 4 oz	110
Tofu (precipitated, 4 oz		Almonds, 1 oz	75
with Calcium Salts)	300	Sweet Potato, 1 med	72
Blackstrap Molasses, 1 T	137	Med Orange, 1 med	55
Tahini, 1/2 oz	115	Bread, 2 sl	45

Dairy Products for Comparison

Fruit-flavored, low fat Yogurt, 8 oz with added milk solids	345 mg
low-fat milk, 1 c	300
Cheddar Cheese, 1 oz	204
low-fat Cottage Cheese, 1/2 c	77

* While 1 c Spinach has 167 mg of calcium, spinach is not regarded as a good source of calcium due to its high content of oxalates which diminish calcium absorption.

Reference: **Bowes & Church's - Food Values of Portions Commonly Used,** edited by Jean A. T. Pennington, PhD, RD., 15th Edition, 1989.
Nutrition for the Eighties by Winston J. Craig, PhD, RD, 1992.

Plant Sources of Zinc

Soy Bean Products

	mg		mg
Miso, 1/2 c	4.58	Tempeh, 1/2 c	1.50
Soybean flour, defatted, 1 c	2.46	Soybeans, mature	0.99
Tofu, firm, 1/2 c	1.98	Soy milk, 1 c	0.54

Vegetables, cooked, 1/2 c

Lentils	2.25	Pinto Beans	0.81
Lima beans	0.37	Potato, baked with skin	0.65
Kidney beans	0.95	Collards	0.61
Corn, yellow	0.39	Artichoke, 1 med	0.43
Black beans	0.96	Squash	0.35

Nuts

Pecans, dry roasted, 1 oz	1.61	Almond, whole, 1 oz.	0.95
Cashews, dry roasted, 1 oz.,		Walnuts, english, 14 halves	0.78
18 pieces	1.59	Sesame butter, 1 T	0.69
Cashew butter, 1 oz	1.47	Almond butter, 1 T	0.49

Seeds

Sunflower, 1oz.	1.44	Sesame, 1 T	0.70
Pumpkin, 1/2 oz., 71 seeds	1.06		

Grains

Ralston cereal, 3/4 c	1.06	Whole wheat, 1 sl	0.42
Oatmeal cereal, 3/4 c	1.00	Mixed grain, 1 sl	0.30
Wheat bran, 2 T	1.00	White, 1 sl	0.15

Reference: Bowes & Church's - Food Values of Portions Commonly Used, edited by Jean A. T. Pennington, PhD, RD., 15th Edition, 1989.

Plant Sources of Iron

Soybean Products, 1/2 c

Tofu, firm	13.19	Tempeh	1.88
Tofu	6.65	Soy milk, 1 c	1.38
Miso	3.78		

Cereal, 3/4 c

Cream of wheat	9.0	Ralston, cooked	1.24
Bran Flakes	8.1	Oatmeal, cooked	1.08
All Bran	4.5	Grits, white hominy	1.02
Rice, white, enriched, 1 c	1.8	Rice, brown, 1 c	1.00

Other Vegetables, cooked, 1/2 c

Soybeans, mature	4.42	Lima beans	2.25
Lentils	3.30	Black-eyed peas	2.14
Potato, baked with skin, 6.5 oz	2.75	Artichoke. 1 med	1.62
Kidney beans	2.60	Peas, green	1.24
Navy beans, canned	2.42	Brussel Sprouts	0.94
Garbanzos	2.37	Broccoli	0.89
Soybeans, green	2.25	Squash	0.32

Leafy Vegetables, 1/2 c

Spinach, cooked	3.21	Dandelion greens	0.94
Swiss chard, cooked	1.99	Mustard greens	0.84
Turnip greens	1.59	Kale, cooked	0.59
Collards	0.95	Lettuce, Romaine	0.31

Seeds

Pumpkin, 1/2 oz., 71 seeds	2.12	Sesame, whole, 1 T	1.31
Sunflower, 1 oz.	1.92		

Fruit

Raisins, seedless, 2/3 c	2.08	Tomato Juice, 1/2 c	0.80
Avocado, 1 med	2.04	Apricots, raw, 3 med	0.58
Prune juice,, 1/2 c	1.51	Grapes, 1 c	0.41
Papaya nectar, 8 oz.	0.86	Banana, raw, 1 med	0.35

Nuts

Cashews, dry roasted, 1 oz.,		Walnuts, black, 1 oz.	
18 pieces	1.70	14 halves	0.87
Cashew butter, 1 oz.	1.43	Walnuts, english, 14 halves	0.69
Sesame butter, 1 T	1.34	Pecans, dry roasted, 1 oz.	0.62
Almond, whole, 1 oz.	1.30	Almond butter, 1 T	0.59

Breads, 1 slice	**mg**		**mg**
Mixed grain	0.82	White bread	0.68
Whole wheat	0.80	Cracked wheat	0.67

Animal products for Comparison

T-bone steak, 3.5 oz.	2.54	Halibut, 3 oz.	0.91
Hamburger, lean, 3.5 oz.	2.35	Bacon, 3 med pieces	0.31
Chicken, 3.5 oz.	1.21	Ham, 1 oz.	0.28
Egg, whole, 1 large	1.04	Milk, 2%, 8 oz.	0.12

Reference: **Bowes & Church's - Food Values of Portions Commonly Used,** edited by Jean A. T. Pennington, PhD, RD., 15th Edition, 1989.

Plant Sources of Protein

Legumes, 1/2 cup cooked	grams		
Soybeans	14.25	Garbanzos,	7.25
Lentils	9.0	Black Eyed Peas	7.0
Split Peas	8.25	Mung Beans	7.0
Red Kidney	8.0	Pinto Beans	7.0
Navy Beans	8.0	Lima Beans	6.0
Great Northern Beans	7.5		

Nuts, 2 oz.			
Peanuts, dry roasted	14.0	Brazil Nuts, dried	8.2
Walnuts dried	13.8	Pumpkin seeds	6.8
Pistachios	11.6	Pine nuts	6.6
Almonds	11.2	Pecans, dried	4.4
Cashews, dry roasted	8.6		

Vegetables, 1/2 cup cooked			
Artichoke, medium	10.4	Collards	2.5
Potato with skin	5.0	Corn	2.5
Green Peas	4.0	Turnips	2.5
Spinach	3.0	Kale	2.0
Avocado, medium, raw	2.5	Tomato Puree	2.0
Broccoli	2.5		

Spreads, 2 T			
Peanut Butter	8.0	Sesame Butter	5.0
Cashew Butter	5.0	Almond Butter	4.8

Bread		grams	
Pita, whole wheat, 1-6" diameter	6.3	Whole wheat,1 sl.	3.0
Pita, white, 1-6" diameter	5.5	French, 1 sl. (1oz)	2.7
English Muffin	4.0	White , 1 sl. (1oz)	2.0
Whole wheat, homemade, 1 sl.	3.9		

Plant Sources of Protein

Crackers	grams		
Triscuits, 7 crackers	3.0	Saltines, low sodium,	
Wheat thins, 24 crackers	2.0	3 crackers	1.6

Meat Analogues, 1 patty			grams
Prime Patties, Frozen,			
Morningstar Farms	19.5	Chik Patties,	
Staklets, 1 piece	12.3	Morningstar Farms	7.3
Garden Vege Patties,		Leanies, Worthington,	
Morningstar Farms	11.2	1 link	7.3
Frichik, Worthington,		Bacon simulated meat	
2 pieces	9.9	product-1-strip	0.9

References:

1. **Bowes and Church's, Food Values of Portions Commonly Used**, 15th edition, 1989
2. **Nutritive Value of Foods**, USDA, Home and Garden Bulletin #72

Fats that Heal, Fats that Kill

Fats that Heal, Fats that Kill, The complete guide to fats, oils, cholesterol and human health, Udo Erasmus, PhD, *alive* books, 1993

Popular books on nutrition that tackle fats, oils, and cholesterol contain many contradictory statements of 'fact'. The reason is that most writers are not knowledgeable in this field. Some of their 'facts' tell only half the story, the part about the fats that kill. Some of their 'Facts' about fats and oils are the half-truths that industries disseminate in order to market fat and oil products for profit. Also, authors often copy each others' mistaken 'facts' because they have not invested the time and effort required to extract truths from the research literature. This book departs from that lazy practice.

All aspects of how fats, oils, cholesterol, and essential nutrients affect our health are covered in this book, including:

- the properties of fats, fatty acids, sugars, and cholesterol; the healing and the killing fats;
- how fats and oils are made into marketable consumer products; the health effects of applying technical skills (processing) to foods without regard for human health;
- the body's ways of dealing with fats and foods; fats and cholesterol found in foods; how food preparation affects health; research findings;
- how to make and use oils with human health in mind; new and therapeutic products; other important nutrients;
- degenerative diseases;
- the politics of health; and
- a consideration of the basis of human health.

You will end up with a broad understanding of the topic, have specific, detailed information at your fingertips, and gain insights that will make it easier to optimize health and avoid degenerative diseases. This book separates fact from advertising fiction, and equips you to assess future developments in the field.

We highly recommend this book as a reference for beginning and maintaining positive lifestyle changes.

You may obtain a copy of this book by contacting any major bookstore, most health food stores or directly from the publisher at 1-604-435-1919 or Fax: 604-435-4888.

Importance of Fats

Fats in our diets are necessary in reasonable amounts for good health. They provide a good source of food energy and also help make the food taste good. Fats also help us from getting hungry too soon after a meal by delaying rapid emptying of the stomach. They also carry the fat soluble vitamins A, D, E, and K. Essential fatty acids are required for growth, reproduction, and maintenance of the health of tissue membranes and skin.

One example of the importance of good fats involves Linoleic acid. Linoleic acid (LA), an essential fatty acid, is one of the important polyunsaturated fats because of its role in prostaglandin metabolism and heart disease. Prostaglandins are potent substances having a vital role in many tissues. Prostacyclin, a prostaglandin synthesized in the walls of blood vessels, inhibits blood clotting, lowers blood pressure, and relaxes coronary arteries. Thromboxane-A2, a prostaglandin made by the platelets, produces opposite effect by stimulating clotting, increasing blood pressure, and constricting coronary arteries. Read Dr. Erasmus's book, **Fats that Heal, Fats that Kill** discussed on page 52, to understand more about the healing fats.

The balance between these two Prostaglandins regulates blood clotting and bleeding times. Higher amounts of thromboxane-A2 would result in clot formation, restricting blood flow and contributing to the blocking of blood vessels. Diets high in linoleic acid lead to decreased levels of thromboxane-A2 which would favor reduced clotting and reduced coronary thrombosis. Good sources of linoleic acid include nuts, seeds, vegetable oils, and soybeans. Smaller amounts of LA are found in other legumes and grains.

Prostacyclin production decreases with smoking and age. Dietary cholesterol also decreases prostacyclin formation and thereby increases the risk of clot formation. Linoleic acid also increases the working capacity of the heart and the blood flow rate through the coronary arteries as well as decreasing serum triglycerides, serum cholesterol, and sodium induced hypertension. Studies of vegetarians have shown that their blood levels of linoleic acid are 20% higher than non-vegetarians.

While fat is only one of the three energy yielding classes of food, it does contain the most calories per gram. Fat also appears to be intimately associated with the health or disease of the heart and blood vessels. It would be most advantageous to our health, well-being and longevity to decrease the total fat intake in our diet by eliminating the harmful fats and consuming only the beneficial fats in the recommended amounts.

All Fats Are Not Equal

Cholesterol: A fat-like substance found in body cells. Cholesterol differs from fat in that cholesterol may be present in all animal tissue, while fat deposits are mainly found under skin and around organs. Cholesterol in high concentrations is unwanted for it may be deleterious to overall health and well-being. Cholesterol is needed to form hormones, cell membranes, and other body substances. The body will naturally produce enough cholesterol to meet its needs without incorporating cholesterol into the diet.

Fat: Even though all fat contains 9 calories per gram (more than twice the 4 calories contained in a gram of Carbohydrate or protein) the type of fat consumed plays an equally important role to the quantity of fat consumed. Fat can be solid (butter, margarine, lard or shortening) or liquid (vegetable oils). The difference in the fat is due to its fatty acid composition. Fats are a mixture of mono, poly, and saturated fatty acids.

Fatty Acids: The basic chemical unit of fat is the fatty acid. Fatty acids are made up of chains of carbon atoms to which hydrogen atoms are attached. Fatty acids are categorized into saturated, monounsaturated, or polyunsaturated based on how many hydrogen atoms are attached in relation to the maximum they can hold. **Essential Fatty Acids** cannot be manufactured by the body therefore must be acquired from our food sources. Overall they are involved with deriving energy from food and moving that energy around so our bodies can utilize it.

Hydrogenated Fat: A fat which is commercially processed from unsaturated liquid oil. By adding hydrogen to the oil (hydrogenation) the oil becomes more saturated. Examples of hydrogenated fat are spreadable fats such as margarine, shortening, and peanut butter.

HDL-C: Known as the "good" cholesterol. Substances made up of proteins and lipids (fats). The HDL has a higher percentage of protein to fat and is thought to help rid the blood of excess cholesterol. Higher HDL levels are desired because of its association with lower rates of heart disease. Caloric restriction has been shown to raise HDL levels.

LDL-C: Known as the "bad" cholesterol. LDL-C is made up of protein and lipid, however, the lipid component is greater than that of the protein component. LDL's are associated with a elevated risk of coronary heart disease because they are associated with high level of blood cholesterol. Caloric restriction has been shown to lower LDL levels.

<u>Lipids</u>: The term lipids is the technical name for substances commonly referred to as fats. Lipids include fatty acids (saturated and unsaturated), cholesterol and triglycerides.

<u>Mono-Unsaturated Fats</u>: These fats are usually liquid at room temperature. Examples are olive, peanut, sesame and canola oils, as well as oils from most nuts and seeds. Monounsaturated fats appear to have positive effects on blood fat levels, by lowering total blood cholesterol, lowering LDL or bad cholesterol, and showing little or no effect on HDL.

<u>Poly-Unsaturated Fats and Oils</u>: These fats and oils are commonly liquid at room temperature and are primarily of plant origin. Examples are soybean, corn, cottonseed, safflower, and sunflower oils. Polyunsaturated fats tend to reduce total cholesterol by lowering LDL-C and HDL-C. Long term effects of diets rich in polyunsaturated fats are uncertain at this time, however some studies have actually shown an increased cancer risk with diets high in polyunsaturated fats.

<u>Saturated Fats</u>: Fats that are usually solid at room temperature. Saturated fats are primarily from animal sources. Examples are red meat, poultry products, dairy (butter, cheese) and lard. Note that palm oil, coconut oil, cocoa butter and partially hydrogenated vegetable oils too are saturated fats. Saturated fats raise total blood cholesterol by increasing both LDL-C and LDL-C. Saturated fats are more related to high lipid levels in the blood than are foods high in cholesterol. However foods high in both cholesterol and saturated cause more damage to the arteries than when saturated fat is found alone such as in plant foods.

<u>Trans-Fatty Acids</u>: Appear to be the most harmful to blood cholesterol because they raise LDL-C and lower HDL-C. The Trans fatty acids (TFA) are found in hydrogenated vegetable oils such as margarines and shortenings and in many commercially made products such as cookies, crackers, chips, and fried foods such as French fries. Unfortunately, the TFA are not required to be included on the ingredient list found on food labels. Although the amount of these fats may be small in some products, the only defense for consumers is to avoid products that contain partially hydrogenated vegetable fat or margarines.

<u>Triglycerides</u>: The primary type of fat that is found in the body and visible in the blood.

Reference: Harvard Heart Letter (adapted), Vol 4, # 8, April, 1994.

Plant Sources of Fat

	Total Fat grams	Sat Fat grams	Mono Fat grams	Poly Fat grams	Chol Fat Mg
Nuts and Seeds - 1/4 c					
Peanuts,					
dry roasted	17.6	3.1	8.0	4.0	0.0
Sesame seeds	17.5	2.5	7.0	8.0	0.0
Pecans	17.0	1.0	11.0	4.5	0.0
Sunflower seeds	16.8	3.2	3.0	9.5	0.0
Almonds	16.0	1.0	10.0	3.5	0.0
Peanut Butter,					
2 T	15.3	2.8	7.8	5.0	0.0
Walnuts	13.5	1.5	4.0	8.0	0.0
Cashews	13.0	2.5	8.0	2.0	0.0
Pumpkin seeds	13.0	2.5	4.0	6.0	0.0
Vegetable Oils - 1 T					
Corn	13.6	1.7	3.9	8.0	0.0
Cottonseed	13.6	3.5	3.0	7.1	0.0
Safflower	13.6	1.2	2.3	10.1	0.0
Soybean	13.6	2.0	3.7	7.9	0.0
Sunflower	13.6	1.4	3.3	8.9	0.0
Coconut	13.6	11.8	1.6	0.2	0.0
Palm	13.6	6.7	5.6	1.3	0.0
Olive	13.5	1.8	10.6	1.1	0.0
Peanut	13.5	2.3	6.9	4.3	0.0
Margarine - 1T					
Veg. shortening	12.8	3.9	7.1	1.8	0.0
Hard (stick)	11.4	2.1	5.7	3.6	0.0
Soft (tub)	11.4	1.8	4.8	4.8	0.0
Salad Dressings -1 T (with egg or dairy except for Italian and French)					
Mayonnaise	11.0	1.6	3.7	5.7	8.0
Blue Cheese	8.0	1.5	2.2	4.3	3.0
Italian	7.1	1.0	2.0	4.1	0.0
French	6.4	1.5	1.5	4.9	0.0
Thousand Island	5.6	0.9	1.6	3.1	4.0
Mayo, LoCal	3.0	0.5	0.7	1.6	4.0

Soy Products - 1/2 c

Miso	6.5	0.9	1.3	3.65	0.0
Tofu, (2½" x 2¾" x1")	5.0	0.7	1.0	2.9	0.0

Beans - 1/2 c

Soybean	5.0	0.65	0.95	2.65	0.0
Chickpeas	2.0	0.2	0.45	0.95	0.0
Lima	0.5	0.1	0.05	0.25	0.0
Lentils	0.5	0.05	0.1	0.25	0.0
Peas	0.5	0.05	0.05	0.15	0.0

Animal Fats- 1 T (Animal Sources for Comparison)

Beef fat	12.8	6.4	5.9	0.5	14
Chicken fat	12.8	3.8	6.3	2.7	11
Lard	12.8	5.0	6.4	1.4	12
Butter	11.5	7.2	3.9	0.4	31

Meat, Poultry, Fish - 2 oz.

Ground beef	11.7	4.6	6.7	0.4	51
Beef rump	8.9	3.5	5.1	0.3	47
Beef liver	4.5	1.6	1.9	0.0	273
Chicken, w skin	6.2	1.7	3.2	1.3	48
Turkey, w/o skin	1.8	0.6	0.7	0.5	39
Tuna in oil	4.6	1.2	0.4	0.4	117
Shrimp	0.9	0.1	0.4	0.4	117

Eggs

Egg yolk	5.6	1.7	3.2	0.7	274
Egg white	trace	0.0	0.0	0.0	0.0

Dairy Products

Whole milk, 8 oz	8.2	5.1	2.4	0.2	34
2% milk, 8 oz	4.7	2.9	1.4	0.2	18
Skim milk, 8 oz	0.6	0.4	0.1	0.0	5
Cottage cheese, 1/2 c	5.2	3.3	1.5	0.2	17
Cheddar cheese, 1 oz.	9.4	6.0	2.7	0.3	30

Reference: **Bowes & Church's - Food Values of Portions Commonly Used,** ed.by Jean A. T. Pennington, PhD, RD., 15th Edition, 1989. **Nutritive Value of Foods,** USDA, Home & Garden Bulletin # 72

Better Than Milk Combo
Barley Nut Waffles
Very Berry Fruit Soup
"Instant" Whipped Topping
Scrambled Tofu "Eggs"
Breakfast Banana Crisp

A
Breakfast
Bash

Featuring

Waffles, french toast, scrambled "eggs", fruit
soups, and more. Breakfast is the most
important meal of the day. It can also be the
healthiest when it is low in fat and cholesterol
free. Start your day out right. Try a wide
selection of fabulous and delightfully healthy
recipes.

HEARTY "MULTI-GRAIN" WAFFLES

2¾ c	Water		1/4 c	Honey
1½ c	Old fashioned oats		2 T	Sunflower seeds
1 c	Rolled barley		1 T	Canola oil
3/4 c	Cornmeal		2 tsp	Maple flavoring
2/3 c	Wheat germ		2 tsp	Vanilla
1/2 c	Better Than Milk™ powder		1 tsp	Salt
1/4 c	Pecans or walnuts			

Combine all ingredients in a blender and process until smooth and creamy. Let stand to thicken while waffle iron is heating. If your waffle iron has a temperature control knob, set a little below the regular waffle setting to allow waffles to bake a few minutes longer than egg waffles. Blend batter again briefly and pour into a waffle iron which has been coated with no-stick cooking spray. Bake waffles 11 minutes or until golden brown. Set waffles on a cooling rack a few minutes before serving.

Tip: Store extra waffles in the refrigerator or freezer. To reheat, just toast in an oven or toaster until hot and crispy.

Yield: 10 (4 inch square) waffles

BARLEY NUT WAFFLES

2 c	Water		1/4 c	Corn meal
1½ c	Rolled barley		1/4 c	Pure maple syrup
1/2 c	Old fashioned oats		1 T	Canola oil
1/2 c	Better Than Milk™ powder		2 tsp	Vanilla
1/2 c	Almonds, slivered		1 tsp	Maple flavoring
1/2 c	Wheat bran		1 tsp	Salt
1/4 c	Raw wheat germ		1/2 tsp	Walnut flavoring

Combine all ingredients in a blender and process on high speed until smooth. Pre-heat a waffle iron, coat surface with a no-stick cooking spray and pour batter into the center of the waffle iron. Spread batter out to the edges. Gently close the lid and cook 10 minutes. (Don't peak.) Serve with fruit soup, nut butter and applesauce or your favorite topping.

Yield: 8 (4 inch square) waffles

LIGHT 'N CRISPY
OAT WAFFLES

2 ¼ c   Water
2 c   Quick oats
1/3 c   Barley flour
1/4 c   Raw wheat germ
1/4 c   Cornmeal
1/4 c   Raw cashew pieces

1/4 c   Sucanat
1 T   Canola oil
2 tsp   Vanilla, natural
1½ tsp Maple flavoring
3/4 tsp Salt

In a blender, combine all ingredients and process on high speed until smooth and creamy. Allow to sit about 5 minutes while you pre-heat the waffle iron. Spray the waffle iron with no-stick cooking spray and then pour batter into the center of the iron and fill out to the edges. Bake 12 minutes. Cool on a baker's rack several minutes before serving for crispier waffles.

Yield: 8 (4 inch square) waffles

SOY-OAT WAFFLES

1 c   Soaked soybeans (1/2 c dry)
5 c   Water
4½ c   Quick oats
1/2 c   Cornmeal
1/2 c   Seven grain cereal, uncooked
1/3 c   Date sugar

1/4 c   Whole wheat flour
1/4 c   Pecans or walnuts
1 T   Canola oil
1 T   Vanilla
2 tsp   Salt
2 tsp   Maple flavoring

Cover soybeans with water and soak overnight. (This step can be done in advance and you can keep drained soybeans in your freezer until needed.) Drain and discard water, then proceed with the recipe. In a blender, combine half of all ingredients at a time and process until smooth. Mix both batters together in a large pitcher for pouring convenience. Bake waffles 11 minutes. Set waffles on a cooling rack a few minutes before serving.

Yield: 16 (4 inch square) waffles

CASHEW-BANANA
FRENCH TOAST

1 c	Water	1 T	Frozen O.J. concentrate
2/3 c	Raw cashews	1/2 tsp	Salt
1/2 med	Ripe banana	1/2 tsp	Vanilla
1/4 c	Unbleached flour	1/4 tsp	Cinnamon (opt)
1 T	Honey	8 slices	Whole grain bread

Combine all ingredients, except bread, in a blender and process on high speed until smooth and creamy. Pour mixture into a shallow bowl. Lightly oil or coat a non-stick griddle or frying pan with no-stick cooking spray. Quickly dip and coat both sides of sliced bread with the batter. Fry over med-lo temperature. Avoid turning until first side is well "set" and golden brown. If French toast seems too "soggy", lightly toast bread before dipping into batter. Or, as another method, dip frozen bread slices. Older bread which has become dry also works great in this recipe. Serve with fruit soup, applesauce, "all-fruit" jam or topping of choice.

Yield: 8 slices

CASHEW-APPLE
FRENCH TOAST

1 c	Water	1 T	Apple juice concentrate
2/3 c	Raw cashews	1/2 tsp	Salt
1/2 med	Apple	1/2 tsp	Vanilla
1/4 c	Unbleached flour	1/4 tsp	Cinnamon
1 T	Honey	8 slices	Apple or raisin bread

Combine all ingredients, except bread, in a blender and process on high speed until smooth and creamy. Pour mixture into a shallow bowl. Lightly oil or coat a non-stick griddle or frying pan with no-stick cooking spray. Quickly dip and coat both sides of sliced bread with the batter. Fry over med-lo temperature. Avoid turning until first side is well "set" and golden brown. If French toast seems too "soggy", lightly toast bread before dipping into batter. Or, as another method, dip frozen bread slices. Older bread which has become dry also works great in this recipe. Serve with fruit soup, applesauce, "all-fruit" jam or topping of choice.

Yield: 8 slices

VERY BERRY FRUIT SOUP

12 oz	Chiquita® "Raspberry Passion" (frozen juice concentrate)	3 T	Cornstarch (or) tapioca powder
2 tsp	Vanilla	4 c	Frozen mixed berries
16 oz	Peaches, canned unsweetened drained (reserve juice)		(Blueberries, strawberries blackberries, raspberries)
1 c	Pineapple chunks, unsweetened drained (reserve juice)	2	Bananas, sliced

Combine the juice concentrate, vanilla, and the reserved fruit juice from the cans of pineapple and peaches in a large saucepan. Add cornstarch and stir to dissolve starch. Bring to a boil over med-hi heat, stirring mixture constantly. Reduce heat, continue stirring and simmer until juice thickens and clears. Stir in the frozen and canned fruits. Return to a boil and cook 2 or 3 minutes longer. Remove from heat and allow to cool 5 min. Add sliced bananas before serving. Serve over waffles, pancakes or toast. Garnish with coconut and/or "Instant" Whipped Topping (recipe on p 64) if desired.

Yield: 12 c

TROPICAL FRUIT SOUP

12 oz	Dole® "Pineapple-Banana" (frozen juice concentrate)	4 c	Aloha Blend® deluxe (frozen mixed fruit)
1¼ c	White grape juice	2	Bananas, sliced
2 tsp	Vanilla	2	Kiwi, sliced
3+ T	Cornstarch or tapioca starch		

Combine the juice concentrate, white grape juice, vanilla, and cornstarch in a large saucepan. Stir to dissolve starch. Bring to a boil, stirring constantly. Reduce heat to simmer and continue stirring until mixture clears and thickens. Cut frozen fruit into smaller chunks. Add frozen fruit to the juice mixture and cook a few minutes more. Stir in sliced bananas and kiwi last before serving. Serve over waffles, pancakes or toast. Garnish with coconut and/or Whipped Topping (see recipe on page 64) if desired.

Yield: 10 c

"INSTANT" WHIPPED TOPPING

1½ c	Water	1/3 c	Canned coconut milk
2/3 c	Better Than Milk™ powder		"lite" (unsweetened)
1/2 c	Blanched almonds (w/o skins)	2 tsp	Vanilla, (natural)
3½ T	Emes Kosher-Jel®, plain	1/4 tsp	Salt
3 T	Honey or powdered sugar		Ice

In a blender, combine the water, milk powder, almonds and Emes Jel and process until the almonds are liquefied completely. Add remaining ingredients and process briefly. Finally, begin adding ice slowly through the lid spout and continue processing on high speed to make a total volume equal to 5 cups. Turn blender off and wait briefly. Mixture should now be light and fluffy. Best served immediately. If stored, and mixture becomes too firm, hand whip or beat gently with an electric beater before serving.

Yield: 5 c

MILLET PORRIDGE

4 c	Water	1/2 c	Coconut, grated
1 c	Millet	1/2 c	Chopped dates
1 tsp	Salt	2 tsp	Vanilla, natural

In a saucepan, combine water, millet and salt. Bring to a boil, stirring constantly. Reduce heat, cover and simmer 30 minutes. Add remaining ingredients and simmer 10 minutes more. Garnish with granola if desired.

Variation: Add 1 c diced apples.

Yield: 6 c

PRACTICALLY PERFECT STUFFED PRUNES

1 bag Sunsweet®"Orange Essence" prunes   2 c English walnut halves

Press walnut halves into the hollow side section of each prune and enjoy!

Tip: To serve as hors d'oeuvres, place prunes on a paper doily and a silver platter.

Yield: 40 stuffed prunes

FRUIT-FILLED
SWEET ROLLS AND BRAIDS

DOUGH:

1 c	Warm water	1 tsp	Salt
2 T	Honey	1-1½ c	Whole wheat flour
2 tsp	Yeast	1 c	Unbleached white flour
1/2 c	Whole wheat flour	1/4 c	Quick oats
4 tsp	Canola oil	1 tsp	Vital wheat gluten

In a bowl, combine water, honey, yeast and 1/2 c flour to make a "sponge". Let rest 15 minutes. Stir in oil and salt then remaining ingredients. Turn out onto a lightly floured surface and knead well, about 10 minutes. Cover and let rise 10 minutes. Then proceed with recipe below.

FILLING:

1 c	Dates (or favorite dried fruit)	1/2 c	Raisins or currants
3/4 c	Water	1 tsp	Maple sprinkles(opt)
1/2 c	Pecans or walnuts, chopped	1/4 tsp	Cinnamon

In a saucepan, simmer dates in water until soft. Cool. Transfer to a blender and process on medium speed until smooth. Set remaining ingredients aside.

SWEET ROLLS: Place dough on a floured surface and roll it out into a 9 x 15 rectangle and about 1/4 inch thick. Spread date purée over flattened dough to within 1/2 inch of edges. Sprinkle generously with nuts, raisins, maple and/or cinnamon flavorings. Roll up and pinch seams together. Cut into 1 inch slices and place on a cookie sheet sprayed with non-stick cooking spray. Let rise 15 minutes or until double. Bake at 350° F, 25 to 30 minutes. While hot from the oven, brush rolls with apple or white grape juice concentrate to give rolls a "glazed" look.

Yield: 16 rolls

DATE-NUT BRAID: Place dough on a floured surface and roll it out into a 9 x 15 rectangle and about 1/4 inch thick. Transfer dough rectangle to a cookie sheet sprayed with no-stick cooking spray. Spread date purée down center third of the flattened dough. Sprinkle generously with nuts, raisins, maple and/or cinnamon flavorings. Using shears or a sharp knife, cut diagonal strips in dough, at 2-inch intervals on each side of filling. Starting at one end, fold strips alternately from each side to make a criss-cross braid. Tuck under any excess dough at the end. Let rise until double. Bake at 350° F, 35 minutes.

Yield: 16 inch bread braid

SCRAMBLED TOFU "EGGS"

1 lb	Fresh tofu, firm	1 T	Nutritional yeast flakes
1/2 c	Onions, chopped	1/2 tsp	Salt (scant)
1/2 c	Mushrooms, sliced	1/2 tsp	Onion powder
1/4 c	Bell peppers, chopped	1/4 tsp	Garlic powder
2 T	Fresh chives, sliced	1/8 tsp	Turmeric (or less for a
1 T	Canola or olive oil		lighter yellow color)
2 tsp	Chicken-Style Seasoning		

Crumble tofu into chunks and set aside to drain. In a large skillet, sauté fresh vegetables in oil until soft. Add tofu to skillet. Combine spices and sprinkle evenly over tofu. Mix well. Cook scrambled "eggs" over medium heat 5-10 minutes or until liquids evaporate and yellow color becomes prominent.

Yield: 4 c

CREAMED TOFU "EGGS"
Over Toast

1 recipe	Scrambled Tofu "Eggs" (see above)	1 recipe	Jiffy Mushroom Soup (see p 201)

Prepare Scrambled "Eggs" according to directions, with or without vegetables added. In a large saucepan, prepare Jiffy Mushroom Soup. Add "eggs" to the soup and mix well to combine both recipes. Reheat and serve over toast, English muffins, biscuits or rice as preferred.

Yield: 7 c

HASHBROWNS

4 c	Raw potatoes, shredded	1 T	Nutritional yeast flakes
2 T	Olive oil	1½ tsp	Garlic salt
2 T	Dried parsley	1/2 tsp	Chicken-style seasoning
1 T	Onion powder	1/2 tsp	Spike® (or)
1 T	Fresh chives		Nature's Blend (p 67)

Rinse shredded potatoes in a colander and drain well. Mix all ingredients together. Pour hashbrowns into a non-stick frying pan and cook over medium heat 10 to 15 minutes stirring every 2 minutes until browned.

Yield: 4 c

NATURE'S BLEND
ALL PURPOSE HERBAL SEASONING

2 T	Granulated onion	1 tsp	Parsley
2 T	Beef-Style Seasoning	1 tsp	Savory
2 T	Sesame seeds	1 tsp	Coriander
4 tsp	Garlic salt	1/2 tsp	Marjoram
2 tsp	Basil	1/2 tsp	Sucanat
1 tsp	Oregano	1/4 tsp	Ground orange peel

Combine all dried herbs in a jar or an air tight container and shake to mix well. Keep out of light or store in the refrigerator.

Yield: 1 1/8 c

"QUICK" VINEGARLESS KETCHUP

1½ c	Tomato sauce	2 T	Fruit-Fresh®, powder
1 c	Tomato paste		(or) 1/8 tsp citric acid
1/2 c	Pineapple juice	1½ tsp	Salt
1/4 c	Fresh lemon juice	1 tsp	Onion powder
1 tsp	Lime juice	1/2 tsp	Garlic salt
3 T	Date butter (p 211)	1/2 tsp	Paprika
2 T	Pineapple/orange juice	1/4 tsp	Worcestershire sauce (opt)
	(frozen concentrate)		(Vegetarian brand)
2 T	Honey		

Combine all ingredients in a blender and process until smooth. Refrigerate. Freeze extras not used within two weeks.

Variation: For a thicker ketchup, decrease tomato sauce to 1 c and increase tomato paste to 1½ c.

Yield: 4 c

COUNTRY BISCUITS
"Yeast raised"

1½ c	Warm water	1½ c	Whole wheat pastry flour
1 T	Rapid-rise yeast	2/3 c	Soy Supreme®, powder
6 T	Canola oil (1/3 c + 1 T)		(May also use Soyagen)
2 c	Unbleached white flour	2 tsp	Salt

In a large bowl, combine water, yeast and oil. In a separate bowl, combine dry ingredients. Pour wet ingredients into dry ingredients and stir quickly but as little as possible until dough is well moistened and holds together. Mixture will be a bit sticky and look "fluffy". Turn out onto a well floured board. Push together into a ball but do not knead mixture. With a floured rolling pin, roll out 1 inch thick and cut with a biscuit cutter. Place biscuits side by side or up to 1/2 inch apart on a cookie sheet coated with a no-stick cooking spray. Let rise in a warm oven 1/4 inch only. (No more than this or biscuits will have a bun texture.) Do not remove biscuits from oven and turn heat on to 425° F. Bake until golden brown or about 10 to 12 minutes.

Note: For a crisp crust, place biscuits in a paper bag, sprinkle with water and place in a warm oven before serving.

Yield: 2 dozen

SAUSAGE-STYLE GRAVY

2½ c	Water	1/4 c	Cornstarch
3/4 tsp	Salt	1 T	Beef-style Seasoning
1 c	Water	3/4 c	Vegan Sausage Crumbles
1/2 c	Raw cashews	1 T	Fresh chives

Combine 2 ½ c water and salt in a large saucepan. In a blender, combine 1 c water, cashews, cornstarch and beef-style seasoning and process until smooth and creamy. Add blender ingredients to the pot of salt water and bring to a boil stirring constantly. Add sausage crumbles and cook until thick and creamy. Add chives and cook one more minute. Serve over biscuits or toast.

Variation: For a burger-style gravy, replace Sausage Crumbles with Burger Crumbles or Ground Meatless.

Yield: 5 c

BREAKFAST SCONES

1 c	Quick oats	4 tsp	Active dry yeast
1 c	Hot water	1/2 c	Warm water
1/4 c	Canola oil	1½ c	Whole wheat flour
1/4 c	Better Than Milk™ powder	1¼ c	Unbleached white flour
2 T	Brown sugar or Sucanat	1/2 c	Raisins or currants (opt)
1 tsp	Salt		

Combine oats, hot water, oil, milk powder, sweetener and salt in a bowl and soak about 30 minutes. Dissolve yeast in the warm water and add to the oat mixture. Combine the two flours. Take out 1/4 c of the flour mixture and spread it out on a clean counter or a kneading board. Add remaining flour and raisins to the oat mixture and stir to form a large ball. Place dough on the floured surface and knead briefly and gently to coat all sides with flour. Roll dough out with a rolling pin to 3/4 inch thickness or into a 10 inch diameter circle. Coat a cookie sheet with no-stick cooking spray. Cut dough with a biscuit cutter, shape into scones and position each one about 1 inch apart on the cookie sheet. Let scones rise about 10 minutes. Bake at 350° F, 25 to 30 minutes or until lightly browned and scones sound hollow when tapped. Cool. Store in an air tight container.

Tip: Scones can be made ahead several days. Wrap in foil and reheat before serving. Scones are also great in lunches to go or traveling.

Yield: 18

HOMEMADE MUESLI

6 c	Low sugar "flake" cereal	1/2 c	Raw sunflower seeds
	(multigrain, bran or corn flakes, etc)	1/2 c	Pecans, chopped
2 c	Barley flakes or rolled oats	1/2 c	Coconut flakes (opt)
1/2 c	Raisins		(Unsweetened)
1/2 c	Dates, chopped		

Choose your favorite "flake" cereal or any combination of several low fat and low sugar dry cereals in a bowl. Then add all remaining ingredients and store in an air-tight container. Serve with milk alternative beverage of choice. If a sweeter cereal is desired, add fresh fruits such as bananas and peaches or drizzle with honey or brown rice syrup.

Yield: 11 c

"HEART SMART" GRANOLA

6 c	Quick oats	1/2 c	Honey
1 c	Oat bran	1/2 c	Water
1 c	Better Than Milk™ powder	2 tsp	Vanilla, natural
1/3 c	Sliced almonds or walnuts	1 tsp	Maple flavoring(opt)
2 T	Sesame seeds		

Combine oats, oat bran, milk powder, nuts and seeds. In a separate bowl, combine honey, water and flavorings. Pour liquids over oat mixture and mix until evenly moistened. Coat two cookie sheets with no-stick cooking spray and spread granola out evenly over both cookie sheets. Do not mash or press granola down. Bake at 225° F 1½ hours, stirring every 30 minutes. Cool completely before storing.

Variation: Replace half the water with apple juice for a fruitier flavor. May reduce honey to 1/3 c but replace it with equal proportions of water.

Yield: 9 c

FRUIT-SWEETENED GRANOLA

DRY INGREDIENTS:

6 c	Rolled grains, any combination (Oats, barley, wheat)	1 c	Almonds, sliced or slivered
1 c	Whole grain flour	1 c	Sesame seeds
1/2 c	Pecans or walnuts, chopped	1 c	Coconut flakes (opt)

BLENDER INGREDIENTS:

3/4 c	Water	2 med	Bananas, ripe
1/2 c	Frozen apple juice (Concentrate)	1 T	Vanilla
		1½ tsp	Maple flavoring
1/2 c	Raw cashews	1 tsp	Salt
1/2 c	Dates		

Combine dry ingredients in a large bowl. Combine blender ingredients and process until smooth and creamy. Pour liquid over dry ingredients. Stir and mix together with hands until entire mixture is evenly moistened and crumbly. Spread granola out on cookie sheets. Bake 2 to 3 hours at 225°F, stirring mixture every 45 minutes until lightly browned. Cool completely before storing. Granola becomes more crisp as it cools.

Yield: 12 c

HONEY GRANOLA

DRY INGREDIENTS:

3 c	Quick oats	1 c	Wheat Germ
2 c	Rolled barley flakes	1 c	Almonds, sliced
1 c	Rolled wheat flakes	1/2 c	Pecans, chopped
1 c	Better Than Milk™ powder	1/2 c	Sesame seeds
1 c	Whole wheat flour	1 c	Coconut, shredded (opt)

LIQUID INGREDIENTS:

3/4 c	Hot water	1 T	Vanilla
3/4 c	Creamy "spun" honey	1 tsp	Maple flavoring
1/2 c	Canola oil	1/2 tsp	Salt (opt)

Combine dry ingredients in a large bowl. Combine liquid ingredients and pour over dry ingredients. Stir and mix together with hands until entire mixture is evenly moistened and crumbly. Spread granola out on 2 cookie sheets. Bake for 2 to 3 hours at 225° F, stirring mixture every 45 minutes until dry or very lightly browned. Remove from oven and cool completely before storing. Granola becomes more crisp as it cools.

Yield: 10 c

BREAKFAST BANANA CRISP

4 c	Water	1½ tsp	Salt
1 c	Millet	1 tsp	Grated lemon zest
12 oz	Pineapple juice	3 T	Tofu milk powder
	(Frozen concentrate)	4 c	Sliced Bananas
12 oz	Water	4 c	Granola, low fat
1 T	Cook's® Vanilla, powder		
	(or use 1½ tsp clear vanilla)		

In a saucepan, combine 4 c water and millet. Bring to a boil. Reduce heat, cover and simmer 20-25 minutes until millet is soft. Remove from heat. Combine pineapple juice concentrate and water for a 1:1 ratio dilution. In a blender, combine half of the cooked millet, juice mixture, vanilla, salt lemon zest and milk powder and process on high speed until creamy. Pour mixture out into a bowl and repeat procedure for the remaining half of ingredients. Place 2 c granola on the bottom of a 9" x 13" pan. Layer enough bananas over top of granola to cover. Pour 1/3 millet cream over the bananas. Repeat layering of bananas and cream procedure two more times. Top with remaining 2 c granola.

Yield: 12 c

BETTER MILK COMBO

1/2 c	Better Than Milk™ powder	1 c	West Soy® "Plus" milk
3 T	DariFree® potato milk powder	5 c	Water

In a blender, combine all ingredients and process until well mixed. Refrigerate until cold before serving. Stir again each time before serving.

Note: Decrease water to 4½ c for a richer flavor. May also use any brand "ready to drink" soy milk. For a "creamier" milk taste, process milk powders in the blender with 1 c "warm" water before adding remaining 4 c water and soy milk.

Yield: 6 c

BASIC NUT MILK

1 c	Water	4 c	Water
3/4 c	Raw nuts, (cashews	1 tsp	Vanilla
	almonds, pecans, etc.)	1/4 tsp	Salt
1 or 2 T	Honey		

In a blender, combine 1 c water with nuts and process on high speed several minutes until completely liquefied or no longer "gritty". Stop blender and add remaining ingredients. Blend briefly. Pour into a pitcher and chill and stir again before serving.

Tip: Pour milk through a cheese cloth to remove extra pulp to produce a thinner consistency. Use pulp in casseroles, cookies or pie crusts.

Yield: 6 c (scant)

CAROB-PECAN MILK

1 recipe	Basic "Pecan" Milk (see above)	1/2 tsp	Maple flavoring
3 T	Sucanat	1/2 tsp	Coffee substitute
1/4 c	Carob powder		(optional)
1/3 c	Better Than Milk powder (opt)		i.e. Roma, Caffix

Combine above ingredients in a blender and process until well mixed.

Note: Add 3 cups Dari-Free or Better than Milk to above recipe to decrease fat grams per serving.

Yield: 6 ½ c

Sweetheart's Banquet

Featuring

French Cuisine. Prepare a candlelight dinner for two, ideal for any special occasion. Show your valentine how much you care by sharing a beautifully presented meal and by expressing your concern for the health of the one you love.

NON-DAIRY OAT CRÊPES

2 c	Tofu or soy milk	1 T	Canola oil
3/4 c	Whole wheat pastry flour	1 tsp	Honey
3/4 c	Quick oats	1/2 tsp	Salt
1 T	ENER-G® Egg Replacer		

Combine all ingredients in a blender and process until smooth. Let stand 10 minutes. Cook according to electric crêpe pan instructions. Or, coat a 10 inch non-stick frying pan with no-stick cooking spray. Preheat pan over med-hi heat. Remove pan from heat and pour a scant 1/3 c batter into the middle of the pan. Quickly tilt the pan in a circular motion until the batter evenly forms an 8-inch crêpe. Return the pan to the heat for about 1 minute or until the bottom of the crêpe is lightly browned. Flip the crêpe over and lightly brown the other side for about 30 seconds.

Yield: 12 crêpes

ASPARAGUS-ALMOND CRÊPES

5 c	Frozen asparagus "cuts" or "tips"	1 T	Onion powder
1 med	Onion, chopped	1 T	Nutritional yeast flakes
1/2 c	Water	1 tsp	Salt
4 c	Almond cream (see p 77)	1 T	Fresh lemon juice
1/2 c	Flour		Paprika to garnish
2 T	McKay's® Chicken-Style Seasoning		

Simmer asparagus and onion in water for 10 minutes or until onion is translucent. Meanwhile, prepare almond cream. Combine almond cream, flour, seasonings, and lemon juice and mix together well. Reserve 1/2 c milk sauce and set aside to be used later for topping. Add remaining milk sauce to cooked asparagus, bring to a boil and cook 1 or 2 minutes until thick. Spoon filling into crêpes and roll up. Place seam side down in a baking dish sprayed with no-stick cooking spray. Cook reserved milk sauce until thick. Pour sauce down center of crêpes. Garnish with paprika and serve.

Yield: 12 crêpes

ALMOND CREAM

3 1/2 c	Water	1 tsp	Vanilla
2/3 c	Blanched almonds (w/o skins)	1/4 tsp	Salt

In a blender, combine enough water to cover almonds (about 1 c) and process until thoroughly liquefied. Add remaining water (plus or minus to make a total volume of 4 c), salt and vanilla and blend well.

Yield: 4 c

SPINACH-POTATO CRÊPES

1 c	Fresh cooked spinach	1 tsp	Seasoned salt
1 c	Raw shredded potatoes	1/2 tsp	Savory
1/2 c	Onions, chopped	1/2 tsp	Chicken-style seasoning
1 clove	Garlic, minced	1/2 c	Jack Cheese Sauce
2 T	Olive oil		Paprika to garnish

Drain cooked spinach, squeeze out excess liquid, chop finely and set aside. Shred and rinse potatoes. Drain well. Using a non-stick frying pan, sauté potatoes, onions, and garlic in oil. While the vegetables are cooking, add seasoned salt, savory and chicken flavored seasoning. When vegetables are tender, add spinach and continue cooking over med-lo heat 5 minutes longer. Stir in 1/2 c cheese sauce (see recipe below) and mix until well blended. Spoon filling into crêpes and roll up. Place seam side down in an oblong baking dish. Garnish with more cheese sauce and paprika. Serve immediately or cover with foil and keep in a warm oven until ready to use.

Variation: If preferred, replace spinach with chopped broccoli florets.

Yield: 12 crêpes

JACK CHEESE SAUCE

1 c	Water	1½ T	Fresh lemon juice
1 c	Cooked brown or white rice	1½ tsp	Salt
1/2 c	Raw cashews, rinsed	1 tsp	Onion powder
1 T	Nutritional yeast flakes	1/4 tsp	Garlic powder

In a blender, combine water, rice and cashews and process until smooth and creamy. Add remaining ingredients and blend well.

Yield: 2 c

"CHICKEN"-MUSHROOM CRÊPES

3 c   Creamy Mushroom Sauce *
3/4 c Sour Cream Supreme *
2 T   Olive oil
2 c   Chic-Ketts®, diced
1 c   Spanish onions, chopped

2 cloves   Garlic, minced
1 c   Fresh mushrooms, sliced
1/2 tsp   Beef-style seasoning
1/2 c   Jicama, julienned
Paprika to garnish

Prepare Mushroom Sauce and Sour Cream Supreme (* see recipes following) and set aside. Sauté Chic-Ketts, onions, garlic, mushrooms and beef-style seasoning together in olive oil until vegetables are tender. Combine mushroom sauce and sour cream. Pour 2½ c sauce mixture over Chic-Ketts and vegetables. Reserve remaining sauce and set aside. Add jicama and stir all together well. Spoon filling into crêpes and roll up. Place seam side down in an oblong baking dish coated with no-stick cooking spray. Pour reserved mushroom sauce down center of crêpes. Cover with foil and bake at 325° F, 10 to 15 minutes. Garnish with paprika before serving.

Yield: 12 crêpes

CREAMY MUSHROOM SAUCE

1½ c   Onion, chopped
2 T   Olive oil
2 c   Fresh mushrooms
1 c   Water
1/4 tsp Onion salt
3 c   Water

2/3 c   Unbleached white flour
1/3 c   Better Than Milk™ powder
2 tsp   Nutritional yeast flakes
2 tsp   Chicken-style seasoning
1½ tsp   Salt
1/2 tsp   Sweet basil, dry

Sauté onions in oil until golden. Coarse chop mushrooms and add to the onions with 1 c water and onion salt and simmer until mushrooms are tender. Set aside 1c sautéed mushrooms. In a blender, combine 3 c water, flour, milk powder, and seasonings and process until smooth and creamy. Add reserved 1 c mushrooms to the blender and "flash blend" ingredients together a few times. Pour blender ingredients into a saucepan and bring to a boil stirring constantly until thickened. Stir remaining onion and mushroom mixture into sauce and mix all together well.

Yield: 4 c

SOUR CREAM SUPREME

1¼ c	Mori-Nu® Tofu, firm, 10.5 oz box		1 tsp	Honey
1/4 c	Sunflower oil		1/2 tsp	Salt
2 ½ T	Fresh lemon juice			

In a blender, process all ingredients until smooth and creamy.

Yield: 1½ c

CHAMPAGNE CHICKEN

1/2 roll	Chic-Ketts (16 oz size)		2 ½ c	Fresh mushrooms
1 or 2 T	Olive oil			

Sauté Chic-Ketts in oil until nicely browned. Add mushrooms and sauté until tender.

GRAVY:

3 c	Water		3 T	Bragg® Liquid Aminos
1/2 c	Raw cashews, rinsed		1½ T	Nutritional yeast flakes
1/3 c	Better Than Milk™, powder		1 T	Onion powder
3 T	Cornstarch		1 T	Chicken-style seasoning

In a blender, process cashews with only 1 cup of the water until very smooth. Add remaining water and other ingredients and continue blending until thoroughly mixed. Pour over Chic-Ketts and mushroom mixture and simmer until thickened.

CHAMPAGNE:
1/4 c   Non-alcoholic champagne (Catawba)

Pour Catawba into gravy/Chik-Ketts mixture and mix well. Serve hot with rice.

Yield: 8 c

GREEN BEANS ALMONDINE

1 lb Fresh or frozen green beans	1 T Nutritional yeast flakes
(opt) Salt or garlic salt to taste	1 T Sesame seeds
1/3 c Sliced or slivered almonds	

Snap or french cut green beans. Simmer, covered, in a large skillet with a small amount of water until tender. Sprinkle lightly with salt if desired. Meanwhile, prepare almonds by placing them on a cookie sheet in the oven and toasting lightly at 250° F, or in a frying pan without oil over med-lo heat, stirring often until light brown. Watch carefully to prevent burning. When beans have completed cooking, add yeast to water remaining in the skillet and stir until dissolved. Add more water if necessary until it has the appearance of melted butter. Spoon green beans into a shallow serving dish and garnish with almonds and sesame seeds.

Yield: 4 c

RICE-BARLEY PILAF

3 c	Water	1/4 c	Toasted wheat germ
1 c	Brown rice	1/2 tsp	Beef-style seasoning
1 tsp	Salt	1/2 tsp	Chicken-style seasoning
1/3 c	Barley, whole grain	2 T	Fresh parsley, snipped
1 c	Onion, finely chopped	1/3 c	Sliced almonds, lightly toasted
1 c	Celery, finely chopped	2 T	Toasted sesame seeds
1 c	Carrots, shredded	(opt)	SoyCo® Lite & Less™ - Grated
2 T	Olive oil		Parmesan Cheese Alternative

In a medium saucepan, bring water to boiling. Add rice and salt; return to boiling. Reduce heat, cover and simmer 15 minutes. Then add barley to the rice and continue cooking 15 minutes more. Do not drain. Meanwhile, sauté onions, celery, and carrots in olive oil until tender. Combine undrained rice-barley mixture, vegetables, wheat germ, beef and chicken-style seasonings. Pour into a large casserole dish coated with no-stick cooking spray. Bake uncovered at 350° F, 20 minutes or until grains are tender and lightly browned. Fluff with a fork and stir in parsley. Garnish with almonds, sesame seeds, and (opt) SoyCo Parmesan Cheese Alternative for added flavor.

Yield: 6 c

FRENCH ONION SOUP

2 lg	Spanish onions, sliced	2 T	Bragg® Liquid Aminos
3 T	Olive or canola oil	2 T	Beef-style seasoning
4 c	Water	1 env	Lipton® Onion Soup Mix
1/2 c	Ginger ale	1 T	Flour, browned
1/2 tsp	Worcestershire sauce -		Alpine cheese *
	(no anchovy-vegetarian brand)		

In a saucepan, sauté onions in oil until golden brown. Combine all liquid ingredients and set aside. Combine all dry ingredients in a separate bowl. Slowly pour liquids into dry ingredients stirring until well mixed. Pour into onions and simmer 5 minutes stirring frequently until thoroughly blended. Fill soup mugs and top with a slice of toasted french bread and Alpine cheese (see recipe below) and broil 1 to 2 minutes until cheese is bubbly. Or, toast bread on a cookie sheet. Remove from oven and place a slice of Alpine cheese over bread. Return to oven and bake at 350° F, 5 minutes or until cheese is melted and bubbly. Drop one slice of bread into each bowl and serve immediately.

Yield: 7 c

ALPINE CHEESE

1 c	Water	1 T	Nutritional yeast flakes
1 c	Cooked white or brown rice	1 T	Fresh lemon juice
1/2 c	Raw cashews, rinsed	1½ tsp	Salt
1/2 c	Ginger ale	1 tsp	Onion powder
3 T	Emes Kosher-Jel®, plain	1/4 tsp	Garlic powder

In a blender, combine water, rice, cashews, ginger ale and Emes and process on high speed until smooth and creamy. Add remaining ingredients and blend well. Pour into a container coated with no-stick cooking spray. Refrigerate 2 to 4 hours until set. Gently shake out of container and slice as needed.

Yield: 2 ½ c

VEGETABLE BOUQUET
SALAD

12	Cherry tomatoes, halved	4 T	Fresh parsley, chopped
3	Celery stalks, thinly sliced	2 T	Green onion, diced (opt)
3	Carrots, thinly sliced	1 head	Leafy lettuce
2	Cucumbers, thinly sliced	2 c	Alfalfa sprouts

Combine all vegetables except lettuce and sprouts in a large bowl. Chill. Arrange lettuce leaves on a salad plate with the leafy edges facing out. Mound vegetables in center of plate or arrange vegetables in a decorative flower design. Garnish with alfalfa sprouts and additional parsley sprigs. Serve with French, Raspberry Vinaigrette or Thousand Island Dressing (recipes following).

Yield: 12 c

FRENCH DRESSING

1/2 c	Water	1/2 tsp	Salt
3 T	Frozen apple juice concentrate	1/2 tsp	Paprika
3 T	Fresh lemon juice	1/2 tsp	Onion powder
2 T	Tomato purée	1/2 tsp	Garlic, granules
2 T	Orange juice	1/8 tsp	Dill weed (opt)
1/4 tsp	Mixed herbs or salad herbs	1 T	Cornstarch

Mix all ingredients except cornstarch in a blender. Pour mixture into a saucepan. Add cornstarch and stir to dissolve. Bring to a boil to thicken. Remove from heat and chill before serving.

Yield: 1 c

RASPBERRY VINAIGRETTE

Add to one 1.05 oz package Good Seasons ® Fat-Free Italian Dressing Mix:

1/2 c	Water	1/4 c	White grape / raspberry
1/4 c	Fresh lemon juice		(frozen juice concentrate)

Combine all ingredients and stir until well mixed. Refrigerate 30 minutes before using. Stores well up to 2 weeks.

Yield: 1 c

THOUSAND ISLAND DRESSING

1 c	Soy Mayonnaise (p 167)	1/2 c	Quick Vinegarless Ketchup
1/3 c	*Pas* Sweet Pickle Relish,		(see p 67)
	vinegarless	1/2 tsp	Onion powder

Combine all ingredients and chill before serving.

Yield: 2 c (scant)

HOT HERBED GARLIC BREAD

Prepare or purchase "whole wheat" french bread. Slice diagonally into 1 inch wide pieces. Spread the following mixture on each slice.

5 T	Spectrum Naturals®	2 stems	Green onion, finely
	"Non-dairy" Spread™		sliced
1 T	Fresh parsley, minced	1/4 tsp	Garlic powder
2 tsp	Fresh basil, minced (or 1/2 tsp dried)	1/8 tsp	Salt or to taste

Wrap loaf in foil and bake at 400° F, 15 minutes. Open foil and bake an additional 3 to 5 minutes for a crispy crust.

Yield: 1 c

CAROB PUDDING PARFAIT

1¼ c	Mori-Nu® Tofu, x-firm, (10.5 oz)	1/4 c	Carob powder
1 c	Almond Mylk™ (vanilla flavor)	3 T	Cornstarch
1/2 c	Sucanat®	1 tsp	Vanilla

In a blender, combine all ingredients and process until smooth. Pour mixture into a saucepan and simmer until thick. Cool. Refrigerate until set. Spoon alternate layers of pudding and "Instant" Whipped Topping (see p 86) into a parfait glass. Finish layering process with whipped topping on the top layer. If desired, garnish with chopped nuts or a cherry etc.

Variation: Add sliced bananas between the layers of Carob Pudding and "Instant" Whipped Topping for a delicious Carob-Banana Pudding Parfait.

Tip: Mori-Nu® "Lite" Tofu also works well in this recipe.

Yield: 6 parfaits

FRENCH TARTS

TART PASTRY:

1 c	Barley or whole wheat pastry flour	1/4 c	Hot water
1 c	All purpose flour	3 T	Orange juice
1/4 c	Wheat germ	1 T	Honey
1 tsp	Salt	1/2 c	Raw cashew butter
1/4 c	Canola oil		

Combine the flours, wheat germ and salt. In a separate bowl, mix oil, water, orange juice and honey together. Add the cashew butter and stir together until well blended. Pour into the flour mixture and stir until dough is moist. Knead into a ball. Roll out ball between 2 pieces of wax paper. Remove wax paper and cut dough into circles 1 inch larger than tart tins. Press pastry circles into tart tins and crimp edges. Bake at 350° F, 10 to 12 minutes. Cool.

CUSTARD:

2½ c	Water	5 T	Cornstarch
1/2 c	Cooked rice	1/4 c	Grated coconut
1/3 c	Blanched almonds (w/o skins)	1 tsp	Vanilla
1/3 c	Honey	1/4 tsp	Salt
3 T	Better Than Milk™ powder		

In a blender, combine 1/2 the water, rice, almonds, coconut and process until completely smooth. Add remaining water and ingredients and blend well. Pour into a saucepan and bring to a boil, stirring constantly until thick. Fill tart tins 3/4 full and chill. When chilled, garnish with thinly sliced fresh fruits of choice. Pour Berry Shine Glaze (see recipe below) over fruit.

BERRY SHINE GLAZE:

2/3 c	Frozen apple juice concentrate	4 tsp	Cornstarch
1/3 c	Strawberries or raspberries		

In a blender, process all ingredients on high for one minute until creamy. Pour into saucepan and cook over medium-high heat stirring constantly until thick and clear. Cool until lukewarm and pour over fresh fruit. Chill before serving.

Yield: 24 Serving size:

BLUEBERRY YUM YUM

BLUEBERRY FILLING:

4 c	Fresh or frozen blueberries	1/2 c	Water
1 ½ c	Grape juice (frozen) concentrate	1/2 c	Cornstarch
2 T	FruitSource®		

In a saucepan, combine berries, grape juice and FruitSource and bring to a boil. Reduce heat to simmering point. Dissolve cornstarch in water and pour into saucepan, stirring constantly. Cook until mixture thickens and clears. Remove from heat. Refrigerate until cold.

YUMMY FILLING:

3/4 c	Water	1/3 c	Mori-Nu® Tofu, x-firm
1/3 c	Better Than Milk™, powder	2 T	FruitSource
1/4 c	Almond slivered	1 tsp	Natural vanilla flavoring
2 ½ T	Emes Kosher Jel®, plain	1/8 tsp	Salt
1/2 c	Better Than Cream Cheese (Tofutti® or any vegan brand)	2 c	Crushed ice (approx)

In a blender, combine water, milk powder, almonds and Emes. Process until completely liquefied. Add remaining ingredients, except ice, and blend until smooth. Add ice through the lid spout and continue blending until mixture become thick and fluffy.

QUICK GRAHAM CRUST:

1 ½ c	Graham cracker crumbs	3 T	Spectrum® Naturals Spread
1/2 c	Freshly ground pecans		(Margarine alternative)

Combine crust ingredients (adding a little water if necessary) and press into a 9 inch pie pan. Bake at 350° F, 10 minutes. Cool before adding fillings.

METHOD #1
To assemble, pour alternate layers of Blueberry filling and Yummy filling into the graham cracker crust, ending with Yummy filling. Garnish with blueberries or graham cracker crumbs.

METHOD #2
Spoon alternate layers of graham cracker crumbs or granola, Blueberry filling and Yummy filling into parfait glasses, ending with Yummy filling. Garnish with blueberries and mint leaf on top.

Yield: One 9 inch pie (or) 12 parfaits

"INSTANT" WHIPPED TOPPING

1½ c	Water	1/3 c	Canned coconut milk
2/3 c	Better Than Milk™ powder		"lite" (unsweetened)
1/2 c	Blanched almonds (w/o skins)	2 tsp	Vanilla, (natural)
3½ T	Emes Kosher-Jel®, plain	1/4 tsp	Salt
3 T	Honey or powdered sugar		Ice

In a blender, combine the water, milk powder, almonds and Emes Jel and process until the almonds are liquefied completely. Add remaining ingredients and process briefly. Finally, begin adding ice slowly through the lid spout and continue processing on high speed to make a total volume equal to 5 cups. Turn blender off and wait briefly. Mixture should now be light and fluffy. Best served immediately. If stored, and mixture becomes too firm, hand whip or beat gently with an electric beater before serving.

Yield: 5 c

Siew Mai
Baked "Egg" Rolls
Vegetable Fried Rice
Lemon Wonton Soup
Sweet and Sour "Chicken"

A
Taste
of
The Orient

Featuring

A selection of Asian recipes for you
to enjoy which are popular in the
countries of Singapore, China,
Philippines, Guam, and Thailand.

VEGETABLE FRIED RICE
"CHINA"

2 c	Mock duck or braised gluten	2 c	Sugar snap peas, frozen
2 c	Firm tofu, cubed	2 c	Carrots, julienned
1/2 tsp	Sesame oil	1 c	Baby corn, sliced
2 tsp	Soy sauce or Bragg™ aminos	1 tsp	Salt (or) 2 T Bragg™
2 tsp	Cornstarch dissolved in 2 T water	6 c	Cooked brown rice
1 c	Onion, diced	1/4 c	Green onion, diced
2 cloves	Garlic, minced	1/2 c	Roasted cashews
1 T	Olive oil, or water	2 T	Sesame seeds, toasted
1½ c	Jicama, julienned	(opt)	Cherry tomato/parsley

Shred duck or gluten into small bite-size pieces and cube tofu. Place mixture into a non-stick wok or an extra large non-stick frying pan. Combine sesame oil, soy sauce and cornstarch-water. Pour sauce over duck-tofu mixture and set aside 5 minutes to marinate. Sauté mixture until tofu is nicely browned. Add onion, garlic and olive oil and stir-fry entire mixture together over medium heat until onion is transparent. Stir gently to avoid breaking up the tofu cubes. Add jicama, peas, carrots, baby corn and seasoning to the wok mixture and stir-fry 2 to 3 minutes until vegetables are crisp-tender. Stir in the pre-cooked rice and toss until well mixed. (Note: Rice should be light and fluffy-not sticky in this recipe. Instant brown rice works well too. For improved flavor, cook rice with salt according to directions and/or with chicken-style seasoning.) Prepare a large serving platter with a border of lettuce. Mound rice mixture into the center of the platter and garnish with green onion, cashews and sesame seeds. For added color and appeal, arrange fresh parsley, green onions and cherry tomatoes on top and around the border.　　　　　　　　　Yield: 18c

MOCK DUCK IN BLACK BEAN SAUCE
"SINGAPORE"

3 cloves	Garlic, minced	12 pods	Fresh snow peas
1 med	Onion, thinly sliced	1 can	Button mushrooms
1/4 tsp	Fresh ginger, minced	1 can	Mock duck
1/4 c	Black beans, canned	1/2 tsp	Honey
1 T	Olive oil	3 T	Mushroom water

Sauté garlic, onion, ginger, and beans (drained) in oil. Add snow peas and stir-fry one minute. Drain mushrooms (reserve water) and add to the mixture. Slice duck into strips, then add and mix all together well. Stir in honey and water, cover and simmer briefly. Serve with rice or noodles.　　　　　Yield: 5 c

SWEET AND SOUR CHICKEN
"CHINA"

1/2 roll	Chic-Ketts™ (16 oz size)	1 c	Red & green bell peppers
1/4 tsp	Sesame oil	1 med	Carrot
2 tsp	Soy sauce or liquid aminos	1/2 sm	Cucumber
2 tsp	Cornstarch	3 sm	Roma tomatoes
2 T	Water	2 c	Sugar snap peas
1 tsp	Olive oil	1/4 tsp	Salt or to taste
1 recipe	Sweet and Sour Sauce	1 stem	Green onion, diced

Tear Chic-Ketts into large bite-size pieces. Combine sesame oil, soy sauce, cornstarch and water and mix with Chic-Ketts. Allow to marinate for 5 minutes. In a large, non-stick frying pan, brown marinated Chic-Ketts in olive oil and set aside. In a large saucepan, prepare Sweet and Sour Sauce (see recipe below). Cut peppers into chunky pieces. Cut carrot into thin diagonal slices. Add bell peppers and carrots to sauce. Cover and simmer until vegetables are tender. Peel cucumber, then quarter lengthwise. Remove seeds, divide strips in half again and then cut strips into 1 inch sticks. Quarter the tomatoes. Add the cucumber, tomatoes, peas and salt to the Sweet and Sour Sauce. Mix well, cover and simmer briefly. (Peas will lose color if over cooked.) Stir in Chic-Ketts, cover and turn off heat. Remove from heat after 5 minutes. Pour Sweet and Sour "Chicken" into a shallow dish and garnish with a border of lettuce. Sprinkle green onion over the top. Serve with rice.

Note: Tofu, mock duck, homemade gluten or any other vegetarian protein may
be substituted for Chic-Ketts. Yield: 8 c

SWEET AND SOUR SAUCE

2 cloves	Garlic, minced	3 T	Tomato paste
1 1/2 c	Onion, thinly sliced	2 T	Honey or Sucanat®
1 T	Olive oil	1 T	Fresh lemon juice
1 tsp	"Lite" soy sauce	1 T	Cornstarch
1 c	Pineapple juice	3 T	Water
1 c	Pineapple chunks		

In a large saucepan, sauté garlic and onion in oil and soy sauce until onion is transparent. Combine pineapple juice, pineapple chunks, tomato paste, honey and lemon juice and add to the garlic-onion mixture. Cover and bring to a slow boil. Dissolve cornstarch in water and add to the sauce. Stir and simmer until sauce "clears".

Yield: 3c

TOFU FOO YUNG

1 c	Onions, finely sliced		2 T	Bragg Liquid Aminos
1 c	Fresh mushrooms, chopped		1/2 c	Fresh tofu, x-firm
1 c	Snow peas, coarse chopped		3/4 c	Unbleached white flour
1 c	Jicama, julienned		3 T	Nutritional yeast flakes
1/2 c	Bamboo shoots		1 T	ENER-G®Egg Replacer
1 T	Olive oil		2 tsp	ENER-G® Baking Soda
2 c	Bean sprouts, fresh		1/2 tsp	Salt
3½ c	Fresh tofu, x-firm			

In a large skillet or wok, combine onions, mushrooms, peas, jicama, bamboo shoots and olive oil. Sauté over low to medium heat until crisp-tender. Add bean sprouts, stir briefly and remove from heat. In a blender, combine 3½ c tofu and liquid aminos and process until smooth and creamy. Pour out into a large bowl and add 1/2 c tofu, flour, yeast flakes, egg replacer, baking soda and salt. Mash tofu and stir mixture well. Add cooked vegetables to tofu mixture. Coat a cookie sheet with no-stick cooking spray and scoop 1/4 c mixture onto cookie sheet and flatten into a 3 inch circle. Leave a 1 inch space between each one. Bake at 350° F, 30 minutes, flip over and bake 15 minutes more. Serve hot with rice and Mushroom Gravy (recipe below).

Yield: 18 patties

MUSHROOM GRAVY

2 c	Cold water		4 T	"Lite" soy sauce
1/2 c	Fresh mushrooms, diced		2 T	Cornstarch

In a saucepan, combine all ingredients and stir until cornstarch dissolves. Cook over med-lo heat until gravy thickens and clears.

Yield: 2 ¾ c

BROCCOLI-CHEESE
RICE RING

4 c	Cooked rice, unseasoned	1/4 c	Onion, minced
1 tsp	Chicken-style seasoning	1/4 c	Olives, sliced
1/4 tsp	Onion salt	2 T	Mild green chilies,
2 c	Broccoli florets		canned, chopped
1½ c	Pimento cheese (see p 148)	1 T	Pimentos, diced

Combine rice, chicken-style seasoning and onion salt and mix well. Steam broccoli 2 minutes and stir into rice. In a small saucepan, heat cheese until melted. Add onions, olives, green chilies, and pimentos. Pour cheese mixture into rice mixture and stir until evenly coated. Spray a plastic ring mold with no-stick cooking spray. Spoon mixture into the mold, packing lightly. Microwave, uncovered at high power 3½ to 5 minutes or until heated through. If you do not have a rotating tray, rotate mold halfway through cooking time. Cool several minutes and invert onto a round serving platter. May fill center of rice ring with additional steamed broccoli.

Yield: 8 c

PEKING NOODLE STIR-FRY

1 rec	Scrambled Tofu "Eggs" (See recipe on p 66)	1/2 c	Sliced almonds, lightly toasted
8 oz	Vermicelli or linguini noodles, dry, broken in half	2 T	Sesame seeds (or) poppy seeds
1 c	Frozen green "petite" peas (opt)	1/2 tsp	Onion salt (opt)

Prepare "eggs" in a large skillet and set aside. Cook noodles in boiling salted water according to directions on the package. While the noodles are cooking, simmer the green peas in a small amount of water until crisp-tender, (about 2 minutes) and remove from heat and drain. When ready, drain and rinse noodles and toss with a light coating of olive oil. Add noodles to the "eggs" and mix well. Stir in peas, almonds and sesame seeds. Season additionally with onion salt if needed.

Yield: 8 c

ALMOND BROCCOLI
STIR-FRY

4 c	Broccoli, florets	1/2 c	Water
3/4 c	Carrots, thinly sliced	1/8 tsp	Salt

In a large skillet or wok, combine vegetables with water and salt. Cover and bring to a boil, reduce heat and simmer 2 minutes. Remove lid for 30 seconds (to preserve the bright green color of the broccoli), cover again and simmer 2 to 3 minutes more until crisp-tender. Drain water into a bowl and reserve for later use. Cover vegetables and set aside.

1/2 lb	Fresh tofu, extra-firm	2 tsp	Chicken-style seasoning
2 tsp	Olive oil	1 T	Cornstarch
2 c	Onion, thinly sliced	(opt)	Soy sauce to taste
1/2 c	Fresh mushrooms, sliced	1/2 c	Slivered almonds, lightly
1 tsp	Olive oil		toasted
1 c	Reserved stock + water		

Cut tofu into 1/2 inch cubes. In a non-stick frying pan, sauté tofu in 2 tsp oil over medium heat until golden brown on all sides. Add to broccoli. Next, sauté onions and mushrooms in an additional 1 tsp oil until tender and the edges begin to brown. Add to broccoli. Combine reserved cooking water with enough additional water to equal 1 c. Add cornstarch and seasoning and mix well. Pour into frying pan and cook until bubbly and clear. Pour over broccoli mixture. Add almonds and stir-fry to reheat entire mixture before serving.

Yield: 8 c

CABBAGE & WALNUT STIR-FRY

1¼ lb	Cabbage, (½ head)	1/2 c	Water
2 med	Garlic cloves, minced	1/4 c	Fresh parsley, chopped
1 c	Onion, sliced	1/4 c	Walnut pieces
1½ tsp	Olive oil	2 tsp	Chicken-style seasoning

Finely slice and cut cabbage into 1/2 inch pieces and set aside. In a wok or large frying pan, sauté garlic and onion in oil until tender. Add cabbage, water, parsley, walnuts, and seasoning. Stir-fry or simmer about 15 minutes or until cabbage is tender.

Yield: 8 c

SIEW MAI
(Singapore)

1/2 c	Onion, minced	1 T	Sesame oil
1 tsp	Garlic, minced	2 tsp	Dry bread crumbs
1/2 c	Mock duck, finely diced	4 tsp	Cornstarch
1/4 c	Jicama or water chestnuts, diced	1/4 c	Water
1/4 c	Carrot, finely diced (reserve 1 T)	20	Wonton wrappers
1 T	Bragg liquid aminos or		(eggless variety)
	"Lite" soy sauce		

Sauté onion and garlic in a small amount of water until onion is translucent. Add mock duck and jicama or water chestnuts and stir-fry 2 minutes. Add liquid aminos or soy sauce, sesame oil and bread crumbs and mix lightly. Mix cornstarch with water and pour over duck mixture. Remove from heat and stir until well mixed. Lightly moisten round wonton wrapper on the top side. Place about one tablespoon of filling onto the center of each wrapper and press wrapper around the filling. Leave the top open and flatten the base. Press a few diced carrots inside the top for garnish. Place each siew mai on an oiled steamer tray and steam for 7 minutes.

Yield: 20 Pieces

PINAKBET
"PHILIPPINES"

1 c	Firm tofu, cut in strips	2 c	Okra, chopped
4 med	Eggplant, chopped	1 c	Bitter melon (opt)
2 c	Fresh green beans, 2" cuts	1 c	Bell pepper, chopped
2 c	Squash, chopped	1 T	Soy sauce
1 c	Onion, chopped	2 tsp	Salt
2 T	Olive oil	1 tsp	Garlic powder
1/2 c	Water	2 tsp	Cornstarch in 2 T water

Sauté tofu in a non-stick frying pan coated with no-stick cooking spray until lightly browned and set aside. Sauté eggplant, beans, squash and onion in oil. Add water and cover. Cook until vegetables are crisp-tender. Add okra, bitter melon (opt), bell pepper and seasonings and simmer until all vegetables are tender. Add cornstarch-water to thicken sauce if desired. Gently stir in tofu strips. Serve with rice and/or crispy noodles.

Yield: 12 c

PAO
"SINGAPORE"

DOUGH:

1 c + 2 T	Warm water	2 T	Oil
1½ T	Yeast	2 c	Whole wheat flour
2 T	Brown sugar or honey	2½ c	All purpose flour
1 tsp	Salt		

Combine water, yeast and sugar in a bowl and let stand a few minutes until yeast begins to bubble. Add salt and oil to yeast mixture and stir to dissolve the salt. In a separate bowl, combine the two kinds of flour and set 1/2 c aside for later use. Pour yeast mixture into the bowl of flour. Stir with a big wooden spoon until the mixture is too difficult to work. Turn dough out unto a lightly floured surface and knead for about 8 to 10 minutes. Sprinkle additional reserved flour on the surface and onto hands if necessary to prevent sticking. Add more flour only when necessary to make a firm smooth dough. (The dough should be firmer than dough for baking bread.) Place dough in a large bowl, cover it with a damp cloth and let it rise until double in size. Punch the dough down with your fist. Return to the floured surface and knead until smooth. Divide into two parts. Shape each part into a long roll about 1 inch in diameter. Cut each roll into 14 small pieces. Form each roll into a ball. Cover all the rolls as you form them. Start with the first ball that you formed and flatten each ball with the palm of your hand. Roll each ball out into a circle, 3 1/2 inches in diameter. Place 2 tablespoons of Pao Filling (recipe below) into the center of each circle, form into a bun, and pinch top edges together. Place each bun on a piece of wax paper, cover and let buns rise 30 minutes.

PAO FILLING:

1 can	Mock duck, minced	1 c	Jicama, minced
1 can	Mock abalone, minced	4-5 tsp	Soy sauce
1/2 c	Onion (or green onion), minced	3 T	Cornstarch
1 tsp	Sesame oil		

Sauté minced mock duck, mock abalone, and onion in oil. Add jicama and soy sauce and stir-fry briefly. Stir in cornstarch and mix well. Let it cool.

TO STEAM: Arrange buns in a steamer, one inch apart. Bring water to a boil. Steam 12 minutes. Transfer steamed buns to a rack or cloth to cool.

TO BAKE: Arrange buns one inch apart on a cookie sheet coated with no-stick cooking spray. Bake in a pre-heated oven at 350° F, 15 minutes. Cover and cool. If you desire the baked Pao to be as soft as the steamed Pao, store overnight in a plastic zip-lock bag. Yield: 28

FRESH SPRING ROLLS
(POPIAH)
"SINGAPORE"

2 doz   Lumpia wrappers

FILLING:

3/4 lb	Firm tofu, finely diced	1 to 2 c	Green beans, french cut
1 T	Olive oil	1/4 head	Cabbage, finely sliced
1 clove	Garlic, minced	1/2 head	Bangkuang (jicama), minced
1/4	Onion, finely chopped		(or use water chestnuts)
1	Carrot, finely julienned	2 c	Fresh bean sprouts

SEASONING:
1 T   Nutritional yeast flakes
1 T   Soy sauce or Bragg® Liquid Aminos
2 tsp   McKay's Chicken-Style Seasoning (or) use salt to suit taste
1/3 c   Sweet flour sauce (or) molasses seasoned with salt or soy sauce

METHOD:
Brown tofu in a non-stick frying pan with olive oil. Remove tofu and set aside. Sauté garlic and onion. Add carrots, green beans and cabbage, cover and cook 2 or 3 minutes over med-lo heat stirring frequently. Stir in Bangkuang, sprouts and tofu. Add yeast flakes, soy sauce and chicken style seasoning and mix well. Remove from heat. Steam wrappers. Spread 1 tsp sweet sauce down the center of the wrapper. Put a lettuce leaf over the sweet sauce and spoon the filling onto the lettuce. Roll up and cut in half or in thirds. Serve on a bed of lettuce.

Tip: For a healthy sweet sauce, mix date butter with water, salt or soy sauce to taste, and a flour paste of equal parts flour and water. Cook over medium heat until thickened.

Yield: 24

BAKED "EGG" ROLLS

1 tsp	Crushed garlic	1 c	Vegan Burger Crumbles (or)
2 T	Canola oil		Mock duck, chopped
4 c	Carrots, finely julienned	1 T	Instant Clear Jel
4 c	Cabbage, finely sliced	3 T	Water
2 c	Bamboo shoots, julienned	28	Dairy-free egg roll skins
2 T	Soy sauce or liquid aminos		

Sauté garlic in oil. Add carrots, cabbage, bamboo shoots, soy sauce and burger. Stir-fry until crisp tender. Combine Clear Jel and water and mix with beaters until mixture is smooth, then set aside. Place approximately 3 T of filling on each egg roll skin. Roll up firmly halfway, tuck ends under, then continue to roll to the edge. Use a small dab of the clear Jel mixture under the edge to "glue" the end of the wrapper shut. Place on a cookie sheet coated with no-stick cooking spray. Leave space between each egg roll. Spray each egg roll with Pam®. Bake at 350° F, 15 minutes. Remove from oven and turn egg rolls over and spray again. Bake an additional 15 minutes. Serve with Sweet & Sour Dip (see recipe below).

Yield: 28

SWEET & SOUR DIP

1/4 c	Onion, minced	2 T	Honey or brown sugar
1 tsp	Canola oil	1 T	Lemon juice
1 c	Tomato sauce		(or 1/8 tsp citric acid)
1/4 c	Pineapple juice	1/4 tsp	Salt
3 T	Cornstarch		

In a small saucepan, sauté onion in oil or 1 T water until transparent. Combine remaining ingredients in a bowl and stir until cornstarch is dissolved. Add to saucepan and cook over medium heat until clear. Add more pineapple juice or water if sauce is too thick.

Yield: 2 c

RICE VERMICELLI
(BEE HOON) or (PANCIT)
"PHILIPPINES"

1/2 roll	Chic-Ketts™ (16 oz size)	5 c	Cabbage, thinly sliced
1 can	Mock duck, diced	6 c	Rice vermicelli, presoaked
12 oz	Firm tofu, cubed	2 c	Baby corn, sliced
1/4 tsp	Sesame oil	2 c	Fresh bean sprouts
2 tsp	Soy sauce or liquid aminos	4 c	Fresh greens (i.e. spinach)
2 tsp	Cornstarch in 2 T water	4 T	Soy sauce or liquid aminos
3 cloves	Garlic, minced	1 T	Chicken-style seasoning
1 c	Onion, chopped	3 T	Nutritional yeast flakes
1 tsp	Olive oil	2 T	Vegetarian Oyster Sauce(opt)
2 c	Green beans, french cut	2 T	Toasted sesame seeds
2 med	Carrots, julienned		

Marinate Chic-Ketts™, mock duck and tofu 5 minutes in sesame oil, soy sauce and cornstarch dissolved in water. In a non-stick wok, sauté mixture until browned. Pour into a bowl and set aside. Sauté garlic and onion in olive oil until onions are transparent. Add to the mixture which was set aside. Layer the next 7 ingredients (green beans to fresh greens) in the wok in the order given. Sprinkle with water, cover and let cook over medium heat 3-5 minutes. Add seasonings and toss until well mixed. Gently stir in the prepared vegetarian protein, tofu, garlic and onion mixture. Garnish with sesame seeds and serve.

Yield: 16 c

CHICKEN KELAGUEN
"GUAM"

1½ c	Chic-Ketts™	2 T	Celery, chopped
1 tsp	Canola oil	2 T	Bell pepper, chopped
1/4 c	Onions, diced	1/4 c	Green onion, chopped
1½ T	Fresh lemon juice	1 c	Fresh coconut, grated
1/2 tsp	Salt	2 T	Pimentos, chopped (opt)

Mash Chic-Ketts with a fork. Sauté Chic-Ketts in a non-stick frying pan with oil until golden. Pour into a bowl and chill. Combine onion, lemon juice and salt in a separate bowl and pour this over the mashed Chic-Ketts. Mix slightly. Add the chopped vegetables and coconut and mix thoroughly. If needed add more salt to taste. Garnish with pimentos if desired. Serve cold.

Yield: 3½ c

LEMON WONTON SOUP

WONTONS:

3 c	Zucchini, shredded	1 T	Cilantro, minced
1 c	Onion, finely chopped	1½ tsp	Sesame seeds
1 c	Fresh mushrooms, diced	1 tsp	Chicken-style seasoning
1/3 c	Red bell pepper, finely diced	1/2 tsp	Salt
2 tsp	Canola oil	36	Round Wonton "eggless"
1 tsp	Sesame oil		wrappers
2 T	Mild green chilies, chopped		

Sauté zucchini, onions, mushrooms and peppers in oils until tender. Add chilies, cilantro, sesame seeds and seasonings and mix well. To assemble wontons, cut into circles if necessary and brush surface of wonton wrapper with water. Place 2 or 3 teaspoons of filling onto center of the wrapper. Fold the top edge of the wrapper over to meet the opposite edge and press both edges together to seal. Continue until all filling and wrappers are used. Bring a pot of water to boil. Drop several wontons into the boiling water at a time and cook until they float to the surface, or about 3 minutes. Occasionally wontons break apart while boiling and will be wasted. Lay cooked wontons in a casserole dish sprayed with no-stick cooking spray until ready to use.

BROTH:

7 c	Water	1/8 tsp	Sesame oil
1/4 c	Vegetable broth powder	1 c	Snow peas, julienned
1½ T	Fresh lemon juice	1/4 c	Green bell pepper, julienned
1½ tsp	Lemon zest, grated	2 T	Cilantro, chopped

In a large pot, combine water, vegetable broth powder, lemon juice, zest and sesame oil. Bring to a boil. After 3 minutes, add snow peas and turn off heat. To serve, place about 6 wontons in a shallow soup bowl with 1 c broth. Garnish with bell peppers and cilantro.

Yield: 36 Wontons in broth

VEGETABLE WILD RICE
& MUSHROOM SOUP

2 c	Fresh mushrooms, sliced	2 T	'Lite' soy sauce
1 c	Onion, chopped		(or) Bragg Liquid Aminos
1/2 c	Celery, thinly sliced	1 T	Beef-style seasoning
3 med	Garlic cloves, minced	1 T	Chicken-style seasoning
2 T	Olive oil	2 tsp	Maggi Seasoning
3 qt	Water	1 tsp	Garlic & Herb seasoning
2 c	Cabbage, finely sliced	1 tsp	Onion salt
1 c	Brown & Wild Rice, dry	1 tsp	Liquid smoke flavoring (opt)
1 c	Carrots, sliced	1 c	Frozen petite green peas
3 T	Nutritional yeast flakes	1/4 c	Fresh chives, sliced

Sauté mushrooms, onion, celery and garlic in oil until tender. Add remaining ingredients, except peas and chives. Cover and simmer 25 minutes. Add peas and chives and simmer 2 to 3 minutes more. Serve hot.

Yield: 16 c

BEAN THREAD SALAD
(YAM WOON SEN)
"THAILAND"

8 oz pkg	Transparent bean thread	1 T	Bragg® Liquid Aminos
	(oriental noodles)	2 tsp	Honey
1c	Onion, finely sliced	1/2 tsp	Garlic purée
2 med	Tomatoes, cut in wedges	1/2 tsp	Lime juice (opt)
1 med	Cucumber, peeled & cubed	1/3 c	Green onion, diced
1/4 c	GranBurger®	1/4 c	Chinese parsley or
1/4 c	Water		cilantro
1 tsp	Beef-style seasoning	1/2 c	Roasted crushed peanuts
3 T	Lemon or tamarind juice		

Bring 1½ quarts water to a boil. Remove from heat and add noodles. Soak 10 minutes or until soft. Drain well. Cut into 6 inch lengths. Slice onion into rings and then cut rings in half. Prepare tomatoes and cucumber and set aside. Rehydrate GranBurger in water and beef-style seasoning. Combine juice, liquid aminos, honey, garlic purée and optional lime juice, to make an "oriental dressing" then set aside. Place noodles on a large platter over a bed of leafy lettuce. Arrange onion, tomatoes, cucumber and GranBurger evenly over noodles. Pour dressing over mixture. Toss lightly. Garnish with a topping of green onion, parsley, and peanuts.

Yield: 8 c

TOFU "COTTAGE CHEESE" SALAD

2 c	Fresh tofu, x-firm	1½ tsp	Onion powder
1/2 c	Tomatoes, diced (opt)	3/4 tsp	Salt
1/2 c	Cucumbers, diced (opt)	1/4 tsp	Garlic salt
1/4 c	Onions, finely diced (opt)	1/3 c	Sour Cream Supreme
1/4 c	Fresh chives, minced	1/8 tsp	Citric acid

Squeeze excess water out of tofu by pressing block between hands. Crumble tofu into a bowl and add vegetables (opt) , chives, and seasonings. Add citric acid to Sour Cream Supreme (see p 145) and gently stir into tofu mixture. Serve on a bed of lettuce and garnish with Paprika.

Variation: Replace Sour Cream Supreme with "Quick and Easy" Ranch Dressing (see page 156).   Yield: 5 c

FUMI SALAD
"JAPAN"

6 c	Cabbage, thinly sliced	1/4 c	Sesame seeds
1 c	Green onions with tops, sliced	1 pkg	Ramen Noodles
1/2 c	Slivered almonds		(Discard broth mix)

Mix cabbage and onions in a large bowl. Chill. Lightly toast the almonds and sesame seeds on a cookie sheet in the oven at 225° F. Cool and add to cabbage. When ready to serve, break the noodles into small pieces, add to the cabbage mixture and toss all ingredients together. Cover with Oriental Dressing recipe below.

Yield: 9 c

ORIENTAL DRESSING

1/3 c	Pineapple juice	2 T	Canola oil
3 T	Apple juice (frozen) concentrate	1 tsp	Sesame oil
2 T	Fresh lemon juice	3/4 tsp	Salt

Mix or shake well and pour over salad when ready to serve. Toss lightly.

Yield: 3/4 c

BANANA CAKE
with
LEMON CHIFFON TOPPING

1 1/3 c	Ripe bananas, mashed	1 c	Whole wheat pastry flour
3/4 c	Fresh tofu, x-soft or silken	1 c	Unbleached white flour
3/4 c	Brown sugar	1 tsp	Baking powder
1/4 c	Canola oil	1/2 tsp	Baking soda
1 tsp	Vanilla	1/2 tsp	Salt

In a blender, combine bananas, tofu, sugar, oil and vanilla and process until smooth and creamy. In a separate bowl, combine remaining dry ingredients. Pour blender ingredients into dry ingredients and mix well. Coat a 9 x 13 baking dish with no-stick cooking spray. Pour batter into prepared dish and bake at 350° F, 40 minutes or until cake springs back to touch. Cool completely. Cut into squares and dollop lemon topping over the top. Garnish with a small lemon twist, a slice of banana, grated coconut or chopped pecans if desired.

Variation: This cake works well in a bundt cake pan also. Bake at 350° F, about 45 minutes.

Yield: 9 x 13 sheet cake

LEMON CHIFFON TOPPING

1½ c	Mori-Nu® Tofu, x-firm , (12.3 oz)	1 tsp	Vanilla, natural
3/4 c	Ripe banana, mashed	1/4 tsp	Lemon zest
3 oz	Pineapple juice (frozen) concentrate	1/16 tsp	Salt
1 T	Fruit Fresh®, powder	1 tsp	Instant Clear Jel
1 T	Powdered sugar, (opt)		(food thickener)

In a blender, combine all ingredients (except the instant food thickener) and process until smooth and creamy. Add the food thickener and blend 15 seconds more until pudding thickens. Chill.

Yield: 2½ c

CARROT-RAISIN COOKIES

2 c	Whole wheat flour	1/2 c	Grated coconut
2 c	All purpose flour	1 c	Grated carrots
1 c	Date sugar	8 oz can	Crushed pineapple
1 c	Raisins	1/3 c	Oil
1 c	Walnuts, chopped	1/3 c	Honey
1 tsp	Baking powder	2 tsp	Vanilla
1/2 tsp	Soda	2/3 c	Frozen apple juice
1/2 tsp	Cinnamon		(concentrate)
1 tsp	Salt		

In a large bowl, mix together all dry ingredients. In a separate bowl combine coconut, carrots, undrained pineapple, and remaining liquid ingredients. Pour mixture into dry ingredients and stir until well mixed. Spoon onto a cookie sheet coated with no-stick cooking spray and shape with oiled fingers. Bake 20 minutes at 350° F. Cool slightly, cover and store.

Yield: 4 doz

OATMEAL COOKIES

1½ c	Water	1/2 tsp	Salt
1/2 c	Walnuts	1/4 tsp	Cardamom
1/2 c	Honey	2 c	Quick rolled oats
1/2 c	Tofu milk powder	1½ c	Whole wheat flour
1/4 c	Molasses	1½ c	Raisins
1 tsp	Vanilla	1 c	Walnuts, chopped
1/2 tsp	Coriander powder	1/2 c	Coconut, shredded

In a blender, combine first nine ingredients (water to Cardamom) and blend until smooth. Combine remaining ingredients in a large bowl. Pour blender ingredients into dry ingredients and stir together until well mixed. Drop by spoonfuls onto a cookie sheets sprayed with no-stick cooking spray. Bake at 375° F, 12 minutes or until lightly browned. (Cookies may seem slightly moist.) Cool on rack.

Yield: 3 doz

COOKIE HAYSTACKS

3 c	Date pieces, softened	1½ c	Walnuts, chopped
1½ c	Raisins	3/4 c	Whole wheat flour
1/2 c	Orange or pineapple juice	1/3 c	Old-fashioned oats
1/8 c	Water	1/2 tsp	Salt
4 c	Unsweetened shredded coconut		

In a blender, combine dates, raisins, juice and water. Blend until smooth. Pour mixture out into a bowl. Add dry ingredients to the blender ingredients and mix lightly. Scoop up with a small ice cream scoop and drop onto an ungreased cookie sheet. Bake at 350° F, 20 to 30 minutes or until browned.

Variation: May use 2 c dates and 3 c shredded coconut.

Yield: 4 doz

MAJA BLANKA
"PHILIPPINES"

4 c	Coconut milk, "Lite", unsweetened	1/2 tsp	Salt
1 c	Honey	1 c	Cornstarch
1 c	Creamed corn	1 c	Water
		1/2 c	Grated coconut, toasted

Boil coconut milk with honey, creamed corn and salt in a deep pot, stirring constantly. Mix cornstarch with water and add to the boiling mixture, stirring until thick. Pour into a jello mold coated with no-stick cooking spray and refrigerate until set. Unmold on a serving platter and sprinkle top with the toasted grated coconut.

Note: To make fresh coconut milk, grate 2 ripe coconuts. Pour 1 quart water over the grated coconut and squeeze the coconut until all the "milk" is squeezed out. Drain coconut in a colander and reserve the milk.

Yield: 7 c

Brunch with "A Twist"

Featuring

An assortment of quiches, potatoes, pastas, breads, and fruits. All have the appearance of a typical morning brunch. However, there is a surprising difference. These recipes taste delicious without adding the usual eggs, cheese, and milk. Give your health a boost. Experience a satisfying meal you can serve and enjoy anytime of day.

MIXED VEGETABLE QUICHE

1 recipe	Potato or Oat Crust	2 T	Water
1 c	Onion, chopped	2 T	ENER-G® Egg Replacer
1 clove	Garlic, minced	1 T	Dry minced onion
1 tsp	Olive oil	2 tsp	Chicken-style seasoning
1 c	Broccoli, finely sliced	1/2 tsp	Salt
1/2 c	Carrots, finely sliced	1/4 tsp	Lawry's Seasoned Salt
1/2 c	Cauliflower, finely sliced	1/4 tsp	Garlic salt
1 c	Cheese Sauce (see below)	1/4 tsp	Spike
2 boxes	Mori-Nu® Tofu, x-firm	1/4 tsp	Basil
	(12.3 oz size)	1/4 c	Pepperidge Farm® (opt)
3 T	Cornstarch		Corn Bread Stuffing Mix

Prepare Potato Crust (see p 109) or Oat Crust (see p 109) and set aside. In a non-stick frying pan, sauté onion and garlic in oil or a small amount of water until onions are translucent and set aside. Steam or microwave vegetables until crisp-tender. Drain if necessary and set aside. Prepare Cheese Sauce. (This step can be done well in advance to save time on the day it is needed.) In a blender, combine (1 c) cheese sauce, tofu, cornstarch, water and egg replacer. Process until smooth and creamy. Pour out into a bowl. Add onions, mixed vegetables and all seasonings, except stuffing mix, to the tofu/cheese sauce mixture and mix well. Pour into a 10 inch quiche dish with the prepared crust. If desired, top with stuffing mix and bake at 350° F, 50 to 60 minutes or until center of quiche is set.   Yield: 10 inch quiche

CHEESE SAUCE

1 c	Cooked rice or millet	1 T	Fresh lemon juice
1 c	Hot water	1 tsp	Onion powder
3/4 c	Raw cashews or almonds	1 tsp	Salt
1/4 c	Carrots, cooked	1/2 tsp	Lawry's® Seasoned Salt
2 T	Nutritional yeast flakes	1/4 tsp	Garlic powder

In a blender, combine rice, water, nuts and carrots and process on high speed until smooth and creamy. Add all other ingredients and blend again briefly.

Yield: 2 ½ c

POTATO CRUST

1/3 c	Mashed potato, cooked	1/3 c	Water
1 c	Unbleached white flour	3 T	Canola oil
1 T	Better Than Milk™ powder	1 tsp	Sesame seeds
1/2 tsp	Salt		

Peel, cube and boil 2 potatoes. Mash enough potatoes to equal 1/3 c and set aside. Combine flour, tofu milk powder and salt. Mix water and oil together and pour into the dry ingredients. Stir until just moistened. Add mashed potatoes to the dough. Knead mixture together until a soft, pliable dough is formed. Let dough rest several minutes. Roll dough out on a floured surface. Then press dough into a 10 inch quiche dish. Flute edges. Press sesame seeds into bottom of crust.

Yield: 2 c

OAT CRUST

1/3 c	Mashed potatoes, cooked	1/2 tsp	Salt
3/4 c	Oat flour	1/3 c	Water
1/4 c	Whole wheat flour	3 T	Canola oil
1 T	Better Than Milk™ powder	1 tsp	Sesame seeds

Peel, cube and boil 2 potatoes. Mash enough potatoes to equal 1/3 c and set aside. Combine flour, tofu milk powder and salt. Mix water and oil together and pour into the dry ingredients. Stir until just moistened. Add mashed potatoes to the dough. Knead mixture together until a soft, pliable dough is formed. Let dough rest several minutes. Roll dough out on a floured surface. Then press dough into a 10 inch quiche dish. Flute edges. Press sesame seeds into bottom of crust.

Yield: 2 c

SPINACH-POTATO QUICHE

1 recipe	Potato or Oat crust	3 T	Cornstarch
1 c	Onions, chopped	2 T	Water
1 c	Fresh mushrooms, chopped	2 T	ENER-G® Egg Replacer
1 clove	Garlic, minced	1 T	Dry minced onion
1 T	Olive oil	1 tsp	Chicken-style seasoning
10 oz	Fresh spinach, coarse chopped	1 tsp	Salt
1 c	Raw potatoes, shredded	1 tsp	Basil
4 oz	Old El Paso® mild Green Chilies	¼ tsp	Lawry's Seasoned Salt
1 c	Cheese Sauce (see p 108)		Paprika to garnish
2 boxes	Mori-Nu® Tofu, x-firm, (12.3 oz size)		

Prepare Potato Crust (see p 109) or Oat Crust (see p 109) and set aside. In a non-stick frying pan, sauté onions, mushrooms and garlic in oil or 2 T water until onions are translucent. Remove from heat. Remove large stems from spinach, cut into 2 inch pieces and place in a large pot with 1 c water. Simmer until tender. Drain, cool and squeeze dry. Add spinach, potatoes and chopped chilies to onion-mushroom mixture, cook 1 or 2 more minutes and remove from heat. Prepare Cheese Sauce. (This step can be done well in advance to save time on the day it is needed.) In a blender, combine (1 c) cheese sauce, tofu, cornstarch, water and egg replacer. Process until smooth and creamy. Pour out into a bowl. Add the spinach-potato mixture, and all seasonings, except paprika, to the tofu/cheese sauce mixture and mix well. Pour into a 10 inch quiche dish with the prepared crust and garnish with paprika. Bake at 350° F, 50 to 60 minutes or until center of quiche is set.

Yield: 10 inch quiche

SAUSAGE-STYLE
MUSHROOM & ONION QUICHE

2 c	Onions, chopped	2 T	ENER-G® Egg Replacer
2 c	Mushrooms, chopped	1 T	Water
1 c	Bell pepper, diced	2 tsp	Beef-style seasoning
2 lg	Garlic cloves, minced	1 tsp	Spike® or Nature's Blend
1 c	Vegan Sausage Crumbles	1 tsp	Basil
2 T	Olive oil	1 tsp	Onion powder
2 c	Mori-Nu ®Tofu, x-firm	1/2 tsp	Salt
3 T	Cornstarch	3 T	Pepperidge Farm® -
2 T	Nutritional yeast flakes		Corn Bread Stuffing, crushed

Prepare Potato Crust (see p 109) or Oat crust (see p 109) and set aside. In a large non-stick frying pan, sauté vegetables and sausage in oil until vegetables are tender. Remove from heat and set aside. In a blender, combine tofu and all remaining ingredients, except stuffing mix, and process until smooth and creamy. Pour over vegetable mixture and stir until well mixed. Pour into a 10 inch quiche dish with the prepared crust. Cover top with stuffing mix and bake at 350° F, 50 to 60 minutes or until center of quiche is set.

Yield: 10 inch quiche

"CHICKEN" DIVAN

4 c	Water	1 T	Canola or olive oil
2 c	Brown rice	2 pkg	Gravy Quik® - chicken flavor
1 tsp	Salt	2 c	Fresh broccoli florets
8 oz	Chic-Ketts®, (1/2 roll)	1 T	Fresh parsley, snipped
1/4 c	Breading Meal # 2	1 T	Sesame seeds, lightly toasted

Cook rice with water and salt. Tear Chic-Ketts into bite-size pieces and moisten with water. Place Chic-Ketts and Breading Meal #2 (see p 114) in a plastic bag and shake to coat Chic-Ketts evenly. Brown Chic-Ketts in oil and set aside. Prepare gravy according to directions on the package except increase water to 1 1/4 cups. (May substitute 1/2 cup water with 1/2 c tofu milk for a richer flavor.) Steam or microwave broccoli 3 minutes or until crisp-tender. Arrange rice on a large platter. Top with the broccoli and Chic-Ketts and pour the gravy over all evenly. Garnish with the parsley and sesame seeds. Serve at once.

Yield: 10 c

SCRAMBLED TOFU
CURRY-STYLE

VEGETABLES:

2 ½ c	Fresh mushrooms, sliced	1 T	Extra virgin olive oil
2 c	Onions, chopped		

In a large frying pan, sauté mushroom and onions in oil until tender. Remove and set aside.

CURRY SAUCE:

3 c	Warm water	1 T	Chicken-Style seasoning
1/2 c	Raw cashew pieces, rinsed	1 T	Onion powder
1/3 c	Better Than Milk™ powder	1 tsp	Curry powder
3 T	Cornstarch	1/2 tsp	Onion salt
1½ T	Nutritional yeast flakes		

Pour one cup of the water into a blender and set the remaining water aside. Add cashews and process on high speed until completely smooth. Add the rest of the water and all remaining ingredients and blend until well mixed.

SCRAMBLED TOFU:

14 oz	Fresh tofu, x-firm	1/2 tsp	Onion powder
1 T	Extra virgin olive oil	1/2 tsp	Salt
1 T	Nutritional yeast flakes	1/4 tsp	Garlic powder
2 tsp	Chicken-Style seasoning	1/8 tsp	Turmeric
1 tsp	Curry powder		

Squeeze excess water out of tofu. Then crumble the tofu into a non-stick frying pan, breaking the pieces into large chunks. Coat with oil. Combine all seasonings (may be done ahead) and sprinkle evenly over the tofu. Heat over medium heat and gently fold seasonings into tofu until well mixed. Avoid breaking tofu into small pieces. Add mushroom and onion mixture. Simmer 3 to 5 minutes, stirring occasionally. Cover with curry sauce and gently stir until heated through and mixture thickens. Serve over rice, noodles, baked potatoes, biscuits or toast.

Yield: 8 c

PASTA PRIMAVERA

2 c	Frozen sugar snap or "petite" green peas	1 tsp	Garlic & Herb seasoning ("salt free" recipe)
1½ c	Carrots, sliced	1 tsp	Onion powder
8 oz	Fettuccine noodles, dry	1 tsp	Parsley, dry
2 c	Water	½ tsp	Basil
1/3 c	Tofutti® Better Than Cream Cheese	½ tsp	Salt
1/4 c	Better Than Milk™ powder	½ tsp	Spike®, regular (opt)
3 T	"Soy Good" Sour Cream (see below)	2 T	Toasted sesame seeds
2 T	Spectrum® "non-dairy" Spread	1 T	Fresh parsley, snipped
2 T	Unbleached white flour		

Simmer peas until crisp-tender. Microwave or steam carrots 2 to 3 minutes. Avoid overcooking. Set aside. Cook Fettuccine noodles according to package in 8 c salted water. Drain, rinse and drizzle with 1 tsp olive oil and stir to coat noodles. While noodles are cooking, combine water, cream cheese, milk powder, sour cream, Spectrum Spread and flour in a blender. Process on medium speed until smooth and creamy. Pour mixture into a saucepan, add dry seasonings and simmer 5 to 10 minutes stirring frequently until thickened. Pour sauce over noodles, add pre-cooked vegetables and toss mixture lightly. May garnish with toasted sesame seeds and fresh parsley if desired. Serve immediately.

Yield: 6 c

"SOY GOOD" TOFU SOUR CREAM

1½ c	Mori-Nu® Tofu, firm (12.3 oz box)	1/4 tsp	Salt
3 T	Sunflower oil	1/4 tsp	Honey
1/4 tsp	Citric acid crystals		

In a blender, combine all ingredients and process until smooth and creamy.

Variation: Add 1 tsp fresh lemon juice for a stronger sour taste.

Yield: 1½ c

BREADING MEAL #2

1/2 c	Flour, wheat or white	1 T	Nutritional yeast flakes
1/4 c	Cracker crumbs, finely blended	1 tsp	Onion powder
1/4 c	Yellow corn meal	1/2 tsp	Salt
2 tsp	Beef or chicken-style seasoning	1/2 tsp	Garlic powder

Mix ingredients together and store in an air tight container. Yield: 1 1/8 c

"QUICK BAKED"
GOLDEN POTATO FRIES

Slice 2 large bakers potatoes lengthwise into 1/2" wide sticks. Spray a cookie sheet with no-stick cooking spray. Spread potatoes out in a single layer. (To enhance flavor, drizzle 1 T olive oil over the potatoes and stir to coat evenly-only if diet permits.) Sprinkle with any combination of dried parsley, herbs, chives, onion salt, garlic salt, Spike, nutritional yeast etc. to your taste. Broil on the top oven rack at 400° F. Stir after 10 minutes and then every 5 minutes for 10-15 minutes more or until tender, and golden brown with crispy edges. You may also want to add onion rings to the fries during the last 5 minutes of baking time. Serve hot and, if desired, with Vinegarless Ketchup (recipe below) on the side.

Yield: 4 c

"QUICK" VINEGARLESS KETCHUP

1½ c	Tomato sauce	2 T	Fruit-Fresh®, powder
1 c	Tomato paste		(or) 1/8 tsp citric acid
1/2 c	Pineapple juice	1½ tsp	Salt
1/4 c	Fresh lemon juice	1 tsp	Onion powder
1 tsp	Lime juice	1/2 tsp	Garlic salt
3 T	Date butter (see note on p 211)	1/2 tsp	Paprika
2 T	Pineapple/orange juice	1/4 tsp	Worcestershire sauce
	(frozen concentrate)		(Vegetarian brand) (opt)
2 T	Honey		

Combine all ingredients in a blender and process until smooth. Refrigerate. Freeze extras not used within two weeks.

Variation: For a thicker ketchup, decrease tomato sauce to 1 c and increase tomato paste to 1½ c.

Yield: 4 c

VERY BERRY
CREAM CHEESE SPREAD

4 oz   *Tofutti* Better Than Cream Cheese
1/4 c   All-fruit jam, (blueberry, strawberry or raspberry)

Gently stir and swirl mixture together. Spread on whole wheat bagels or any whole grain bread of choice. Or, spread cream cheese on bread and top with jam.

Yield: 3/4 c

CREAM CHEESY SPREAD

8 oz   *Tofutti* Better Than Cream Cheese   1/8 tsp   Citric acid

Sprinkle citric acid evenly over cream cheese and stir until well mixed. Use mixture to stuff celery, or as a sandwich filling with sliced olives, cucumbers, or onions etc.

Yield: 1 c

DATE AND WALNUT BREAD

1 c	Boiling water	1 tsp	Soda
1 c	Dates, snipped finely	3/4 tsp	Salt
1 T	Canola oil	1/2 tsp	Cinnamon
1/2 c	Brown sugar or Sucanat®	1/2 c	Walnuts, chopped
1¾ c	Whole wheat flour	2 tsp	ENER-G® Egg Replacer
2 tsp	Baking powder	2 T	Water

Pour boiling water over dates and stir until cool. Add oil, and sweetener of choice. Mix well. Add dry ingredients (except Egg Replacer) and stir gently. Whisk Egg Replacer with water until foamy. Fold into batter. Pour into a loaf pan coated with no-stick cooking spray and bake at 350° F, 55 to 60 minutes.

Yield: 1 loaf / 12 slices

TOFU - BANANA BREAD #1

1 1/3 c	Ripe bananas, mashed	1 c	Whole wheat flour
3/4 c	Tofu, extra soft or silken	1 tsp	Baking powder
3/4 c	Brown sugar or Sucanat®	1/2 tsp	Baking soda
1/4 c	Canola oil	1/2 tsp	Salt
1 tsp	Vanilla	3/4 c	Walnut pieces
1 c	Unbleached flour		

In a blender, combine bananas, tofu, sweetener, oil and vanilla and process until smooth and creamy. In another bowl, combine remaining ingredients. Pour blender ingredients into dry ingredients and mix well. Pour into a loaf pan coated with no-stick cooking spray. Bake at 350° F, 52-55 minutes.

Yield: 1 loaf / 12 slices

HAWAIIAN BANANA-NUT BREAD

1 c	Ripe bananas, mashed	2 tsp	Baking powder
1/2 c	Tofu, firm	3/4 tsp	Salt
1/4 c	Canola oil	1/2 tsp	Soda
2 tsp	Vanilla	1/2 tsp	Cinnamon
3/4 c	Brown sugar or Sucanat®	4 oz	Crushed pineapple
1 c	Whole wheat flour	3 tsp	ENER-G® Egg Replacer
3/4 c	Grape Nuts® cereal	4 T	Water
1/2 c	Unbleached white flour	1 c	Walnuts or pecans, chopped

In a blender, combine bananas, tofu, oil, vanilla, and sweetener and process until smooth and creamy. Mix flours, grape nuts, baking powder, salt, soda and cinnamon in a bowl. Add blender ingredients and well drained pineapple to the dry ingredients and stir gently. Whisk Egg Replacer with water 2 or 3 minutes until foamy and fold into mixture. Add nuts last. Pour batter into a loaf pan coated with no-stick cooking spray and bake at 350° F, 55 to 60 minutes.

Variation: To make Hawaiian Banana-Nut Muffins; increase baking powder to 1 T, fill muffin tins 3/4 full, sprinkle additional finely chopped

Yield: 1 loaf / 12 slices

PEACH-NUT BREAD

2½ c	All purpose flour	3/4 c	Honey
1 c	Wheat germ	1/4 c	Dole® "Orchard Peach"
1 T	Baking powder		(frozen juice concentrate)
1/2 tsp	Soda	1/4 c	Canola oil
1/2 tsp	Salt	1 T	Lemon juice
1 c	Chopped walnuts	1 tsp	Vanilla
	(reserve 1/4 c)	1 T	ENER-G® Egg Replacer
16 oz	Canned peaches, juice pack		

Combine dry ingredients and set aside. Drain peaches, mash or chop finely and set aside. Combine honey, frozen juice concentrate, oil, lemon juice, vanilla and Egg Replacer and beat to dissolve Egg Replacer. Stir in peaches. Pour peach mixture into flour mixture; stir just until moistened. Pour into a loaf pan coated with no-stick cooking spray. Sprinkle with reserved nuts. Bake at 350° F, approximately 1 hour and 10 minutes or until a toothpick comes out clean.

Variation: To make Peach-Nut Spice Bread, add 1 tsp cinnamon, 1/4 tsp

Yield: 1 loaf / 12 slices

RASPBERRY BRAN MUFFINS

1 c	All purpose flour	1/3 c	Honey
1 c	Wheat bran	1/4 c	Canola oil
1 T	Baking powder	1½ tsp	ENER-G® Egg Replacer
1/2 tsp	Salt	1 c	Raspberries, fresh
3/4 c	Better Than Milk™		(or whole frozen berries)

Combine dry ingredients. In another bowl combine tofu milk, honey, oil and Egg Replacer. Whisk to dissolve Egg Replacer. Combine liquid and dry ingredients and stir until just moistened. Fold in rinsed and drained raspberries. Coat a muffin tin with no-stick cooking spray. Fill cups 3/4 full. Bake at 400° F, 20 minutes or until lightly browned.

Yield: 1 dozen

RAISIN BRAN MUFFINS
(Yeast-Raised)

1¼ c	Warm water	1¼ c	Whole wheat flour
2 T	Canola oil	1/2 c	Oat bran
2 T	Wonderslim or Lighter Bake	1/2 c	Wheat germ
	(Fat and Egg Substitute)	1/2 c	Date sugar
1 T	Rapid-rise yeast	1/2 c	Dates, diced
1 T	Honey or molasses	1/2 c	Raisins
1 tsp	Vanilla	1/2 c	Pecans, chopped
1/2 tsp	Salt		(opt)

Combine water, oil, Wonderslim, yeast, honey, vanilla and salt. (Set aside while measuring dry ingredients.) Combine remaining ingredients in a separate bowl. Pour liquid ingredients into dry ingredients and stir gently until well mixed. Spray a muffin tin with no-stick cooking spray. Fill muffin tins with batter 3/4 full. Allow to rise in a warm draft-free place until double or about 30 minutes. Bake at 350°F, 25 minutes. Cool 10 to 15 minutes before trying to remove from pan. Set muffins on a cooling rack to cool completely before storing.

Yield: 1 dozen

BRAN MUFFINS

1 1/2 c	Whole wheat flour	1/2 c	Raisins
1 1/2 c	Wheat bran	1/2 c	Dates, chopped
1/2 c	Oat bran	1/2 c	Nuts, chopped
1/2 c	Brown sugar or Sucanat®	1½ c	Tofu milk
1 T	Baking powder	1/4 c	Canola oil
1 tsp	Carob powder	1/4 c	Molasses (opt)
1/2 tsp	Soda	1 T	Lemon juice
1/2 tsp	Salt	1 T	Vanilla

Combine all dry ingredients. In a separate bowl, combine tofu milk, oil, molasses, lemon juice and vanilla. Stir liquid ingredients gently into dry mixture and blend well. Spray a muffin tin with no-stick cooking spray and fill cups 3/4 full. Bake at 400° F, 20 to 25 minutes.

Yield: 1 dozen

BLUEBERRY
OAT BRAN MUFFINS

1 1/2 c	All purpose flour	1/2 c	Honey
1 c	Oat bran cereal	1/3 c	Canola oil
3/4 tsp	Salt	3 T	Applesauce
1/2 tsp	Soda	1 tsp	Vanilla
1 T	Baking powder	1 T	ENER-G® Egg Replacer
1/2 tsp	Grated lemon zest		Water
3/4 c	Tofu milk	3/.	Fresh blueberries

Spray muffin tin with Pam. Combine dry ingredients. In another bowl, combine milk, honey, oil, applesauce, and vanilla. Then add mixture to dry ingredients, stirring only until dry ingredients are moistened. Whisk Egg Replacer with water 2 or 3 minutes until foamy. Fold gently into batter. Rinse, drain, and blot blueberries dry and gently stir into the batter. Fill muffin cups 3/4 full. Bake at 375° F, 20 to 25 minutes or until a light golden brown color.

Variation: For a "diabetic version", reduce oil to 3 T and increase apple-sauce to 1/3 c. Also, decrease honey to 1/3 c and increase vanilla to 1 T.

Yield: 1 dozen

BLUEBERRY PRESERVES

12 oz	White grape juice (frozen) concentrate	6 T	Cornstarch, arrowroot or tapioca powder
12 oz	Water (or less for sweeter jam)	4 c	Frozen blueberries
1 tsp	Fresh lemon juice		

In a saucepan, combine grape juice, water and lemon juice. Add cornstarch and stir to dissolve. Add 1 cup blueberries and bring to a boil. Simmer until juice is thick, clear, and blue in color. Pour in remaining blueberries and remove from heat. Stir to cool mixture. Refrigerate.

Yield: 5 c

RASPBERRY JAM

4 c	Raspberries	5 T	Cornstarch, arrowroot,
12 oz	White grape juice		or tapioca powder
	(frozen) concentrate	1/2 tsp	Fresh lemon juice
12 oz	Water (or less for sweeter jam)		

Purée raspberries in a blender. If desired, may strain puréed raspberries to remove seeds. In a saucepan, combine remaining ingredients and stir until cornstarch is dissolved. Bring to a boil and simmer until juice is clear. Add raspberry purée to juice and continue to cook stirring constantly until jam is thick. Cool and refrigerate.

Yield: 5 c

APPLE BUTTER

1 c	Purple grape juice, unsweetened	1 c	Frozen apple juice
3/4 c	Dark raisins		(concentrate)
1/3 c	Dates, pitted	1/2 tsp	Cinnamon
5 T	Cornstarch	1 1/3 c	Applesauce

Simmer grape juice, raisins and dates until soft. Pour mixture into a blender and process until smooth. In a saucepan, dissolve cornstarch in apple juice. Add grape juice mixture and cinnamon. Simmer, stirring constantly, until clear and thick. Stir in applesauce and refrigerate.

Yield: 4 c

APPLE SPICE BUTTER

| 2 c | Dried apples, packed | 1/2 c | Pineapple juice |
| 2 c | Hot water | 1/2 tsp | Cinnamon |

Soak apples in water 15 minutes. Pour into a blender and add remaining ingredients. Process on high speed until smooth. Chill.

Yield: 3 c

"HEART SMART"
CORN BUTTER

1 c	Cold water	2 T	Canola oil
1/4 c	Yellow corn meal	1 T	Emes Kosher-Jel®, plain
1/2 c	Mori-Nu® Tofu, x-firm	1 T	Cooked carrot (opt for color)
1/2 c	Warm water	1 tsp	Honey
1/4 c	Almonds	1 tsp	Imitation butter flavored salt
3 T	Spicery Shoppe® Natural -	½ tsp	Salt
	Butter Flavor (vegan)	Pinch	Citric acid

Combine cold water and corn meal in a small saucepan and bring to a boil stirring constantly. Reduce heat to low, cover and simmer 10 minutes. Refrigerate mixture until completely cool and "set". In a blender, combine water, almonds, butter flavoring, oil and Emes. Process on high speed until no longer "gritty". Spoon chilled corn meal mush into the blender mixture and all remaining ingredients and process until smooth and creamy. Bits of carrot should not be visible. Refrigerate several hours before serving until "butter" thickens to a spreadable consistency.

Yield: 3 c

ORANGE HONEY BUTTER

Add the following ingredients to 1 cup of cold, pre-set Corn Butter:

2 T Creamy "Spun" honey	1 T	Orange juice concentrate
(SueBee® or similar brand)	1/2 tsp	Grated orange peel

Whip at high speed until fluffy. Refrigerate before serving.

Yield: 1¼ c

ENGLISH TRIFLE

BERRY FILLING:

1 c	Water	1/4 c	Cornstarch
6 oz	White grape/raspberry	2 c	Fresh or frozen berries
	(frozen 100% juice concentrate)		(blueberries, cherries
1 tsp	Vanilla		or raspberries)
1/2 c	Water		

Combine 1 c water, juice concentrate and vanilla and bring mixture to a boil. Combine 1/2 c water and cornstarch and stir until dissolved. Stirring constantly, add cornstarch-water to the boiling juice and continue stirring until mixture thickens and "clears". Add the berries and remove from heat. Set aside to cool.

CREAM FILLING:

10.5 oz box	Mori-Nu™ tofu, firm	1 tsp	Vanilla
1/4 c	Fructose	1/4 tsp	Salt
1 c	Better Than Milk™	1/4 c	Instant Clear Jel

In a blender, combine tofu, fructose, milk, vanilla and salt and process until smooth. Turn blender speed down to lowest setting, remove the lid and add Instant Clear Jel food thickener. Replace lid, increase speed to highest setting and process briefly until mixture is thick.

CRUNCHY FILLING:

2 c   Granola or graham crackers crushed until crumbly

PROCEDURE:

Layer above ingredients into parfait glasses in the following order:
1. Granola or graham crackers.
2. Berry filling

3. Cream filling
4. Repeat

End top layer with granola or graham crackers and a dollop of berry filling.

Yield: 8 parfaits

FRESH FRUIT
with
PUDDING COMPOTE

12 c   Fresh or frozen fruit combinations
        (Peaches, bananas, strawberries, grapes, blueberries, pineapple and
        kiwi)

2 c	Water	1/2 c	Spun "creamy" honey
1 c	Tofu, soft silken	1/2 c	White flour or tapioca
1 c	White rice, cooked	1 T	Fresh lemon juice
1 c	Coconut Milk "Lite",	2 tsp	Vanilla
	(unsweetened)	(opt)	Fresh mint leaves

In a blender, process water, tofu, rice, and coconut milk until smooth and creamy. Add remaining ingredients and blend until well mixed. Pour mixture into a saucepan and bring to a boil, stirring constantly until thick. Refrigerate pudding until cold before serving. Arrange half of fruit in a large serving bowl. Layer 3/4 of pudding mixture over fruit. Cover with remaining fruit. Spoon remaining pudding on top center, allowing fruit to show around the border. Place a whole strawberry or small cluster of grapes on top. Garnish with mint leaves if desired.

Yield: 16 c

Garbanzo Olive Salad
Italian Bread Sticks
Almond Cheesecake Delight
Fat-Free Italian Dressing
Tofu Lasagna

Italian
At It's
Best

Featuring

This dinner evokes the spirit of Italian cooking at it's very best - with healthful sauces and "cheese" for the pasta, fresh vegetables, whole wheat garlic bread, and special desserts you won't forget.

TOFU LASAGNA

BASIC ITALIAN SAUCE:

2 T	Olive oil	1 tsp	Salt
1 med	Onion, chopped	3 cans	Hunt's® "Special" Sauce
1/2 sm	Bell pepper, chopped	6 oz	Tomato paste
2 cloves	Garlic, minced	6 oz	Water or "olive broth"
2 T	Sucanat® or honey	1 c	Vegan Burger Crumbles®
1½ T	Nutritional yeast flakes	4 c	Assortment of vegetables, ie
1 T	Dry minced onion		sliced olives, mushrooms,
2 ½ tsp	Italian seasoning		fresh steamed spinach,
2 tsp	Beef-Style Seasoning		grated carrots or zucchini

Sauté onion, bell pepper, and garlic in olive oil or water. Add seasonings, sauces, liquids, Burger Crumbles (may also use sausage flavored crumbles) and vegetables of choice and simmer 10 minutes. Or if preferred, add vegetables as a separate layer during the assembling process.

NOODLES:
It is not necessary to cook the noodles in this recipe. Just allow 1/2" spaces between the noodles when arranging them in the baking dish to provide enough room for the noodles to expand. May use whole grain or spinach noodles as desired but you may need to allow extra baking time.

RICOTTA-STYLE FILLING:

1 3/4 lb	Tofu, x-firm, (28 oz)	2 tsp	Basil
1/4 c	Fresh lemon juice	2 tsp	Honey
2 1/2 T	Olive oil	1 1/4 tsp	Salt
1 T	ENER-G® Egg Replacer	1 tsp	Garlic powder

Squeeze excess water out of tofu. Crumble tofu in a large bowl until tofu resembles ricotta cheese. Stir in remaining ingredients.

METHOD:
Coat a large oblong baking dish with no-stick spray. Pour a thin layer of sauce in the bottom of the dish. Assemble thin layers of ingredients in this order:
1. Noodles 2. Filling 3. Sauce 4. Olives, mushrooms, spinach, carrots etc.
Make at least 2 layers (better with 3). Bake at 350°F, 50 to 60 minutes. Garnish top with Parmesan and/or Mozzarella cheese (recipes on page 127). Cook 10-15 more minutes until cheese is bubbly. Cool 10 minutes. Serve.

Note: I prefer using SoyCo® Lite & Less™ Parmesan Cheese Alternative.

Yield: 18 c

NON-DAIRY PARMESAN CHEESE

MIX:

1/3 c Nutritional yeast flakes   1/2 c Ground almonds, w/o skins

ADD:

2 T   Better than Milk™ powder   1 tsp Garlic powder
2 tsp McKay's® Chicken-Style Seasoning   1 tsp Onion powder

SPREAD OR SPRAY EVENLY:

2 tsp Fresh lemon juice mixed with 1 tsp water

Mix with hands until crumbs are very small. Toast on a cookie sheet at 200° F, stirring every 30 minutes until dry and crispy. Avoid browning. If desired, return toasted "parmesan cheese" to the blender and process until mixture resembles fine crumbs. Store in a closed container. Keeps for many weeks in the refrigerator.

Yield: 3/4 c

MOZZARELLA CHEESE

1 c   Water   4 tsp   Fresh lemon juice
1 c   Cooked rice, brown or white   1½ tsp   Salt
3/4 c Tofu, x-firm   1 tsp   Onion powder
1/2 c Raw cashews, rinsed   1/4 tsp Garlic powder
4 T   Emes Kosher-Jel®, plain

In a blender, combine all ingredients and process on high speed, stopping and stirring as necessary, until completely smooth and creamy (3 - 5 minutes). The sauce will heat up and appear "shiny" when completed. Pour into a container coated with no stick cooking spray. Refrigerate 2 to 4 hours until set. Gently shake out to slice cheese.

Note: To grate cheese easily, freeze mixture at least 2 hours first. For a creamy sauce to pour over vegetables or noodles; do not refrigerate mixture after blending, but heat and serve immediately. Or, if using previously "set" leftover cheese, heat mixture slowly over lo-med heat, stirring frequently until melted.

Tip: May substitute cashews with slivered blanched almonds (w/o skins).

Yield: 3 c

SPAGHETTI FLORENTINE
with
BETTER 'N MEATBALLS

4 c	Fresh spinach, stems removed	2 jars	Spaghetti sauce, vegan
1 c	Onion, chopped	1 T	Nutritional yeast flakes
2 med	Garlic cloves, minced	1 tsp	Beef-Style seasoning
1 c	Vegetarian Burger,	1/2 c	Olives and/or mushrooms,
	(frozen or canned)		sliced
16-18	Better 'n Meatballs (see below)		

Steam or simmer spinach in a small amount of water until tender. In a larg
pot, sauté onion and garlic in a small amount of water or olive oil. Ad
spinach and remaining ingredients, except meatballs, and simmer 5 to 1
minutes. Serve with spaghetti noodles and Better 'n Meatballs (recip
below) on the side.

Yield: 10 c

BETTER 'N MEATBALLS

1 pkg   Morning Star Farms® Better 'n Burgers   (4 patties per pkg)

Thaw burgers completely. Lightly oil or spray hands with a no-stick cooking
spray. Break off pieces of the patties and re-shape into 16 to 18 1-inch balls.
Arrange on a cookie sheet and bake at 350° F, 10 to 15 minutes.

Tip: For a quick appetizer, try Better 'n Meatballs with the Barbecue
Sauce on page 166. Serve with fringed toothpicks.

Yield: 16 to 18

BAKED EGGPLANT PARMESAN

1 lg	Eggplant	1/2 tsp	Marjoram
2 c	Corn bread stuffing mix	1/2 tsp	Thyme
1/2 tsp	Paprika	1/2 tsp	Salt
1/2 tsp	Onion powder	1/2 c	Garbanzo Mayonnaise
1/2 tsp	Garlic salt		

Wash eggplant (peeling is optional). Slice eggplant into 1/2 inch thick pieces. In a blender, process stuffing mix and spices to make fine crumbs. Coat both sides of eggplant with Garbanzo Mayonnaise (see recipe below) and then dip into the corn bread stuffing mixture. Spray a cookie sheet with no-stick cooking spray. Spread eggplant out evenly and bake at 375° F, at least 20 minutes. Slices need to be turned to have them evenly browned. Place a single layer of eggplant slightly overlapping in a casserole dish. Pour Italian sauce (p 126) or spaghetti sauce over center strip of eggplants. Garnish with grated Mozzarella and Parmesan cheese (recipes on page 127). If available, you may prefer using SoyCo® Lite & Less™ "Grated Parmesan Cheese Alternative". Bake at 350°F, 10 to 15 minutes until sauce is bubbly. Serve while hot.

Yield: 18 to 20 slices

GARBANZO MAYONNAISE

2 c	Water	1 tsp	Salt
1/2 c	Raw cashews, rinsed well	1/2 tsp	Onion salt
6 T	Garbanzo flour	1/2 tsp	Garlic powder
1/4 c	Fresh lemon juice	2 T	Instant Clear Jel®
4 tsp	Frozen apple juice concentrate		

In a blender, combine all ingredients except Instant Clear Jel. Process until very smooth. While blender is running, add Clear Jel 1 tablespoon at a time through the lid spout to thicken mayonnaise. Use as soon as possible. The thickened state is temporary (about 6 hours). For a long term effect, use 2 to 2½ T cornstarch and cook until thick. Refrigerate.

Yield: 2 ½ c

ITALIAN-STYLE
GROUND MEATLESS BALLS

1 c	Vegetarian burger (or)		1 c	Firm tofu
	1 c GranBurger®, ground and		1 c	Black olives
	rehydrated in 3/4 c hot water		2 T	Nutritional yeast flakes
1 c	Mashed potatoes, cooked		1 T	ENER-G® Egg Replacer
1 c	Onion, minced		1 T	Beef-Style seasoning
1 c	Pecans or walnuts, chopped		2 tsp	Basil
1/2 c	Quick oats		1 tsp	Garlic powder
1/2 c	Wheat germ		1 tsp	Italian seasoning
1 env	Lipton® "Onion-Mushroom" Soup Mix			
1/2 c	Seasoned bread crumbs or Pepperidge Farm Stuffing®			
2 T	Olive oil			

Combine Vegeburger (or GranBurger), mashed potatoes, onion, nuts, oats, wheat germ, soup mix, bread crumbs and oil. Set aside. In a blender, combine tofu, olives and seasonings and process until well mixed. Stir blender ingredients into dry ingredients. Shape into 1 inch balls and place on cookie sheet coated with no-stick cooking spray. Bake at 350° F, 35-40 minutes. Turn half way through cooking time to assure even browning. Serve with spaghetti sauce.

Yield: 5 c / 40 to 60 balls

CARROTS WITH ORANGE SAUCE

1 lb	Fresh carrots		2 T	Honey
1/2 c	Unsweetened pineapple juice		1/2 tsp	Orange zest (opt)
1 T	Cornstarch		1/3 c	Water
3 T	Frozen orange juice concentrate		1/4 tsp	Salt

Julienne carrots or slice diagonally. Microwave, steam or cook carrots in a small amount of water. Carrots should remain crisp-tender for improved flavor and color. In a saucepan, combine half the pineapple juice with cornstarch and stir until dissolved. Add remaining pineapple juice, orange juice, honey, orange zest, water and salt and bring to a boil stirring constantly. Cook until thick and clear. Pour orange sauce over carrots and serve.

Yield: 4 c

BROCCOLI IN LEMON SAUCE

Prepare lemon sauce and bell pepper garnish.

LEMON SAUCE:

2 T	Canola oil	1 T	Fresh lemon juice
1 T	All purpose flour	1/2 tsp	Lemon rind, grated
1/2 c	Better Than Milk™	1/4 tsp	Salt

Combine oil and flour in a small saucepan. Blend well. Add remaining ingredients. Cook over medium heat, stirring constantly, until thickened.

Note: For a creamier sauce, prepare Better Than Milk in double strength proportions of powder and water.

BELL PEPPER GARNISH:

1/8 c	Red bell pepper, slivered	1 tsp	Fresh lemon juice
1 tsp	Canola oil		

Sauté peppers in oil and lemon juice about 2 minutes. Set aside.

STEAMED BROCCOLI:
1 lb   Fresh broccoli spears

Steam broccoli just until tender. Do not overcook. Pour lemon sauce over broccoli and garnish with sautéed red bell pepper.

Yield: 6 c

GARBANZO-OLIVE SALAD

Iceberg or romaine lettuce	Carrots
Fresh spinach leaves	Bell peppers
Canned garbanzos	Red onion rings
Black olives	Artichokes, canned
Cherry tomatoes	Alfalfa sprouts

Combine any of the above ingredients to your own preference. Serve with "Lite" or "Fat Free" Italian Dressing (recipe on page 132).

Yield: Variable

"LITE" ITALIAN DRESSING

Add to one 0.7 oz package of Good Seasons "Lite" Italian dressing mix:

3 T Fresh lemon juice
3 T Pineapple juice concentrate

1/3 c Water (+ 2 T opt)
1/4 c Light olive oil

Mix together and close container. (Add an additional 2 T of water if you prefer a thinner and milder dressing.) Shake well and refrigerate. Shake again before serving.

Yield: 1 c

SPINACH & PASTA SALAD

1 c Spiral or bow tie pasta
8 c Fresh spinach, cleaned
1 c Red cabbage, finely sliced
1 c Green onion, 1 inch diagonal slices

1 c Artichoke hearts (opt)
2 T Fresh cilantro, snipped
1 c Fat-Free Italian Dressing
     (see below)

Cook pasta according to directions, rinse and chill. Break spinach leaves and remove any large stems. Chop sliced cabbage into 1 inch pieces. Add remaining ingredients and toss lightly.

Yield: 12 c

"FAT-FREE" ITALIAN DRESSING

Add to one 1.05 oz package Good Seasons® "Fat-Free" Italian Dressing Mix:

1/4 c Fresh lemon juice
2 T   Frozen apple juice concentrate

6 T   Pineapple juice
1/3 c Water

Mix together in an air-tight container. Close lid and shake well. Refrigerate 30 minutes before using. Shake again before serving.

Variation: For a stronger Italian flavor, decrease water to 1/4 c.

Yield: 1 1/8 c

MINESTRONE SOUP

1 c	Onion, chopped	1 tsp	Onion powder
1/2 c	Celery, sliced	1/2 tsp	Coriander
2 med	Garlic cloves, minced	1/16 tsp	Oregano
1 T	Olive oil	1 small	Bay leaf
6 c	Water	1½ c	Kidney or red beans, canned
1 T	Chicken-style seasoning	2 c	Diced tomatoes, canned
2 tsp	Basil, (or) 2 T fresh basil	3/4 c	Macaroni, elbow or shell
1½ tsp	Lawry's® Seasoned Salt	2 c	Zucchini, sliced or quartered
1½ tsp	Sucanat	1 c	Carrots, sliced
1 tsp	Onion powder		

In a large saucepan, sauté onion, celery and garlic in oil until tender. Add water, seasonings and beans. Bring to a boil. Lower heat, cover and simmer about 20 minutes. Add tomatoes and macaroni, cover and simmer about 10 minutes. Add zucchini and carrots and simmer 5 to 10 minutes more or until pasta and vegetables are tender. Remove bay leaf before serving.

Yield: 14 c

ITALIAN BREAD STICKS

7 oz	Warm water	1 c	Unbleached white flour
2/3 c	Raw cashews, rinsed	1/2 tsp	Italian seasonings, (opt)
1 T	Canola or olive oil	1/2 tsp	Salt
1 T	Rapid-rise active yeast	1 tsp	Garlic purée,
1 T	Honey		(mixed in 1 T water)
1 c	Whole wheat pastry flour	1 T	Sesame seeds

In a blender, combine water, cashews, and oil and process on high speed until smooth and creamy. Pour blended mixture into a bowl and stir in yeast and honey. Wait 5 minutes. In a separate bowl, combine flours, Italian seasoning (opt) and salt. Pour the blender mixture into the flour and stir until a dough forms. Knead lightly. Pinch off pieces of dough (about 1/4 c) and roll between hands to form a long thin roll about 1/2 inch thick. Coat a cookie sheet with no-stick cooking spray and lay each bread sticks down 1 inch apart. Twist each bread stick into desired shape. Lightly brush with warm water (or opt garlic water) and sprinkle with sesame seeds and pat into dough gently. Pre-heat oven to 350° F. Let rise 10 minutes or until double in size. Bake 15 to 20 minutes or until golden brown, light and crispy.

Yield: 1 dozen

GARLIC BREAD

Spread garlic butter (recipe below) generously on fresh whole grain french bread. Sprinkle with granulated garlic powder and herbs of choice. Wrap with foil and bake at 400° F, 15 minutes until warm and moist. For a crispy crust, open foil at the top and bake an additional 5 minutes.

GARLIC BUTTER

1 c	Cold water	1 T	Emes Kosher-Jel, plain
1/4 c	Yellow corn meal	1 T	Cooked carrot (opt for color)
1/2 c	Mori-Nu® tofu, x-firm	2 tsp	Garlic powder
1/2 c	Warm water	1 tsp	Honey
1/4 c	Almonds	1 tsp	Imitation butter flavored salt
3 T	Spicery Shoppe® Natural -	½ tsp	Salt
	Butter Flavor (vegan)	Pinch	Citric acid
2 T	Canola oil		

Combine cold water and corn meal in a small saucepan and bring to a boil stirring constantly. Reduce heat to low, cover and simmer 10 minutes. Refrigerate until completely cool and "set". In a blender, combine water, almonds, butter flavoring, oil and Emes. Process on high speed until no longer "gritty". Spoon chilled corn meal mush into the blender mixture and all remaining ingredients and process until smooth and creamy. Bits of carrot should not be visible. Refrigerate several hours before serving until "butter" thickens to a spreadable consistency.

Yield: 3 c

QUICK & EASY GARLIC BUTTER

10 oz	Spectrum® "non-dairy" Spread	1/4 tsp	Salt
1 tsp	Garlic powder (or) 2 tsp garlic purée		

Combine ingredients and stir until well mixed. Spread on bread as needed and wrap loaf in foil. Bake at 400° F, 15 minutes. For a crispy crust, open foil at the top and bake an additional 5 minutes.

Yield: 1¼ c

ITALIAN-STYLE PIZZA

CORN MEAL CRUST:

1 T	Dry active "rapid" yeast	1 tsp	Salt
1 T	Honey or brown sugar	2 T	Gluten flour
1¼ c	Warm water	3/4 c	Yellow corn meal
1½ T	Olive oil	2 ½ c	Unbleached flour

Dissolve yeast and honey in water. Yeast should bubble in 5 to 10 minutes. When ready add oil and salt. Beat in gluten flour by hand. Stir in cornmeal. Add flour gradually and with oiled hands knead dough gently forming dough into a ball. Place in oiled bowl and let rise 20 to 30 minutes until double. Punch down and knead briefly. Divide dough into two equal parts. Spray two pizza pans with no-stick cooking spray and sprinkle with cornmeal. Using a lightly floured rolling pin, roll dough out to 1 cm thick and 1/2 inch wider than the pizza pan. Transfer to pan and leave edges thicker to form a border.

ITALIAN PIZZA SAUCE:

1 tsp	Garlic, purée	1/2 tsp	Onion powder
1 T	Olive oil	1/2 tsp	Parsley
14 oz can	Italian plum tomatoes	1/4 tsp	Basil
6 oz	Hunt's® tomato paste	1/2 tsp	Salt
1 1/2 tsp	Sucanat®	2 tsp	SoyCo® Grated-
3/4 tsp	Ground oregano		Parmesan Cheese

Sauté garlic in oil. Add tomatoes with juice and mash until smooth. Stir in tomato paste. Add remaining ingredients and simmer 15 minutes.

METHOD:

Spoon pizza sauce over entire crust. For added flavor, sprinkle additional commercial pizza seasonings over sauce. Cover with grated Mozzarella Cheese, (recipe on page 127), your choice of favorite vegetable toppings and SoyCo® Lite & Less™ "Grated Parmesan Cheese Alternative". Bake at 450°F, 10 minutes. Reduce heat to 375° F, and continue baking 15 to 20 minutes until crust is lightly browned and toppings are cooked.

NOTE: When short on time, may substitute Italian Pizza Sauce with your favorite commercial brand pizza sauce.

Yield: Two 12 inch pizza -12 slices

ONE OF A KIND
MINI PIZZAS

Whole wheat pita bread, uncut
Garlic purée (opt)
Pizza sauce
Pizza seasoning
Soy parmesan cheese, grated
Soy mozzarella cheese, (see p 127)

Vegan sausage crumbles (opt)
Vegetables of choice
(olives, mushrooms, onions,
tomatoes etc)
Parsley

Personalize each mini pizza with choice of above ingredients. Turn pita bread up side down and if desired, spread with a thin layer of garlic before covering "crust" with pizza sauce. Season with pizza seasoning or any vegetable herb seasoning mix. Sprinkle with mozzarella and parmesan cheese, vegan crumbles and add veggies of choice. Cover with additional mozzarella and/or parmesan cheese. Garnish with parsley. Arrange pizzas on a cookie sheet or pizza stone and bake at 375° F, 15 to 20 minutes or until crust is crispy and veggies are tender.

Variation: Replace pita bread with whole wheat English muffins.

Yield: Variable

PISTACHIO ICE CREAM

1 c	Soy milk, full strength	1/4 + 1/8 tsp	Almond flavoring
1/2 c	Soy milk, powder	1/16 tsp	Green food coloring
1/3 c	DariFree, powder	1 qt	Ice cubes
1/4 c	Fructose	1 c	Pistachio nuts,chopped

In a blender, combine soy milk, milk powders, fructose, flavoring, and coloring. Blend until well mixed. Add ice cubes and blend until smooth. Pour into a bowl and stir in nuts. Freeze if necessary before serving.

Yield: 1 quart

FROSTED GRAPES

Wash and freeze red seedless grapes. Cut into clusters and arrange on a decorative platter. Serve immediately before grapes lose their "frosty look".

Yield: Variable

FROZEN FRUIT
ICE CREAM

Freeze any combination of fruits you like. In a blender, process 4 cups fruit with 6 T Better Than Milk™ powder. Add a small amount of 100% fruit juice, only if necessary to assist the blending process. Serve at once as soft ice cream or return to freezer 1-2 hours for hard ice cream. Scoop up, garnish with toppings and serve immediately.

Toppings: Sprinkle with grated coconut, chopped nuts, carob chips, sunflower seeds, or fresh chopped fruit for added flavor.

Variation: May add 1/4 c almond butter for extra creaminess.

Yield: 3 c

CARROT CAKE

1/2 c	Canola oil	2 c	Whole wheat pastry flour
1½ c	Sucanat	1 c	Oat or unbleached flour
8 oz	Canned crushed pineapple	1½ T	Ener-G Baking Powder
	("In its own juice" undrained)	1½ T	Ener-G Baking Soda
3 c	Carrots, finely grated	1 tsp	Salt
1/4 c	Grated coconut, unsweetened	1 tsp	Coriander
1/2 c	Water	1/4 tsp	Cardamom (heaping)
2 tsp	Vanilla, natural	1/2 tsp	Cinnamon (heaping)
1 c	Raisins	1/2 c	Walnuts, chopped (opt)

In a large bowl, combine oil, Sucanat and crushed pineapple, undrained, and mix together well until the Sucanat is completely dissolved. Add carrots, coconut, water, vanilla and raisins and mix until well blended. In a separate bowl, combine remaining ingredients. Then add gradually to the wet ingredients, mixing until well blended. Spray 2 cake pans or one oblong baking pan with no-stick cooking spray and lightly flour before adding batter. Bake at 350° F, 30 to 35 minutes if using cake pans or 45 to 55 minutes for the oblong pan. Cool. Top with frosting of choice. (See next page)

Yield: 9 x 13 sheet cake (or) double 9 inch layered cake

"BETTER THAN CREAM CHEESE" FROSTING

12 oz	Tofutti® Better Than Cream Cheese	1½ tsp	Instant Clear Jel
6 T	Powdered sugar		(food thickener)
3 T	Vanilla, powdered or natural	1/3 c	Pecans, chopped

Using an electric beater, whip cream cheese with sugar and vanilla until smooth and fluffy. Sprinkle the Instant Clear Jel into the mixture while beating on medium speed and continue 15 seconds until thickened. Stir in nuts. Spread on completely cooled cake. May garnish with additional pecans.

Note: Double recipe to frost a layered cake.

Yield: 2 c (scant)

ORANGE FLUFF TOFU WHIPPED TOPPING

1 box	Mori-Nu® Tofu, x-firm	1/4 c	Powdered sugar
1/3 c	Orange juice concentrate	1 tsp	Vanilla, natural
1/3 c	Water	2 T	Instant Clear Jel
1/4 tsp	Salt		(food thickener)

In a blender, combine all ingredients except Instant Clear Jel. Process until smooth and creamy. Set the blender on medium speed, remove the lid spout and add Clear Jel one tablespoon at a time until thickened. Chill before spreading on cake. May garnish with choice of sliced orange wedges, orange twists or grated orange peel and fresh mint leaves.

Note: Double recipe to cover a layered cake.

Yield: Approx 2 c

ALMOND CHEESECAKE DELIGHT

CRUST:

1 c	Freshly ground pecans	1/8 tsp	Salt
1 c	Graham cracker crumbs	3 T	Water
3 T	Vital wheat gluten (Do-Pep)		

Process raw pecans in a food processor or blender until they are finely ground. Combine pecans with remaining ingredients. Work mixture with hands until the water has evenly moistened the dry ingredients and mixture is slightly sticky. Pour into an 8 inch pie pan or spring form mold and press mixture out to edges evenly. Bake 10 minutes at 325° F. Set aside to cool.

FILLING:

1/2 c	Water	1/4 c	Better Than Milk™ powder
1/2 c	White grape/peach juice, (frozen concentrate)	2 ½ T	Emes Kosher-Jel®, plain
		2 T	Honey, fructose or sugar
1/2 c	Slivered almonds, (w/o skins)	1 T	Fresh lemon juice
1 c	Fresh tofu, x-firm	1 T	Natural vanilla
1 c	Cooked white rice, packed	1/8 tsp	Salt
1/4 c	Unbleached white flour		

Combine water, juice (Welch's 100%), and almonds in a blender and process on high speed until almonds are completely liquefied and mixture does not taste "gritty". Add remaining ingredients and process until smooth and creamy. It may be necessary to stop and stir mixture as needed during processing. Pour blender ingredients into a saucepan and heat over med/lo stirring constantly until thickened. Pour mixture into a pre-baked and cooled crust. Refrigerate 2 to 3 hours until set. Serve with berry topping of choice. (Recipes follow)

Yield: 4 c

BLUEBERRY TOPPING

3 c	Blueberries (fresh or frozen)	1/4 c	White grape juice (frozen concentrate)
1/4 c	FruitSource® or honey	1½ T	Cornstarch

Bring 2 c blueberries and FruitSource® or honey to a boil in a heavy saucepan. Mix the (Welch's 100%) white grape juice and cornstarch together and stir until dissolved. Pour the cornstarch-juice mixture into the boiling berries, stirring constantly. Reduce heat, continue stirring and simmer until mixture is thick and clear. Remove from heat. Gently stir in remaining blueberries. Chill.

Yield: 3 c

STRAWBERRY-RASPBERRY TOPPING

1 c	Birds Eye® frozen raspberries	1 T	Cornstarch
1/4 c	White grape juice, frozen concentrate	2 c	Fresh strawberries
3 T	FruitSource® or 2 T honey		

Combine thawed raspberries with their juice, (Welch's 100%) white grape juice, FruitSource® and cornstarch in a blender and process until smooth. Strain the puréed mixture through a sieve to remove seeds. Pour into a saucepan and simmer, stirring constantly until thick and clear. Cool. Slice strawberries and stir into mixture. Refrigerate until needed.

Yield: 3 c

LEMON CUSTARD PIE

3/4 c	Pineapple chunks	3 T	Fresh lemon juice
1/2 c	Water	2 c	Pineapple juice
1/2 c	Raw cashews, rinsed	1/3 c	Fructose
1/2 c	Minute® Tapioca	1 tsp	Vanilla, natural
1/4 c	Welch's white grape/peach (frozen) 100% juice concentrate	1/4 tsp	Lemon zest
		1/8 tsp	Salt
1/4 c	Better than Milk™ powder	Pinch	Turmeric

In a blender, combine pineapple chunks, water, cashews, tapioca, juice concentrate, milk powder, and lemon juice. Process on high speed until smooth and creamy. Add remaining ingredients and blend again until well mixed. Pour mixture into a heavy non-stick sauce pan or double boiler pan and bring to a boil stirring constantly. Reduce heat slightly and simmer until thick and tapioca dissolves. Cool 5 minutes. Pour into a "9 inch" graham cracker or granola crust. Refrigerate until set, about 6 hours. Garnish with lightly toasted shredded coconut before serving if desired.

Yield: 9 inch pie

LEMON CHIFFON PIE

1/2 c	Water	2 c	Pineapple juice
1/2 c	Raw cashews, rinsed	1/3 c	Fructose
1/2 c	Pineapple chunks	3 T	Fresh lemon juice
1/4 c	Welch's white grape/peach	2 tsp	Vanilla, natural
	(frozen) 100% juice concentrate	1/2 tsp	Lemon zest
1/4 c	Better Than Milk, powder	1/8 tsp	Salt
3 T	Emes Kosher-Jel®, plain	Pinch	Turmeric

In a blender, combine water, cashews, pineapple chunks, juice concentrate, milk powder and Emes. Process until completely smooth and creamy. Add remaining ingredients and blend again until well mixed. Pour mixture into a saucepan and simmer, stirring constantly until yellow color develops. Cool to lukewarm. Fill a "9 inch" graham cracker or granola crust half full, transfer crust to your refrigerator shelf and fill to the top with remaining filling. (This procedure will avoid spilling since the filling is in a very liquid form before it is chilled and set.) Refrigerate until set, about 6 hours. Garnish with lightly toasted shredded coconut or fresh mint leaves if desired.

Yield: 9 inch pie

GRANOLA PIE CRUST

2 c	Granola	2 T	Water (more or less as needed)
1 T	Unbleached white flour		

In a blender, combine granola and flour and grind until only fine crumbs are left. Moisten with water, pour into a pie pan and pat into shape.

Yield: 1½ c

La Fiesta Grande Mexican Food

Featuring

Tasty low-fat recipes bursting with all the natural flavors of Mexico without the added hot spices and oils.

QUESADILLAS

2 doz   Corn tortillas
3 c   Enchilada sauce, (see below)
2 c   Mozzarella cheese, grated (p 127)

1 c   Olives, sliced
4 oz   Old El Paso®
        green chilies, chopped

ENCHILADA SAUCE:

1/2 c   Onion, diced
2 med   Garlic cloves, minced
1 tsp   Olive oil
15 oz   Tomato sauce
1 1/8 c Water

1½ T   Chili Powder Substitute
        (see p 148)
1 tsp   Cumin
1/2 tsp Salt

In a saucepan, sauté onion and garlic in oil until translucent. Add remaining ingredients and simmer 30 minutes. Pour 1/2 of the sauce into a shallow round bowl.

PREPARATION: Dip tortillas in enchilada sauce and transfer to a non-stick frying pan. Cover tortilla with 3 T Mozzarella grated cheese, 2 T olives and 1 tsp chilies. Dip another tortilla in the sauce and place on top. Fry over medium heat until soft and slightly crispy. Flip and fry other side the same way. Serve with additional enchilada sauce, sour cream recipe of choice (see p 145 or p 147) and guacamole recipe (see p 154).

Yield: 12 Quesadillas

"CHICKEN" ENCHILADAS

2 c   Creamy Mushroom Sauce
1 c   Sour Cream Supreme
1¼ c   Cashew Jack Cheese
1 c   Chic-Ketts™ cubed

2 tsp   Olive oil
1 c   Onion, minced
1/4 c   Green chilies, chopped
1 doz   Tortilla shells

Prepare Creamy Mushroom Sauce (see p 145), Sour Cream Supreme (see p 145) and Cashew Jack Cheese (see p 145 but do not add the Emes Jel for this recipe). Combine the required amounts of mushroom sauce, sour cream and cheese in a large bowl. Sauté Chic-Ketts in oil and add to the sauce mixture. Stir in onions and chilies and mix all together well. Fill shells, roll up and place in a baking dish, seam side down. Then add a little water to thin sauce enough to spoon remaining mixture over top. Bake at 350° F, about 30 minutes.

Yield: 12 enchiladas

144

CREAMY MUSHROOM SAUCE

1½ c	Onion, chopped	2/3 c	Unbleached white flour
2 T	Olive oil	1/3 c	Better Than Milk™ powder
2 c	Fresh mushrooms	2 tsp	Nutritional yeast flakes
1 c	Water	2 tsp	Chicken-style seasoning
1/4 tsp	Onion salt	1½ tsp	Salt
3 c	Water	1/2 tsp	Sweet basil, dry

Sauté onions in oil until golden. Coarse chop mushrooms and add to the onions with 1 c water and onion salt and simmer until mushrooms are tender. Set aside 1c sautéed mushrooms. In a blender, combine 3 c water, flour, tofu milk powder, and seasonings and process until smooth and creamy. Add the reserved 1 c mushrooms to the blender and "flash blend" ingredients together twice. Pour blender ingredients into a saucepan and bring to a boil stirring constantly until thickened. Add remaining onion and mushroom mixture and mix well.   Yield 4 c

SOUR CREAM SUPREME

1¼ c	Mori-Nu® Tofu, firm (10.5 oz box)	1 tsp	Honey
1/4 c	Sunflower oil	1/2 tsp	Salt
2 ½ T	Fresh lemon juice		

In a blender, combine all ingredients and process until smooth and creamy.
Yield: 1½ c

CASHEW JACK CHEESE

1 c	Water	1 T	Fresh lemon juice
4 T	Emes Kosher-Jel®, plain	1½ tsp	Salt
1 c	Cooked rice, brown or white	1 tsp	Onion powder
1/2 c	Raw cashews, rinsed	1/4 tsp	Garlic powder
1 T	Nutritional yeast flakes		

In a blender, combine water, Emes Jel, rice and cashews. Process on high speed until completely smooth and creamy. Add seasonings and blend again until well mixed. Pour into a container coated with no-stick cooking spray. Refrigerate several hours until set. Gently shake out of container to slice cheese as needed. To grate cheese easily, freeze mixture at least 2 hours first. Or, for a creamy sauce to serve over vegetables, slowly heat and melt cheese over lo-med heat stirring frequently.   Yield: 2 c

TEX-MEX
"CHEESE" ENCHILADAS

ENCHILADA SAUCE:

1 c	Onions, diced	2 ½ T	Chili Powder
5 med	Garlic cloves, minced		Substitute (p 148)
2 tsp	Olive oil	2 tsp	Cumin
2 cans	Tomato sauce (15 oz each)	1 tsp	Salt
2 ½ c	Water		

In a 2 quart saucepan, sauté onions and garlic in oil until translucent. Add remaining ingredients and simmer 30 minutes.

FILLING:

2 lb	Fresh tofu, firm	1½ tsp	Onion powder
3 T	Soy sauce or liquid aminos	3/4 tsp	Cumin
1½ T	Tomato paste	2 tsp	Olive oil
1½ T	Peanut butter		

Freeze tofu ahead of time to change tofu into a "bean curd". Thaw tofu and squeeze the excess water out. Tear the bean curd into bite-size pieces. Combine soy sauce, tomato paste, peanut butter, onion powder and cumin and mix with the tofu pieces. Pour into a large non-stick frying pan or skillet and brown in oil, turning often. Proceed with recipe.

1½ c	Mozzarella cheese, grated (see p 127)	2 T	Old El Paso® mild green chilies, chopped
1 c	Olives, sliced		
1/2 c	Onion, chopped	15	Corn tortillas

Stir the grated cheese, olives, onions and chilies into the tofu mixture.

PREPARATION: Spray a 9x13 casserole dish with no-stick cooking spray. Fill the bottom of the dish with enough enchilada sauce to cover. Heat tortillas in a frying pan over med heat until softened. Lay 1/3 c filling at the edge of the shell and roll it up tightly and place seam side down in rows. Continue procedure until pan is filled. Cover with sauce and bake uncovered at 350° F, about 25 minutes or until bubbling. Garnish with additional grated mozzarella cheese and olives if desired and return to oven 5 more minutes. Serve with "Soy Good" Tofu Sour Cream. (See p 147)

Yield: 15 enchiladas

"SOY GOOD"
TOFU SOUR CREAM

1½ c	Mori-Nu® Tofu, firm (12.3 oz box)	1/4 tsp	Salt
3 T	Sunflower oil	1/4 tsp	Honey
1/4 tsp	Citric acid crystals		

In a blender, combine all ingredients and process until smooth and creamy.

Variation: Add 1 tsp fresh lemon juice for a stronger sour taste.

Yield: 1½ c

MEXICAN ENCHILADAS

FILLING:

2 c	Pimento Cheese, grated (see p 148)	1½ c	Onion, chopped
1/4 c	Mild green chilies, chopped	1/4 c	GranBurger®
1/2 c	Black olives, sliced	1/4 c	Warm water

Rehydrate Granburger in water. Combine all ingredients.

SAUCE:

2 cans	Hunt's® Ready Sauce, "Special"	2 T	Olive oil
6 oz	Tomato paste	1 T	Garlic purée
1 c	Water	1 tsp	Garlic powder
1½ T	Mild chili powder (or substitute *)	1 tsp	Cumin
1 tsp	McKay's® Beef-style seasoning		

Combine Special Sauce and tomato paste. Stir in remaining ingredients.
(* see Chili Powder Substitute recipes on page 148)

SHELLS:

15	Fresh corn tortillas (Frozen tortillas break easily)

PROCEDURE:

Fill bottom of baking dish with enough sauce to cover. Heat tortillas one at a time in a frying pan until softened. Spoon 1/4 c filling into tortilla shells, roll them up and place enchiladas seam side down in rows. Cover with remaining sauce and sprinkle with grated Cashew Jack Cheese (see p 145) or Pimento Cheese (see p 148) and olives. Bake uncovered at 325° F, 20 to 25 minutes.

Yield: 15 enchiladas

PIMENTO CHEESE

1 1/4 c	Water		4 oz	Pimentos, canned
1 c	Cooked rice		2 T	Lemon juice
4 T	Emes Kosher-Jel®, plain		2 tsp	Onion powder
1/2 c	Tofu, x-firm		2 tsp	Salt
1/2 c	Raw cashews, rinsed		1/2 tsp	Garlic powder
3 T	Nutritional yeast flakes			

In a blender, combine water, rice, Emes Jel, tofu and cashews. Process on high speed until completely smooth and creamy. Add remaining ingredients and blend well. Pour into a container coated with no-stick cooking spray. Refrigerate several hours until set. Gently shake out to slice cheese.

Note: To grate cheese easily, freeze mixture at least 2 hours first. For a creamy sauce to serve over vegetables or noodles, do not refrigerate mixture after blending, but heat and serve immediately. Or, if using previously "set" leftovers, heat mixture slowly until cheese melts.

Yield: 3 c

CHILI POWDER SUBSTITUTE

2 T	Paprika		1 tsp	Ground cumin
1 T	Parsley flakes		1 tsp	Ground oregano
1 T	Dried bell pepper		1/2 tsp	Ground dill
1 T	Basil		1/2 tsp	Savory
1 T	Onion powder		1/4 tsp	Garlic powder
2 sm	Bay leaves			

Grind all in a blender until fine and powdery.

Yield: 1/2 c

TAMALE PIE

FILLING:

2 c	Onion, chopped		1 c	Cut corn
1/2 c	Green or red bell peppers, chopped		15 oz	Canned tomatoes, diced
			2 tsp	Chili Powder substitute*
2 T	Olive oil		1 tsp	Beef-Style seasoning
1/2 c	Vegetarian burger, canned or frozen type		1/2 tsp	Cumin
			1/2 tsp	Onion salt
2 oz	Old El Paso® mild green chilies, chopped		1/2 c	Soy cheese, grated (opt)
			1/4 c	Black olives, sliced
2 c	Canned beans, any combination of kidney, black and pinto beans			

Sauté onions and bell peppers in olive oil until tender. Stir in burger and chilies. Add the beans, corn and tomatoes and mix well. Add the chili powder, beef-style seasoning, cumin and onion salt, stir until mixture begins to simmer and remove from heat. The cheese and olives will be added later.

CRUST:

2½ c	Cold water		1½ tsp	Chili Powder substitute*
1½ c	Yellow corn meal		1 tsp	Salt
2 oz	Old El Paso® mild green chilies, chopped			

In a non-stick saucepan, combine above ingredients and bring to a boil, stirring constantly. Reduce heat, simmer and stir frequently until thick and sides pull away from the pan, about 5 minutes. Coat a 10 inch deep dish pie pan with no-stick cooking spray and pour about 2/3 of the corn meal mixture into the bottom of the pan. Spray a rubber spatula with no-stick cooking spray and press mixture over the bottom and sides of the pan. Pour filling into the pie pan and level. Sprinkle (opt) grated soy cheese over the filling. Top with sliced black olives. Drop remaining corn meal evenly over the filling and with fingers gently spread crust out to the edges. Flute the edges if desired. Bake at 350° F, 45 to 50 minutes or until golden brown.

*Note: Recipe for Chili Powder Substitute is found on page 148. If using store bought chili powder, reduce amounts listed in recipe by half.

Yield: 10 inch pie

VEGETABLE FAJITAS

2 c	Onion, sliced		1 c	Yellow summer squash
10 slices	Green bell pepper,			sliced diagonally
	2 inch long strips		1 c	Zucchini, sliced diagonally
6 slices	Red bell peppers,			and julienned
	2 inch long strips		(opt)	Salt, liquid aminos or
1 med	Garlic clove, minced			"lite" soy sauce
2 T	Olive oil		1 doz	Flour tortillas, wheat or
8 oz	Fresh spinach, trimmed			white, 8 inch
1/2 c	Fresh mushrooms, sliced			

Toppings: Limes, sour cream, (p 145 or 147) guacamole, (p 154) and salsa, (p 154)

In a large non-stick skillet, sauté onions, peppers and garlic in oil. Add 2 T to 1/4 c water and remaining vegetables, cover and simmer about 15 minutes or until vegetables are tender and water has evaporated. Season to taste. Wrap tortillas in 2 pkgs of foil and place in a warm oven until ready to serve, then transfer to a covered tortilla dish.

Tip: For a full course Mexican dinner, serve vegetable fajitas with a side dish of Spanish rice and refried beans or frijoles.

Yield: 12 fajitas

HAYSTACKS

Crispy Corn Chips *	Chopped onions
Seasoned Brown Rice *	Sliced olives
Chili Beans *	Huevos Rancheros Salsa *
Pimento Cheese, grated *	Guacamole *
Shredded lettuce	"Soy Good" Sour Cream *
Diced tomatoes	Ranch-Style Dressing *

Stack the above ingredients in the order given. For example, serve chips and/or rice on the plate first. Spoon beans on top next. Sprinkle cheese over beans. Add any or all of the other ingredients up to the top.

* See recipes consecutively on pages 151, 151, 151, 148, 154, 154, 145 or 147, and 155.

Note: For "quick" Haystacks, replace any of the above homemade ingredients for commercial products of choice.

CRISPY CORN CHIPS

6 Corn tortilla shells   Pam® "Olive Oil" type
Salt to taste

Place 6 corn tortillas in a stack. Cut into quarters, then cut quarters in half to make 8 wedge shaped stacks of chips. Arrange chips, one layer thick, on a baking sheet. Spray chips lightly with "Pam"® no-stick cooking spray and sprinkle with salt or seasoned salt. Bake in a preheated oven at 450°F, 8 to 10 minutes watching carefully to avoid browning.

Yield: 48 chips

SEASONED BROWN RICE

2 c	Water	1/2 tsp	Chicken-Style Seasoning
1 c	Uncooked brown rice	1/2 tsp	Salt
1 T	Dried onion flakes		

Combine ingredients and cook in a rice cooker or cook on the stove top until rice is tender and water is absorbed, about 45 min.

Yield: 4 c

CHILI BEANS

3 c	Dried pinto beans	1 qt	Diced tomatoes, canned
1½ c	Red kidney beans, canned	1 c	GranBurger® (or) 2 c
1½ c	Canned black beans, canned		Vegan Burger Crumbles
1 tsp	Salt, or to taste	1 T	Honey or Sucanat®
2 c	Onion, chopped	1 T	Cumin
1 c	Red or green bell pepper, chopped	1 T	Mild chili powder (or)
3 lg	Garlic cloves, minced		Chili Powder Substitute
1 T	Olive oil	2 tsp	Beef-Style Seasoning

Sort, wash, and soak pinto beans overnight. Drain. In a large pot, simmer beans for 2 to 3 hours in only enough water to keep the beans covered. When tender, add kidney beans (drained), black beans and salt. In a non-stick frying pan, steam or sauté onions, bell pepper, and garlic in oil. Add sautéed mixture, tomatoes, burger, honey and seasonings to beans and simmer 30 minutes more stirring occasionally. (The longer the beans cook, the better the flavor.) Chili beans are also good cooked in a crock pot, but with limited space, you will find it necessary to cut this recipe in half.

Yield: 12 c

QUICK & SNAPPY
3 BEAN CHILI

1 can	Bush's® Chili Magic, "Traditional Recipe"	1 can	Diced tomatoes, "no salt"
1 can	Red kidney beans, "low-sodium" variety	2/3 c	Vegan Burger Crumbles
		2 T	Dry minced onions
		1 tsp	Beef-style seasoning
1 can	Black beans	1 tsp	Cumin

Lightly drain Chili Magic and pour into a saucepan. Drain kidney beans and add to the saucepan. Do not drain black beans or tomatoes and add next. Stir in burger and seasonings. Cover and simmer chili 5 to 10 minutes. Serve hot.

Tip: Try a dollop of "Soy Good" Tofu Sour Cream (see p 147) or grated Mozzarella Cheese (see p 127) to top off this chili bean recipe.

Yield: 7 c

BAKED
CORN FRITTERS

1 c	Warm water	3/4 c	Yellow cornmeal
2 T	Honey	3 T	Better Than Milk™ powder
1 T	Yeast	1 tsp	Salt
2 T	Canola oil	1/4 c	Canned pimento, diced
1½ c	Unbleached white flour	2 T	Old El Paso® chilies, diced

Combine water, honey, yeast and oil. Let stand 3 to 5 minutes. Stir in flour, cornmeal, milk powder and salt. Add pimentos and green chilies and gently stir until evenly mixed. Spray a "corn mold" pan with a no-stick cooking spray. Fill with batter until 3/4 full. Let rise until double. Bake at 350° F, 15 minutes or until golden brown. Remove from pan and arrange on a cookie sheet bottom side up. Return to oven and bake 5 minutes more to crisp the bottom side.

Note: If using a muffin tin, bake at 350° F, 20 minutes or until lightly browned.

Yield: 12

POSÓLE SOUP

SOUP BASE:

1 T	Olive oil	1 qt	Water
1 clove	Garlic, minced	2 c	Crushed tomatoes, canned
1 stalk	Celery, thinly sliced	1 c	Tomato purée, canned
1 c	Onion, diced	1 c	Cilantro, chopped
1 c	Yellow squash, julienned	1 T	Chicken-Style seasoning
1 c	Zucchini, julienned	1 tsp	Chili powder substitute (opt)
1 c	Carrots, diced		(see p 148)
1½ c	Hominy, canned	1/2 tsp	Salt

In a large pot, sauté garlic, celery, onion, squash and carrots in oil. Add remaining ingredients, (except hominy) and simmer until vegetables are tender. Add hominy just before serving to avoid overcooking. Fill soup bowls about half way and garnish with baked tortilla strips and an assortment of toppings. (See below)

GARNISH:

12	Corn tortillas strips, baked (see below)	1 c	Avocado, cubed
2 c	Purple cabbage, finely shredded	1 c	Olives, sliced
2 c	Tomatoes, diced	2	Limes, quartered
1 c	Green onions, sliced	2	Lemons, wedged
1 can	Black beans, rinsed	(opt)	Soy cheese, grated
1 c	Radishes, minced		

Prepare **baked tortillas strips** ahead. Stack tortillas and cut them into thin strips and then cut the strips in half. Coat a cookie sheet with no-stick cooking spray and spread tortilla strips out evenly. Bake at 250° F until crisp, turning as needed. Add any or all of above toppings to hot soup. Squeeze lemon and/or lime juice over entire soup mixture.

Yield: 3 qts

HUEVOS RANCHEROS SALSA

STEAM:

1½ c	Onion, chopped	1 tsp	Salt
1 c	Bell pepper, chopped	1/4 tsp	Cumin
2 cloves	Garlic, minced	1/4 tsp	Basil
1/4 c	Parsley or cilantro, minced	1/8 tsp	Oregano

ADD:
4 oz   Old El Paso® mild green chilies, chopped and drained.
4 c   Fresh tomatoes, chopped or 1 qt canned diced tomatoes.

Combine all ingredients. Microwave or cook on stove top until vegetables are blanched. Chill and serve with chips, salads or Mexican dishes.

Yield: 7 c

GUACAMOLE

3 med	Ripe avocados	1¼ tsp	Salt or seasoned salt
1/4 c	Tofu or Soy Mayonnaise	1/2 tsp	Garlic powder (opt)
1 c	Onion, minced	1/8 tsp	Cumin (opt)
2 tsp	Fresh lemon juice	1½ c	Tomatoes, diced

Mash avocado to desired consistency. Add mayonnaise of choice (recipes on page 155 or p 167) and remaining ingredients, one at a time, mixing well after each addition. Add tomatoes last, stirring gently. Best if eaten the same day.

Yield: 5 c

SEASONED SALT

1/4 c	Celery salt	2 T	Onion powder
1/4 c	Paprika	2 tsp	Garlic powder
2 T	Salt		

Mix all ingredients well. Store in an air-tight container.

Yield: 3/4 c

TOFU MAYONNAISE

1 c	Water		1/8 tsp	Citric acid crystals
1/2 c	Tofu milk powder		2 ½ T	Instant Clear-Jel® powder
1/2 c	Almonds (w/o skins)			(or)
1/2 c	Firm tofu		3 T	Cornstarch dissolved in
1/3 c	Canola oil			2 tablespoons water
1½ tsp	Salt		1/4 c	Pineapple juice
1/2 tsp	Onion powder		1/4 c	Fresh lemon juice
1/4 tsp	Garlic powder		1 T	Frozen O.J. concentrate

Combine water, milk powder, nuts and tofu in a blender and process on high speed until completely smooth. Reduce blender speed to lowest setting and drizzle oil in slowly. Then add salt, onion powder, garlic powder, and citric acid. Resume a high speed, remove lid spout and add Instant Clear-Jel powder one tablespoon at a time. It may be necessary to stop the blender often and stir mixture to assist the blending process. Continue blending until completely smooth. (Or, add cornstarch/water to mayonnaise mixture, blend briefly and pour out into a saucepan and simmer until thick.) Pour into a bowl and gently stir in pineapple, lemon juice and orange juice concentrate. (Do not add juices to the blender. It must be stirred in by hand .) Refrigerate 1 to 2 hours before serving to enhance flavor.

Yield: 3 c

RANCH-STYLE DRESSING

1½ c	Mori Nu® tofu, firm		1 tsp	Onion powder
1/2 c	Water		1 tsp	Basil
1/4 c	Fresh lemon juice		1/2 tsp	Savory
1/4 c	Sunflower oil		1/2 tsp	Dried parsley
1¼ tsp	Salt		1/16 tsp	Citric acid crystals
1 tsp	Honey		2 T	Fresh chives, minced (opt)
1 tsp	Garlic salt		1 T	Fresh parsley, minced (opt)

Combine all ingredients except fresh herbs in a blender and process until smooth and creamy. Stir in the optional fresh chives and parsley last. Chill before serving.

Yield: 2 ½ c

RANCH DRESSING
"QUICK and EASY"

1 pkg	Ranch® Dressing Mix	1/3 c	Canola oil
	(Original buttermilk recipe)	3 to 4 T	Fresh lemon juice
1¼ c	Mori-Nu® "lite" tofu, firm	3 T	Tofu milk powder
1/2 c	Water		

Combine above ingredients in a blender and process until smooth and creamy. Chill before serving.

Variation: May add 2 T more water and decrease oil to 1/4 c for a lower fat version.

Yield 2½ c

ARROZ MEXICANO
(MEXICAN RICE)

2 T	Olive or Canola oil	1/4 tsp	Basil
1 c	Uncooked brown rice	1/4 tsp	Cumin
2 c	Water	1/4 tsp	Paprika
3/4 c	Stewed tomatoes, drained	1 c	Carrots, diced
1/2 c	Onion, chopped	1/4 c	Bell pepper, diced
1 lg	Garlic clove, minced	1/4 c	Red sweet pepper, diced
1 tsp	Chicken-Style Seasoning	1 T	Old El Paso®chilies, diced
1 tsp	Dried parsley	1 T	Fresh parsley, chopped
3/4 tsp	Salt		

Heat oil in a large saucepan over medium heat. Add the rice and stir-fry several minutes until rice is well coated with the oil. Remove from heat. (This is called "dextrinizing" and although this step is optional, it helps to prevent sticky rice.) In a blender, process "half" the water, tomatoes, onion, garlic, seasonings and herbs. Pour into rice. Stir in the remaining water, cover, and cook over medium heat 30 minutes. Add carrots and bell peppers and continue to cook 15 to 20 minutes until the liquid is absorbed and the rice is tender. Add the chilies and fresh parsley and stir until heated through. Serve immediately.

Yield: 5 c

CORNBREAD
(Yeast-Raised)

1 c	Warm water	1½ c	Unbleached white flour
3 T	Honey	3/4 c	Yellow cornmeal
2 T	Canola oil	3 T	Tofu milk powder
2½ tsp	Yeast	1 tsp	Salt

Combine water, honey, oil and yeast. Let stand 3 minutes. Stir in remaining ingredients and mix well. Pour into an 8" square pan coated with no-stick cooking spray. Let rise 30 minutes or until double. Bake at 350° F, 25 to 30 minutes until golden brown. Cool 10 minutes before trying to remove cornbread from pan.

Variation: For "quick cornbread", replace yeast with 1 T non-aluminum baking powder. Reduce salt to 1/2 tsp. Bake at 375° F, 20 to 25 minutes or until light golden brown.

Yield: 8 inch square pan or 12 muffins

FRESH FRUIT PIE

1 rec	Almond Pie Crust (see below)	1 rec	"Instant" Whipped Topping
1 rec	Fresh Fruit Pie Filling (see p 158)		(see p 158)

ALMOND PIE CRUST

1/2 c	Barley flour	1/4 c	Raw almond butter
1/2 c	All purpose flour	1/4 c	Hot water
1 T	Wheat germ (opt)	2 ½ T	Canola oil
1/2 tsp	Salt		

Combine flours, wheat germ and salt. In a separate bowl, mix the almond butter, water and oil together. Pour into flour and stir until dough is moist. Knead into a ball and until smooth. (It won't get tough from too much handling.) Roll out between two sheets of waxed paper. Carefully remove wax paper and shape crust into pie plate. Pre-bake crust before adding fresh fruit filling. Prick the bottom of the crust with a fork and bake at 350° F, 10 to 12 minutes. Over baking causes the crust to become tough.

Variation: May replace almond butter with raw cashew butter.

Yield: 9 inch crust

FRESH FRUIT PIE FILLING

FRESH FRUIT: i.e. (Strawberries, banana, kiwi, mango, peaches, etc.)

CUSTARD:

1¼ c	Water	2½ T	Cornstarch
1/4 c	Cooked rice	2 T	Tofu milk powder
3 T	Blanched almonds (w/o skins)	1/2 tsp	Vanilla
2 T	Coconut, grated	1/8 tsp	Salt
3 T	Honey		

In a blender combine "half" the water, rice, almonds and coconut and process until smooth. Add remaining water and ingredients. Blend well. Place in saucepan and bring to a boil, stirring constantly. Pour into crust and refrigerate until cool. When chilled, cover with fresh fruits of choice, thinly sliced. Pour Berry Shine Glaze (recipe below) over fruit. Chill again. Top with "Instant" Whipped Topping (recipe below) before serving.

BERRY SHINE GLAZE:

2/3 c	Frozen apple juice concentrate	4 tsp	Cornstarch
1/3 c	Strawberries or raspberries		

In a blender, process all ingredients on high speed until creamy. Pour into a saucepan and bring to a boil, stirring constantly until thick and clear. Cool until lukewarm and pour over fresh fruit. Chill pie until ready to serve.

Yield: 9 inch pie

"INSTANT" WHIPPED TOPPING

1½ c	Water	1/3 c	Canned coconut milk
2/3 c	Better than Milk™ powder		"lite" (unsweetened)
1/2 c	Blanched almonds (w/o skins)	2 tsp	Vanilla, (natural)
3½ T	Emes Kosher-Jel®, plain	1/4 tsp	Salt
3 T	Honey or powdered sugar		Ice

In a blender, combine the water, milk powder, almonds and Emes Jel and process until the almonds are liquefied completely. Add remaining ingredients and process briefly. Finally, begin adding ice slowly through the lid spout and continue processing on high speed to make a total volume equal to 5 cups. Turn blender off and wait briefly. Mixture should now be light and fluffy. Best served immediately. If stored, and mixture becomes too firm, hand whip or beat gently with an electric beater before serving.

Yield: 5 c

VIRGIN PIÑA COLADA

1½ c	Crushed pineapple with juice	2 T	Cream of coconut
1/2 c	Canned coconut milk, unsweetened	3 c	Ice cubes
2 T	Pineapple juice (frozen) concentrate		

Combine all ingredients in a blender. Blend on high speed until drink becomes slushy. Serve immediately.

Yield: 4 c

VIRGIN STRAWBERRY DAIQUIRI

| 10 oz | Frozen strawberries | 6 oz | Water |
| 6 oz | Lemonade concentrate | | |

Combine ingredients in a blender. Process until well mixed. Add ice cubes until blender is full and blend again until mixture becomes slushy.

Note: If using unsweetened strawberries, add honey or fructose, if desired.

Yield: 2 ½ c

La FIESTA "SPLASH" SLUSHY DRINK

2 c	Fresh ripe mango, cubed	1½ c	Water
1 c	Fresh ripe papaya, cubed	1 c	Pineapple juice
1/2 c	Chiquita® "Caribbean Splash"	1 tsp	Fresh lime juice
	(frozen juice concentrate)	1/2 tsp	Coconut flavoring (opt)

In a blender, combine all ingredients and process until smooth. Pour into a large shallow pan, cover and freeze several hours until slushy. Spoon into glasses and garnish with lime wedges.

Variation: Add 1 ripe banana to mixture. Also, may replace mango with ripe peaches.

Yield: 6 c

HOW TO COOK DRY BEANS

Measure desired amount of beans (1 c dry beans yields about 2 ½ c of cooked beans). Wash several times with water, removing any spotted or discolored beans Cover with water and soak overnight. Soybeans and garbanzos cook faster if frozen after being soaked. Other beans need not be frozen after being soaked, but, if you do this, it will shorten their cooking time.

To one cup of beans add 4 c water (for lentils use 3 c only). Bring to boiling point and reduce heat just to keep a constant simmer. Add more boiling water as necessary until beans are at desired tenderness. Lentils may be cooked in less than one hour, and should not be soaked, however, other beans may vary up to two hours or more. Soybeans and garbanzos will take 5 or more hours to be palatable and tender. When tender, add salt to taste, 1/2 tsp (more or less) to each cup of dried beans. Additional seasoning is advised as your taste indicates.

Many people do not eat beans because they cause flatus or gas. This can be overcome by preparing them properly. The substance in beans which produce gas, two unusual starches: stachyose and raffinose, are not broken down by the starch digesting enzymes normally present in the gut. Thus they remain in the digestive tract to come into contact with certain bacteria which react to break them down to carbon dioxide and hydrogen, which are the main components of gastrointestinal gas.

To break down these starches so they can be digested, wash the beans in the morning. Then place them in the amount of water needed for cooking. Let them soak all day. Before going to bed, place them in the freezer. The freezing process breaks up the starch molecules. Cook them in the same water that is now ice, but do not add any salt. Use the meat tenderizer that contains papain, which comes from papaya. This tenderizer contains salt, therefore it takes the place of salt. The papaya enzyme gets through to these starches and breaks them down. They will not cause any gas. If you cannot find meat tenderizer with papain then use six papaya enzyme tablets, crushed. These are equivalent to one teaspoon of meat tenderizer. Papaya enzymes do not contain salt. Therefore you will have to add salt. The INDO meat tenderizer is available in most nutritional centers and is free from harmful additives. Be sure to check the label as not all are acceptable.

Methods to help eliminate the distress from eating beans include the following:

1. Soak overnight, drain, cover with water and cook.
2. Soak overnight, drain and cover with water, bringing to a boil.
   Let set for one hour, then drain, add water and cook.
3. Soak overnight, drain and cover with water. Add 1-2 T fennel seed
   before cooking.
4. Soak overnight, drain and freeze beans. Rinse, add water and cook.

To all white beans at the time of salting add a few sprinkles of garlic salt. Lentils and black beans are good this way also. Simmer for 15 minutes. Red beans and soybeans are tasty with a sauce made of 1 c onions, diced and sautéed in water until tender. Then add 1 clove of minced garlic, 1 T diced pimento, and 2 T tomato paste. For soybeans use 1/2 c tomato paste, more onion and a bit of lemon juice. Simmer together and add to the beans. Cook beans until soupy thickness. A pinch of sweet basil, oregano or Italian seasoning may be added. Garbanzos are excellent when simmered with chopped onions, a little nutritional food yeast and salt.

Cooking Times for Legumes

There are two methods of pre-soaking legumes before cooking. Only lentils and split peas require no soaking before cooking.

1. Long Soak Method: Cover beans with about four times their volume of cold water and let stand to soak for 8 hours or longer.
2. Rapid Soak Method: Cover beans with about four times their volume. Bring to a boil, reduce heat and simmer 2 minutes. Remove from heat. Cover and let stand 1 hour before cooking.

Pressure cooking dramatically decreases the cooking times of dried beans. Use 4 cups water to 1 cup beans. Never fill the cooker more than half full. Add 1 T oil to lessen frothing. Cook beans without salt at 15 lbs pressure.

Item:	Pressure Cooker:	Stove Top:
Lentils	5 - 10 minutes	45 minutes
Navy beans	20 minutes	1 hour
Green split peas	20 minutes	1 hour
Black-eyed peas	30 minutes	2 hours
Kidney beans	60 minutes	3 hours
Pinto beans	60 minutes	3 hours
Garbanzos	70 minutes	4 - 6 hours
Soybeans	70 minutes	4 - 6 hours

Stars & Stripes Sizzler

Featuring

A variety of fun and tasty recipes combined to make your 4th of July picnic delightfully healthy and a smashing success.

BARBECUED VEGETARIAN KABOBS

24 cubes	Marinated tofu	2 sm	Zucchini, 1/4-inch slices
12 pieces	Marinated Chic-Ketts	12	Whole button mushrooms
2 med	Carrots, 1/2 in. diagonal cuts	12	Cherry tomatoes
1 med	Onion, cut in thick wedges	24	Pineapple chunks
1 sm	Bell pepper, 1-inch squares		

Cut "x-firm" fresh tofu, into 2 cm cubes. Cover tofu with Tofu Marinade (see p 165) and marinate in the refrigerator at least 4 to 24 hours before time of barbecue. Prepare Kabob Sauce or Tangy Mayo (page 165) for the Kabob dressing. Prepare the Teriyaki Sauce (page 165). Tear Chi-Ketts (or vegetable protein of choice) into large bite-size pieces and marinate in Teriyaki Sauce at least 20 minutes while preparing the vegetables.

Microwave or simmer carrots and onions in a small amount of water until crisp-tender. Add bell peppers and zucchini and cook 1 minute more. Sauté pre-marinated tofu in a non-stick fry pan with a small amount of left-over marinade. Be careful to brown all sides a few minutes until crispy to prevent tofu from falling off skewer. Set aside. Sauté pre-marinated Chic-Ketts or gluten of choice in 1/3 cup Teriyaki Sauce until the liquid has evaporated and the gluten is nicely browned.

Place vegetables, prepared tofu and gluten on kabob skewers in the following order: (Add or delete any ingredient according to preference.)

1. Chi-Ketts	5. Zucchini	9. Tofu
2. Onion	6. Carrot	10. Pineapple
3. Pineapple	7. Tomato	11. Onion
4. Tofu	8. Bell pepper	12. Mushroom

BARBECUE OPTION:
Place kabobs on a lightly oiled grill 4-6 inches above a solid bed of low-glowing coals. Grill, turning often and basting liberally with Kabob Sauce or Tangy Mayo until vegetables are tender.

OVEN OPTION:
Arrange kabobs on a cookie sheet coated with no-stick cooking spray. Pour Kabob Sauce or brush Tangy Mayo over kabobs and bake at 400° F, 20 to 25 minutes or until lightly browned. Turn once and baste several times with sauce during baking.

Yield: 12 vegetarian kabobs

KABOB SAUCE

1½ c	Tomato sauce	2 T	Honey
2 T	Lemon juice	2 T	Pineapple juice
3 T	Bragg® Liquid Aminos or soy sauce	1/4 tsp	Garlic powder

Mix together and store in refrigerator until ready for use.

Yield: 2½ c

TERIYAKI SAUCE

1/2 c	Water	1¼ tsp	Onion powder
2 tsp	Bragg® Liquid Aminos (or) "lite" soy sauce	1/4 tsp	Garlic powder
		2 T	Honey
1 tsp	Lemon juice	2 T	Brown sugar

Mix together and store in refrigerator until ready for use.   Yield: 3/4 c

TOFU MARINADE

1/4 c	Olive or canola oil	1 T	Sesame oil
1/4 c	Lemon juice	1 tsp	Oregano powder
1/4 c	Bragg® Liquid Aminos (or) "dark" soy sauce	2 med	Garlic cloves, minced

Drain tofu, cube and let stand 15 min. while preparing marinade.   Put the marinade and tofu into a plastic zip-lock bag, remove the air, seal and set the bag in a shallow pan so the tofu is covered by the marinade.

Yield: 3/4 c

TANGY MAYO KABOB DRESSING

1 c	Soy Mayonnaise, (see p 167)	1/2 tsp	Garlic purée
1 tsp	Oregano powder	1/2 tsp	Paprika
1 tsp	Cumin		

Mix together and store in refrigerator until ready for use.

Yield: 1 c

VEGETARIAN "MEATBALLS"
with
BARBECUE SAUCE

MEATBALLS:

2 c	Textured Vegetable Protein *	1/4 c	Vital wheat gluten flour
1 ½ c	Boiling water	1 T	Nutritional yeast flakes
1 T	Soy sauce or Bragg Aminos	1 tsp	Soy or tofu milk powder
1 T	Olive oil	1 tsp	Beef-style seasoning
1/2 c	Onion, chopped fine	1/2 tsp	Garlic powder
1/4 c	Pecans, finely chopped	1/8 tsp	Basil or Italian seasoning
1/4 c	Whole wheat flour	Pinch	Paprika

* (TVP)

Mix TVP with water, soy sauce and oil and let stand 10 minutes. Add remaining ingredients and mix thoroughly. Shape into 1-inch balls. Coat a cookie sheet with no-stick cooking spray and bake at 350° F, 20 minutes, or until lightly browned. Serve with barbecue sauce or spaghetti sauce and pasta.

Yield: 20 balls

BARBECUE SAUCE:

1½ c	Tomato sauce	2 tsp	Fresh lemon juice
3 T	Molasses	1/2 tsp	Liquid smoke
2 T	Tomato paste	1/4 tsp	Onion powder
1 T	Honey	1/8 tsp	Garlic powder
4 tsp	Soy sauce	2 tsp	Instant Clear Jel
	(or) Bragg Liquid Aminos		

In a blender, combine all ingredients, except Clear Jel, and process until well mixed. Set blender on medium speed, remove lid spout and add Clear Jel to blender while in motion. Mixture will thicken in 5 to 10 seconds.

Yield: 2 c

CLASSIC POTATO SALAD

4 or 5 c	Potatoes, (cooked, peeled and cut into 3/4" cubes)	2 T	Fresh parsley, minced
		2½ tsp	Onion powder
1 c	Celery, finely chopped	1½ tsp	Dill weed
1 c	Onions, finely chopped	1 tsp	Salt
1/2 c	Pickles, chopped	1/4 tsp	Garlic powder
1/2 c	Black olives, sliced	1/8 tsp	Turmeric
1 c	Soy Mayonnaise (recipe below)		

In a large bowl, combine vegetables, pickles (vinegarless), olives and mayonnaise and stir gently until well mixed. Combine seasonings and stir evenly into the potato mixture. Serve hot or cold.

Yield: 8 c

SOY MAYONNAISE

1 c	West Soy® Plus™ soy milk	1/2 tsp	Onion powder
2 T	Cornstarch or arrowroot	1/4 tsp	Garlic powder
1/2 c	Water	1/8 tsp	Citric acid
1/2 c	Better Than Milk™ powder	2 T	Instant Clear-Jel®
1/4 c	Slivered almonds, (w/o skins)	1/4 c	Pineapple juice
1/3 c	Canola oil	1/4 c	Fresh lemon juice
1¼ tsp	Salt		

Dissolve starch in soy milk. Simmer over medium heat stirring constantly until thick. Cool. In a blender, combine water, milk powder, and almonds and process on high speed until completely smooth. Reduce blender speed and slowly dribble in oil through the lid spout. Turn the blender off, add the cooled soy milk and spices then blend again until well mixed. Keep the blender running at a high speed and add Instant Clear-Jel powder one tablespoon at a time. It may be necessary to stop often and stir mixture to assist the blending process. Continue blending until completely smooth. Pour into a bowl and gently stir in the pineapple and lemon juice. (Do not add juices to the blender.) Refrigerate 1 to 2 hours before serving.

Yield: 2½ c

PICNIC POTATO SALAD

2 lb   Red potatoes, boiled (about 1 qt)   1 c   Potato Salad Dressing
1 c   Onion, chopped   (see below)
3/4 c   Celery, sliced or diced   1 tsp Salt
1/2 c   Pickles, chopped   1 tsp Dill weed

Cool potatoes and cut into bite size cubes. (Peeling is optional.) Add onion, celery, and pickles. Combine Potato Salad Dressing, salt and dill weed and stir gently into potato mixture. Chill before serving.

Yield: 7 c

POTATO SALAD DRESSING

1 c   Soy milk   1/2 tsp   Salt
1/4 c   Canola oil   2 T   Instant Clear Jel
2 T   Carrot, cooked   (instant food thickener)
1½ tsp   Onion powder   1½ T   Fresh lemon juice

In a blender, combine soy milk, oil, carrot, onion powder and salt. Process on high speed until carrots are liquefied. Add food thickener through the lid spout while blending on low speed. Increase speed as it thickens. Pour out into a bowl and add lemon juice. Stir until well mixed.

Yield: 1½ c

MACARONI SALAD

4 c   Cooked elbow macaroni   1/4 c   Sliced olives, black or green
3/4 c   Red onion, chopped   1/2 c   Soy mayonnaise, (see p 167)
3/4 c   Celery, sliced   1/2 tsp   Garlic salt
3/4 c   Dill pickles, chopped   1/8 tsp   Celery salt

Combine all ingredients and mix lightly. Chill before serving.

Yield: 7 c

MOCK EGG SALAD

1 recipe	Scrambled Tofu "Eggs", without vegetables (see p 66)	1/3 c	Olives, sliced (opt)
		1/3 c	Celery, sliced (opt)
1/2 c	Soy mayonnaise (see p 167)	1/3 c	Pickles, diced (opt)
1/2 c	Onions, chopped (opt)		

Prepare "eggs" according to directions except omitting onions, peppers, mushrooms and chives. Chill. Prepare soy mayonnaise and refrigerate. When chilled, add mayonnaise, onions, olives, celery and pickles (each more or less than specified according to preference), and stir gently into "eggs" until well mixed.

Yield: 4 c

CHOICE COLESLAW

1/2 head	White cabbage	2	Carrots, grated
1/4 head	Red cabbage	1	Red apple, diced
2 stalks	Celery, sliced	1 c	Cooked pasta spirals (opt)

Thinly slice cabbage and place in a large bowl. Add celery, carrots and apple to the cabbage. Cook pasta according to directions, rinse and drain well. Toss in with slaw. Add one recipe Coleslaw Dressing (recipe below) more or less according to taste.

Yield: 10 c

COLESLAW DRESSING

1 c	Crushed pineapple, drained	1/8 tsp	Salt
1/4 c	Honey	1 T	Instant Clear Jel
3 T	Fresh lemon juice	1 c	Soy Mayonnaise *

In a blender, whiz pineapple with honey, lemon juice, and salt. Add Clear Jel through the lid spout while blender is running. Pour out into a bowl. Stir in Soy Mayonnaise (recipe on page 167), then mix with well drained coleslaw. Adjust amount of dressing to your taste.

Yield: 2½ c

BLUE RIBBON BAKED BEANS

1 lb	Dried navy or great northern beans, dry
1 c	Onion, chopped
2 cloves	Garlic, minced
1/4 c	Olive or canola oil
1/4 c	Date butter, brown sugar or Sucanat®
1 c	Ketchup (see recipes on page 171)
1 or 2 tsp	Worcestershire sauce, (vegetarian brand)
6 T	Pure maple syrup
1/4 c	Light molasses
14 oz can	Peeled tomatoes
20 oz can	Unsweetened pineapple tidbits, drained
2 c	Bell peppers, diced
(opt)	Salt or soy sauce to taste

Wash and sort beans. Soak overnight in a large pot of water. Rinse soaked beans well under cold water and place them in a large pot. Cover with water and bring to a boil. Reduce heat and simmer until tender (about 45 minutes to 1 hour). Drain, reserving 3/4 cup cooking liquid.

In a 2-quart casserole dish or Dutch oven, over medium heat, sauté the onion and garlic in oil until onions are translucent (about 5 minutes). Add the date butter, brown sugar or Sucanat and stir over medium-low heat until dissolved. Then stir in the ketchup and the remaining ingredients. Add salt, if desired to taste. Add the drained beans and mix well.

Preheat oven to 300° F. Cover the Dutch oven and transfer it to the oven, stirring occasionally for 2½ hours. Add the reserved bean liquid. Cover and bake 30 minutes more. Remove the cover and bake until the sauce is thick and syrupy (another 10 to 15 minutes). Serve hot.

Tip: Leftovers freeze well or you can divide recipe in half for a smaller yield.

Yield: 4 qts

"SPICY" VINEGARLESS TOMATO KETCHUP

1/2 c	Tomato purée	1 tsp	Salt
12 oz	Tomato paste	1/2 tsp	Basil
1/2 c	Tomato sauce	1/2 tsp	Paprika
3 T	Frozen pineapple juice concentrate	1/4 tsp	Cumin
2 T	Frozen orange juice concentrate	1/4 tsp	Garlic powder
3 T	Lemon juice	1 T	Honey
1 tsp	Calamansi lime or kumquat juice	2 T	Date butter
1/2 tsp	Spike® All Purpose Seasoning		(see p 211)
1 tsp	Onion powder		

Combine all ingredients in a blender and process until smooth. Refrigerate. The flavor improves after 2 days. Freeze extras not used within two weeks. After thawing, blend again before using.　　　　　　　Yield: 4 c

"THICK & ZESTY" VINEGARLESS KETCHUP

12 oz	Tomato paste	1 tsp	Onion powder
1 c	Tomato sauce	1 tsp	Salt
1/4 c	Fresh lemon juice	1/2 tsp	Paprika
1/4 c	Froz. pineapple juice conc.	1/2 tsp	Garlic salt
2 T	Froz. orange juice concentrate	1/8 tsp	Cumin
1 tsp	Lime juice	2 T	Honey
1/4 tsp	Citric acid crystals	3 T	Date butter (p 211)

Combine all ingredients in a blender and process until smooth. Refrigerate. The flavor improves after 2 days. Freeze extras not used within two weeks.

"QUICK" VINEGARLESS KETCHUP

1½ c	Tomato sauce	2 T	Fruit-Fresh®, powder
1 c	Tomato paste		(or) 1/8 tsp citric acid
1/2 c	Pineapple juice	1½ tsp	Salt
1/4 c	Fresh lemon juice	1 tsp	Onion powder
1 tsp	Lime juice	1/2 tsp	Garlic salt
3 T	Date butter (p 211)	1/2 tsp	Paprika
2 T	Pineapple/orange juice	1/4 tsp	Worcestershire sauce (opt)
	(frozen concentrate)		(Vegetarian brand)
2 T	Honey		

Combine all ingredients in a blender and process until smooth. Refrigerate. Freeze extras not used within two weeks.　　　　　　　Yield: 4 c

PEACH-RASPBERRY CRISP

FILLING:

1 qt	Canned or frozen peaches	1 tsp	Lemon juice
1 c	Frozen raspberries, drained	1/4 tsp	Salt
1 can	Dole® "Orchard Peach"	1/4 tsp	Cinnamon *
	(frozen juice concentrate)	1/8 tsp	Nutmeg
3 T	Minute® Tapioca		

Drain peaches and reserve juice. Chop peaches into bite-size pieces. Combine frozen juice concentrate with tapioca. Add lemon juice and salt. Bring juice to a boil over med-low heat, stirring often. Stir in peaches, raspberries, and spices when juice is thick and clear. Pour into a 9 x 13 inch pan coated with a no-stick cooking spray.

TOPPING:

1 c	Quick oats	1/2 tsp	Salt
1/2 c	Unbleached white flour	1/4 tsp	Cinnamon *
1/2 c	Walnuts, chopped	1/3 c	Dates (or) 3 T brown sugar
1/4 c	Old fashioned oats	3 T	Canola oil
1/4 c	Shredded coconut	1 tsp	Vanilla

DATE OPTION:
Combine dry ingredients except dates and set aside. Cook dates over med-low heat with enough left over juice from peaches to cover dates. Simmer until dates become a smooth paste. Process in blender if necessary. Add oil and vanilla to the date mixture. Combine the date mixture and dry ingredients and mix together until topping is moist and crumbly. Cover fruit evenly with the topping. Bake at 350° F, about 20 minutes or just until topping is golden brown. Watch carefully.

BROWN SUGAR OPTION:
Combine dry ingredients except brown sugar. Combine brown sugar, oil and vanilla. Mix the dry and wet ingredients together until crumbly. Add enough reserved peach juice or water to moisten topping. Cover fruit evenly with the topping. Bake at 350° F, 20 to 25 minutes or until golden brown.

Variation: For those who prefer a cinnamon substitute; Combine 2 T ground coriander and 2 tsp ground anise or cardamom. Store in a covered container.

Tip: Serve with "Instant" Whipped Topping (see p 158)

Yield: 2 qts

172

PURPLE PASSION FRUIT SALAD

6 c	Water or fruit juice
1 c	Tapioca pearls, small size (not "Minute" type)
12 oz	Grape juice concentrate or a mixture of
	Grape juice and passion fruit juice concentrates
3 qt	Fruit assortment - canned, fresh, or frozen
	(Peaches, pears, grapes, apples, bananas, blueberries, etc.)

Combine water and tapioca in a large saucepan and cook over low heat about 45 minutes or until clear. Then refrigerate mixture until set. Pour out into a large salad bowl and add grape juice concentrate and stir until well mixed. Add fruit assortment, up to 3 quarts (more or less to your preference) stirring gently after each addition until desired thickness is achieved.

Yield: 5 qts

ALMOND-APPLE BARS

3 c	Quick oats	3 oz	Water (6 T)
1½ c	Old fashioned rolled oats	1½ T	ENER-G Egg Replacer
1½ c	Whole wheat flour	3/4 c	Canola oil
1½ c	Unbleached all purpose flour	3/4 c	Apple juice,
1½ c	Sliced almonds		(frozen concentrate)
3/4 c	Better Than Milk, powder	1/2 c	Honey
3/4 c	Shredded coconut (opt)	2 tsp	Natural vanilla flavoring
1¼ tsp	Salt	1 tsp	Natural maple flavoring

In a large bowl, combine all dry ingredients (1st column). In a separate bowl, combine water and egg replacer and whip until foamy. Add remaining liquids. Add liquid ingredients to dry ingredients and stir until well mixed. Spray a cookie sheet with Pam or a non-stick cooking spray. Press mixture out into the cookie sheet until evenly flattened. Bake at 350° F, 18 to 20 minutes or until lightly browned. Remove from oven and score into desired shapes. Break into pieces when cooled.

Yield: 48 squares

CAROB CHIP COOKIES

1 c	Whole wheat flour		1/4 c	Spectrum® non-dairy Spread®
1/2 c	Unbleached white flour		1/4 c	Wonderslim® or Lighter Bake®
1/2 c	Walnuts, chopped			(Fat and Egg Substitute)
1/3 c	Carob chips		2 tsp	Vanilla
1/4 tsp	Salt		1/2 tsp	Walnut flavoring
1/3 c	Honey			

Combine flour, walnuts, carob chips and salt. In a separate bowl, combine remaining ingredients. Pour liquids into dry ingredients and stir until well mixed. Cookie dough will seem sticky. Drop by spoonfuls onto a cookie sheet sprayed with no-stick cooking spray. Oil fingers and lightly spread dough out into round shapes. Avoid mashing. Bake at 350° F, 18 to 20 minutes. Cookies will become crispier as they cool.

Variation: Replace half (2 T) of Spectrum Spread with equal amounts raw natural nut butter (cashew, almond or peanut). Cookies will be crunchier with this method.

Yield: 15 - 18 cookies

STRAWBERRY TROPIC DRINK

1 can	Frozen pineapple juice, diluted		1 or 2	Ripe bananas
1 can	Frozen apple juice, diluted		2 c	Strawberries
1 can	Frozen orange juice, diluted			

Mix each can of juice concentrate with the amount of water listed on the can. Combine the bananas, strawberries and 1 c of the frozen juice mixture in a blender. Process until liquefied. Add blender mixture to the other juices and stir until well mixed. Chill if necessary and serve.

Yield: 5 qts

QUICK PICNIC PUNCH

64 oz	Apple juice		32 oz	White grape juice
40 oz	Dole® "Orchard Peach" juice			

Combine juices and serve with crushed ice.

Yield: 4 qts

Summertime Breeze

Featuring

Quick and easy recipes to prepare in 30 minutes. A variety of delicious and healthy meals perfect for singles, weekdays, after work or when those unexpected guests drop by.

SAVORY LENTILS
Over Toast

2 c	Brown lentils	1/2 tsp	Savory
6 c	Hot water	1/2 tsp	Coriander
2 T	Olive oil	1½ tsp	Cumin
1 med	Onion, chopped	1 tsp	Thyme
2 med	Garlic cloves, minced	1/2 tsp	Paprika
1 tsp	Basil	1½ tsp	Salt
2 T	Nutritional yeast flakes	1 tsp	Garlic salt
2 tsp	Spike® All Purpose Seasoning	2 tsp	Honey (opt)

Rinse lentils well in water. Drain. In a saucepan, cover lentils with 6 c hot water and set aside. In a small frying pan, sauté onions and garlic in oil. Pour sautéed mixture into the water and lentils. Add all seasonings (except salt and garlic salt). Bring to a boil, cover and simmer 20-30 minutes or until lentils are tender. Finally, stir in salts and honey and continue cooking 1 to 2 minutes. Pour into a serving bowl and if desired, garnish with fresh herbs such as parsley, green onion, chives and chopped tomato. Serve over toasted whole wheat or pumpernickel bread. Garnish with shredded lettuce, carrots, cucumber, chopped tomato, avocado, sliced black olives, onions, roasted sunflower seeds, etc. Top with Ranch-Style Dressing. (Recipe on page 179)

Variation: Serve lentils over brown rice and garnish as above for another delicious and healthy whole-meal idea.

Note: If you suffer from G.I. discomfort after eating legumes, try the following remedy. After thoroughly washing and rinsing the lentils, cover with water, bring to a boil and simmer 2-3 minutes. Remove from heat and let beans soak at least 1 hour or overnight, or all day while at work. Drain and thoroughly wash and rinse lentils again. Drain. Proceed with recipe. Unfortunately, this will also somewhat diminish the delicious flavor of the lentil. Also see page 160.

Yield: 8 c

RANCH-STYLE DRESSING

1½ c	Mori Nu® tofu, firm	1 tsp	Onion powder
1/2 c	Water	1 tsp	Basil
1/4 c	Fresh lemon juice	1/2 tsp	Savory
1/4 c	Sunflower oil	1/2 tsp	Dried parsley
1¼ tsp	Salt	1/16 tsp	Citric acid crystals
1 tsp	Honey	2 T	Fresh chives, minced (opt)
1 tsp	Garlic salt	1 T	Fresh parsley, minced (opt)

Combine all ingredients except fresh herbs in a blender and process until smooth and creamy. Stir in the optional fresh chives and parsley last. Chill before serving.

Yield: 2 ½ c

RANCH DRESSING
"QUICK and EASY"

1 pkg	Ranch® Dressing Mix (Original buttermilk recipe)	1/3 c	Canola oil
		3 to 4 T	Fresh lemon juice
1¼ c	Mori-Nu® "lite" tofu, firm	3 T	Tofu milk powder
1/2 c	Water		

Combine above ingredients in a blender and process until smooth and creamy. Chill before serving.

Variation: May add 2 T more water and decrease oil to 1/4 c for a lower fat version.

Yield 2½ c

QUICK & SNAPPY
3 BEAN CHILI

1 can	Bush's® Chili Magic,	1 can	Diced tomatoes, "no salt"
	"Traditional recipe"	2/3 c	Vegan Burger Crumbles
1 can	Red kidney beans,	2 T	Dry minced onions
	"low-sodium" variety	1 tsp	Beef-style seasoning
1 can	Black beans	1 tsp	Cumin

Lightly drain Chili Magic and pour into a saucepan. Drain kidney beans and add to the saucepan. Do not drain black beans or tomatoes and add next. Stir in burger and seasonings. Cover and simmer chili 5 to 10 minutes. Serve hot.

Tip: Try a dollop of "Soy Good" Tofu Sour Cream (see p 147) or grated Mozzarella Cheese (p.127) to top off this chili bean recipe.

Yield: 7 c

ONE OF A KIND
MINI PIZZAS

Whole wheat pita bread, uncut
Garlic purée (opt)
Pizza sauce
Pizza seasoning
Soy parmesan cheese, grated
Soy mozzarella cheese, (see p 127)

Vegan sausage crumbles (opt)
Vegetables of choice
(olives, mushrooms, onions, tomatoes etc)
Parsley

Personalize each mini pizza with choice of above ingredients. Turn pita bread up side down and if desired, spread with a thin layer of garlic before covering "crust" with pizza sauce. Season with pizza seasoning or any vegetable herb seasoning mix. Sprinkle with mozzarella and parmesan cheese, vegan crumbles and add veggies of choice. Cover with additional mozzarella and/or parmesan cheese. Garnish with parsley. Arrange pizzas on a cookie sheet or pizza stone and bake at 375° F, 15 to 20 minutes or until crust is crispy and veggies are tender.

Variation: Replace pita bread with whole wheat English muffins.

Yield: Variable

TOFU "FISH" STICKS

1 lb   Fresh tofu, extra firm

Slice tofu block vertically into strips 1/4 inch thick, 2 inches wide and 4 inches long.

Broth:
2 c   Water   2 tsp   Onion salt
2 tsp   McKay's Chicken-Style Seasoning

Prepare broth and bring to a boil. Add sliced tofu, reduce heat and simmer 3 to 5 minutes. (Use left over broth as a base in your favorite soup or gravy recipe.)

Breading Meal:
1/2 c   Unbleached white or wh. wheat flour   1 T   Granulated onion
1/2 c   Yellow corn meal   1 T   Parsley, dried
1/4 c   Cracker crumbs, (opt)   1/2 tsp Garlic powder
2 T   Nutritional yeast flakes   1/2 tsp Salt
1 T   McKay's Chicken-Style seasoning
1 T   McCormick "Salt-free" Garlic & Herb seasoning

Dip the tofu into breading meal to coat both sides. Coat a non-stick frying pan with no-stick cooking oil or lightly coat the pan with olive oil and heat to medium temperature. Spray a light coat of Pam® onto one side of the breaded tofu and gently lay the coated side into the pan. Then spray the other side. Fry both sides until golden brown and crispy. For an extra tasty treat, serve with ketchup (see p 190) or tarter sauce (see p 182).

Hint: Tofu "fish" sticks, tarter sauce and a whole wheat bun make a great sandwich too!

Yield: 12 fish sticks

TARTER SAUCE

1 c	Soy mayonnaise (see p 167)	1 tsp	Chicken-Style Seasoning
1/2 c	Fresh onions, minced	1/2 tsp	Onion powder
1/3 c	*Pas* Vinegarless Sweet Pickle Relish	1/16 tsp	Turmeric

Combine all ingredients and chill.

Variation: Onions may be sautéed in a small amount of water for a less crunchy texture.

Yield: 2 c

VEGETARIAN GOULASH

1½ c	Large elbow macaroni	1 T	Olive oil
1½ c	Onions, chopped	2/3 c	Vegan Burger Crumbles
1/2 c	Fresh mushrooms, sliced (optional)	1 tsp	Beef-style seasoning
		29 oz	Stewed tomatoes (2 cans)
1/4 c	Green bell peppers, diced	1/2 tsp	Basil
3 med	Garlic cloves, minced		

Cook macaroni in salted water until tender. Drain and rinse well. While macaroni is cooking, sauté vegetables in oil until soft. Add burger crumbles, cover with beef-style seasoning and brown mixture slightly. Add tomatoes and basil, and simmer about 5 minutes. Stir in cooked macaroni and simmer until heated through. May garnish with parmesan cheese alternative.

Yield: 8 c

GERMAN POTATO CASSEROLE

8 c	Red or white potatoes, diced	1 c	Sauerkraut, drained
2 c	Onion, chopped	1 c	Golden Sauce (recipe below)
6 to 8	Fat-free vegan wieners, sliced	1/2 c	Golden delicious apple
1 T	Canola oil	1 tsp	Onion salt

In a large pot, cover potatoes with water and bring to a boil. Reduce heat, cover and simmer about 5 minutes. Drain. Sauté onions and wieners in oil. Grate apples. In a large bowl, combine potatoes, onions and wieners. Combine remaining ingredients and stir gently into potato mixture. Coat a large casserole dish with no-stick cooking spray. Spread mixture evenly into dish. Bake uncovered at 350° F, 45 minutes to 1 hour.   Yield: 15 c

GOLDEN SAUCE

1 c	Mori-Nu® Tofu, Firm	1½ tsp	Onion powder
1/4 c	Canola oil	1/2 tsp	Salt
1 to 2 T	Cooked carrot	1/4 tsp	Garlic powder

In a blender, combine above ingredients and process until carrots are no longer visible and mixture is smooth and creamy.

Yield: 1 1/3 c

CHEESY HASHBROWN CASSEROLE

32 oz	Frozen hashbrowns, thawed	1 T	Chicken-style Seasoning
1 c	Water	1/2 tsp	Salt
1 c	Pimento Cheese Sauce (p 184)	2 c	Onion, chopped
1/2 c	Tofutti® Sour Cream (or)	1 T	Olive oil
	"Soy Good" Sour Cream (p 147)		

Pour potatoes into a large bowl. In a separate bowl, combine cheese sauce, sour cream, Chicken-style seasoning and salt. Pour over potatoes and mix well. Sauté onion in oil until translucent and stir into potato mixture. Spray a casserole dish with no-stick cooking spray. Spoon potato mixture into dish and spread out evenly. Bake uncovered at 350° F, about 45 minutes.

Yield: 9 x 13 casserole

PIMENTO CHEESE SAUCE

2 c	Water		1 T	Fresh lemon juice
1/3 c	Raw cashews, rinsed		1½ tsp	Salt
1/4 c	Nutritional yeast flakes		1 tsp	Onion powder
4 oz	Pimentos		1/4 tsp	Garlic powder
3 T	Cornstarch			

In a blender, combine half the water, cashews, yeast flakes and pimentos and process on high speed until smooth and creamy. Add remaining water and ingredients and blend until well mixed. Pour out into a saucepan and cook over medium heat until thickened.

Yield: 3 c

TABOULI SALAD

2 c	Water		1/4 c	Olive oil
1 c	Bulgur wheat (# 3)		2 T	Fresh lemon juice
1½ c	Fresh tomatoes, diced		2 lg	Garlic cloves, crushed
1 c	Green onion, diced		1 tsp	Salt
3/4 c	Fresh parsley, minced			

In a saucepan, combine water and Bulgur wheat. Bring to a boil, cover, remove from heat and let sit overnight or 6 to 8 hours. Add tomatoes, onion, parsley, oil and lemon juice and stir gently. Combine garlic and salt and mash together to make a paste. Add this to the other ingredients and stir until flavors are well mixed. Chill 1 or 2 hours before serving.

Yield: 5 c

HUMMUS
(A Middle Eastern Chickpea Puree)

2 ½ c	Cooked garbanzos, drained, (reserve broth)	4 cloves	Garlic
1/2 c	Tahini (sesame seed butter)	1 ½ tsp	Onion powder
7 T	Garbanzo broth or water	1 tsp	Salt
6 T	Fresh lemon juice	4 oz	Green chilies, chopped (Old El Paso preferred)

Combine all ingredients, except chilies, in a blender and process on high speed 1 to 2 minutes until smooth and creamy. Pour out into a bowl and stir in chilies.

Tip: Delicious as a spread on bread and crackers, or as a dip with chips and raw vegetables. Also great in pocket bread stuffed with falafels.

Yield: 3 cups

PEAS & PEANUTS SALAD

3 c	Frozen "petite or early" peas, uncooked (16 oz bag)
1 c	Jicama, julienne style
1/2 c	Onion, chopped
1/2 c	Lightly roasted peanuts, salted or unsalted
1/4 c	Lightly roasted sunflower seeds, salted or unsalted
1/4 c	Pepitas (green pumpkin seeds), raw or lightly roasted
1/2 tsp	McCormick® "Salt free" Garlic and Herb Seasoning
1/2 tsp	Onion salt
1/4 tsp	Garlic salt
1 c	Sour Cream Supreme (see p 186)
4 leaves	Leafy green or red lettuce
1 stem	Green onion for garnish, with top fringed

Rinse frozen peas in a colander and drain well. Pour peas out into a serving bowl. Add vegetables, peanuts, and seeds. Mix seasonings together and sprinkle evenly over the pea salad mixture. Add Sour Cream Supreme and stir all together until well mixed. Border with leafy lettuce and garnish with green onion. Chill until ready to serve.

Yield: 6½ c

SOUR CREAM SUPREME

1¼ c	Mori Nu® firm tofu (10.5 oz box)	1 tsp	Honey
1/4 c	Sunflower oil	1/2 tsp	Salt
2½ T	Fresh lemon juice		

In a blender, process all ingredients until smooth and creamy.

Yield: 1½ c

PICNIC POTATO SALAD

2 lb	Red potatoes, boiled (about 1 qt)	1 c	Potato Salad Dressing
1 c	Onion, chopped		(See below)
3/4 c	Celery, sliced or diced	1 tsp	Salt
1/2 c	Pickles, chopped	1 tsp	Dill weed

Cool potatoes and cut into bite size cubes. (Peeling is optional.) Add onion, celery, and pickles. Combine Potato Salad Dressing, salt and dill weed and stir gently into potato mixture. Chill before serving.

Yield: 7 c

POTATO SALAD DRESSING

1 c	Soy milk	1/2 tsp	Salt
1/4 c	Canola oil	2 T	Instant Clear Jel
2 T	Carrot, cooked		(Instant food thickener)
1½ tsp	Onion powder	1½ T	Fresh lemon juice

In a blender, combine soy milk, oil, carrot, onion powder and salt. Process on high speed until carrots are liquefied. Add food thickener through the lid spout while blending on low speed. Increase speed as it thickens. Pour out into a bowl and add lemon juice. Stir until well mixed.

Yield: 1½ c

QUICK ARTICHOKE PASTA TOSS

2 c	Rotinni (Veggie Spirals) uncooked
1 1/3 c	Zesty Italian Dressing * or "Fat Free" Italian Dressing
8 oz	Canned artichoke hearts in water, drained and quartered
2 c	Broccoli florets
1 c	Fresh small button mushrooms (opt)
1 c	Cherry tomatoes, whole
1 can	Pitted whole black olives, small size
1/8 c	Fresh parsley, snipped

Cook noodles according to directions on package in salted water. While the noodles are cooking, prepare a double recipe of Zesty or Fat Free Italian Dressing * (see recipes below) and set 1 1/3 c aside. Drain and rinse noodles. Pour Italian dressing over hot noodles. Add vegetables and toss until well mixed. Cover and chill salad at least 6 hours before serving.

Yield: 10 c

ZESTY ITALIAN DRESSING

Add to one .6 oz package of Good Seasons® "Zesty Italian" Dressing Mix:

3 T	Fresh lemon juice	1/3 c	Water
3 T	Pineapple juice concentrate	1/4 c	Light olive oil

Mix together in an air-tight container. Close lid and shake well. Refrigerate 30 minutes before using. Shake again before serving.

Yield: 1 c

"FAT-FREE" ITALIAN DRESSING

Add to one 1.05 oz package Good Seasons® "Fat-Free" Italian Dressing Mix:

1/4 c	Fresh lemon juice	6 T	Pineapple juice
2 T	Frozen apple juice concentrate	1/3 c	Water

Mix together in an air-tight container. Close lid and shake well. Refrigerate 30 minutes before using. Shake again before serving.

Note: For a stronger Italian flavor, decrease water to 1/4 c.

Yield: 1 c

MARINATED BEAN SALAD

2 c	Fresh green beans, cooked	1/2 c	Black olives, sliced
1 can	Wax beans, cut	1/4 c	Green bell pepper, diced
1 can	Red kidney beans	1/4 c	Red bell pepper, diced
1 can	Garbanzos or chick peas	1 c	Italian Dressing *
1 c	Onion rings or slices		

Drain beans to remove juice. Combine all vegetables in a large bowl. Prepare Italian Dressing of choice (* recipes on page 187). This step can be done ahead. Pour dressing over vegetables and mix thoroughly. Cover and marinate in refrigerator for several hours or overnight before serving.

Variation: Add 1 can artichoke hearts, quartered

Yield: 8 c

TOFU GREEK SALAD

1 lb	Fresh tofu, x-firm, cubed	1/2 lg	Red onion
3	Tomatoes	1 c	Black olives, pitted
3	Cucumbers	1 c	Herb Dressing *

Cut tofu into 1/2 inch cubes. Core tomatoes and cut into wedges. Peel and slice cucumbers. Chop red onion. Leave the olives whole. Toss mixture with Herb Dressing* (recipe on page 226) or Zesty Italian Dressing* (recipe on page 187) and serve on a bed of leafy lettuce. For improved flavor, marinate tofu and vegetables in dressing 4-6 hours before lightly tossing.

Yield: 10 c

VERY BERRY
CREAM CHEESE SPREAD

4 oz	*Tofutti* Better Than Cream Cheese
1/4 c	All-fruit jam, blueberry, strawberry or raspberry

Gently stir or swirl mixture together. Spread on whole wheat bagels or any whole grain bread of choice. Or, spread cream cheese on bread and top with jam.

Yield: 3/4 c

CREAM CHEESY SPREAD

8 oz   *Tofutti* Better Than Cream Cheese   1/8 tsp   Citric acid

Sprinkle citric acid evenly over cream cheese and stir until well mixed. Use mixture to stuff celery, or as a sandwich filling with sliced olives, cucumbers, or onions etc.

Yield: 1 c

SIMPLY SMASHING STUFFED POTATOES

4 med	Russet potatoes, baked	1/4 tsp	Salt (or more)
1 c	Mori Nu® tofu, soft	1½ T	Dry bread crumbs, fine
1/4 c	Green onion, diced	1½ T	SoyCo® Parmesan Cheese
1½ tsp	Chicken Style Seasoning	1 tsp	Olive oil

Slice baked potatoes in half lengthwise and scoop out pulp, leaving a 1/4 inch shell. Mash potatoes with a mixer. Add tofu, onion and seasonings and beat until light and fluffy. Add more tofu if necessary. Spoon potato mixture back into shells. Combine bread crumbs, grated parmesan cheese, and oil. Sprinkle evenly over potatoes. Place potatoes on an un-greased baking sheet. Bake at 350° F, 15 minutes or until heated through. Garnish with additional sliced green onions.

Yield: 8 stuffed potatoes

"QUICK BAKED" GOLDEN POTATO FRIES

Slice 2 large bakers potatoes lengthwise into 1/2" wide sticks. Spray a cookie sheet with no-stick cooking spray. Spread potatoes out in a single layer. (To enhance flavor, drizzle 1 tsp olive oil over the potatoes and stir to coat evenly-only if diet permits.) Sprinkle with any combination of dried parsley, herbs, chives, onion salt, garlic salt, Spike, nutritional yeast etc. to your taste. Broil on the top oven rack at 400° F. Stir after 10 minutes and then every 5 minutes for 10-15 minutes more or until tender, and golden brown with crispy edges. You may also want to add onion rings to the fries during the last 5 minutes of baking time. Serve hot and, if desired, with Vinegarless Ketchup (p 190) on the side.

Yield: 4 c

"THICK & ZESTY" VINEGARLESS KETCHUP

12 oz	Tomato paste	1 tsp	Lime juice
1 c	Tomato sauce	1 tsp	Onion powder
1/4 c	Froz. pineapple juice conc.	1 tsp	Salt
1/4 c	Fresh lemon juice	1/2 tsp	Garlic salt
2 T	Froz. orange juice concentrate	1/2 tsp	Paprika
3 T	Date butter (see p 211)	1/4 tsp	Citric acid crystals
2 T	Honey	1/8 tsp	Cumin

Combine all ingredients in a blender and process until smooth. Refrigerate. The flavor improves after 2 days. Freeze extras not used within two weeks.

Yield: 3½ c

"QUICK" VINEGARLESS KETCHUP

1½ c	Tomato sauce	2 T	Fruit-Fresh®, powder
1 c	Tomato paste		(or) 1/8 tsp citric acid
1/2 c	Pineapple juice	1½ tsp	Salt
1/4 c	Fresh lemon juice	1 tsp	Onion powder
1 tsp	Lime juice	1/2 tsp	Garlic salt
3 T	Date butter (p 211)	1/2 tsp	Paprika
2 T	Pineapple/orange juice (frozen concentrate)	1/4 tsp	Worcestershire sauce (opt) (Vegetarian brand)
2 T	Honey		

Combine all ingredients in a blender and process until smooth. Refrigerate. Freeze extras not used within two weeks.

Variation: For a thicker ketchup, decrease tomato sauce to 1 c and increase tomato paste to 1½ c.

Yield: 4 c

QUICK RICE PUDDING
with
MANGOS AND CREAM

1/2 c	Canned pear juice	1/3 c	Currants or raisins (opt)
1/2 c	Canned coconut milk	2 c	Fresh or canned fruit
1/2 c	Water		(e.g. mangos, pears,
3 T	Better Than Milk™ powder		peaches, pineapple,
1½ c	Minute® Brown Rice, uncooked		bananas, apricots etc.)

Combine fruit juice, coconut milk, water and milk powder in a saucepan. Bring to a boil. Turn heat down to low setting and stir in rice. Cover and cook 5 minutes. Stir in currants or raisins, cover, and turn heat off. Allow to sit 5 to 10 minutes before removing cover.

TO SERVE HOT:
Spoon into bowls, pour fruit over rice and garnish as desired.

TO SERVE COLD:
Chill 1 to 2 hours before adding fruit and garnishes.

SUGGESTED GARNISHES:
Grated coconut, granola and "Instant" Whipped Topping (see recipe below)

Yield: 5 c

"INSTANT" WHIPPED TOPPING

1½ c	Water	1/3 c	Canned coconut milk,
2/3 c	Better than Milk™ powder		"lite" (unsweetened)
1/2 c	Blanched almonds (w/o skins)	2 tsp	Vanilla, (natural type)
3½ T	Emes Kosher-Jel®, plain	1/4 tsp	Salt
3 T	Honey or powdered sugar		Ice

In a blender, combine the water, milk powder, almonds and Emes Jel and process until the almonds are liquefied completely. Add remaining ingredients and process briefly. Finally, begin adding ice slowly through the lid spout and continue processing on high speed to make a total volume equal to 5 cups. Turn blender off and wait briefly. Mixture should now be light and fluffy. Best served immediately. If stored, and mixture becomes too firm, hand whip or beat gently with an electric beater before serving.

Yield: 5 c

SMOOTHIES

2 to 3 c   Frozen fruit of choice
          (Peaches, bananas, strawberries, blueberries, pineapple etc.)
1 to 2 c   Unsweetened 100% juice of choice
          (Pineapple, apple, fruit blends etc.)
1/2 c   Vegan Yogurt, any flavor (opt)
1/3 c   Better Than Milk™ powder
2 T   Honey, brown rice syrup or fructose (opt)

Combine all ingredients in a blender and process until smooth. Serve immediately.

Note: Ratio of fruit and juice can be adjusted according to your preference of thickness.

Yield: 5 c

FRUIT KABOBS

Place on a skewer fresh cut fruits of choice.
i.e. Bananas, grapes, strawberries, pineapple, kiwi and oranges.

If not serving immediately, dip or brush fruit with pineapple juice to keep bananas and other fruits from turning dark. Enjoy kabobs plain or serve with Fresh Fruit Dressing (see recipe below).

SWEET & SOUR
FRESH FRUIT DRESSING

1 c   Sour Cream Supreme
1/2 c Crushed pineapple, well drained
1/4 c Canned coconut milk, "lite" (unsweetened)
3 T   Better Than Milk™ powder
3 T   Honey

1 T   Frozen pineapple juice, (concentrate)
2 tsp Cook's® Vanilla powder
1 lg   Ripe banana
1 T   Instant Clear Jel

In a blender, combine Sour Cream Supreme (recipe on page 79) with all remaining ingredients, except clear jel, and process until smooth and creamy. If desired, stir crushed pineapple into mixture rather than blending. Add 1 T Instant Clear Jel through the lid spout while blender is running.

Note: May substitute Cook's Vanilla powder with "clear" vanilla.

Yield: 3 c

"SWEET REFLECTIONS"
BANANA-RASPBERRY DESSERT

4 c	Raspberries, unsweetened	4	Ripe bananas
6 oz	White grape juice concentrate	2 tsp	Pineapple juice
1/2 tsp	Fresh lemon juice	2 T	Almonds, slivered
2 T	Cornstarch or arrowroot		

If using frozen raspberries, place unopened raspberry package in a large bowl, add hot water to cover. Set aside to thaw.

Drain thawed raspberries. Measure out 1/2 c raspberries and pour into a blender. Add the grape juice concentrate and lemon juice and process until smooth. Pour out into a saucepan and add cornstarch, arrowroot, or tapioca powder. Stir to dissolve thickener and bring mixture to a boil. Stir constantly and cook until syrup is thick and clear. Cool.

Cut peeled bananas into diagonal slices 1/4 inch thick. Arrange on four individual dessert plates in a sunburst pattern. Brush or drizzle bananas with the pineapple juice.

Mound remaining raspberries in center of bananas, dividing equally. Spoon about 1/4 c raspberry juice syrup over raspberries on each plate, or divide equally.

Before serving, sprinkle desserts with almonds

Yield: 8 servings

Broccoli "Cheese" Soup
"Chicken" Noodle Soup
Cheesy Delight Open Faced Sandwich
Deluxe Lentil Vegetable Soup
Garden Oat Burger

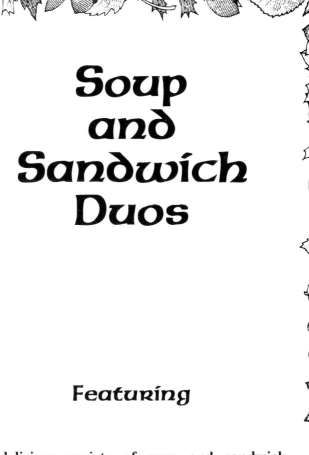

Soup
and
Sandwich
Duos

Featuring

A delicious variety of soup and sandwich recipes sure to please even the choosiest appetites. Try tasty cheese substitutes and healthy "vinegarless" condiments to compliment all your favorite sandwiches. As a special treat, you will enjoy a "sugarless" tofu milk and fruit ice cream. It's delicious and good for you too!

DELUXE LENTIL-VEGETABLE SOUP

1 c	Brown or red lentils	1/2 tsp	Basil
6 c	Hot water	1/2 tsp	Coriander
2 T	Olive oil	1/2 tsp	Paprika
2 med	Garlic cloves, minced	1 tsp	Salt
2 c	Onion, chopped	2 tsp	Honey or rice syrup
1 c	Celery, diced	1 c	Frozen peas (opt)
3 c	Potatoes, cubed	1 can	Diced tomatoes (14.5 oz)
1½ c	Carrots, sliced	1/4 c	Fresh chopped herbs
2 tsp	Beef-style Seasoning		(parsley, chives, or
1½ tsp	Spike® or Nature's Blend (p 67)		green onion, etc.)
3/4 tsp	Cumin		

Place lentils in a bowl with hot water to soften while preparing vegetables. Sauté garlic, onions and celery in oil about 3 minutes. Add potatoes, carrots, Beef-style seasoning, Spike or Nature's Blend, cumin, basil, coriander, and paprika and cook 2 to 3 more minutes over moderate heat stirring constantly. Add water and lentils, cover and simmer 20 to 25 minutes or until vegetables and lentils are tender. Add salt, honey, and (opt) peas, cover and cook a few minutes more. Finally, add tomatoes and fresh herbs reserving a small amount for garnish.

Yield: 15 c

CHICKEN NOODLE SOUP

1 c	Onion chopped	1 T	Dry minced onion
2 med	Garlic cloves, minced	1 tsp	Spike®All Purpose Seasoning
2 stalks	Celery, sliced		(or) Nature's Blend (see p 67)
1 med	Carrot, diced	1 tsp	McCormick® Onion and Herb
1/8 c	Fresh parsley, minced		"Salt-free" Seasoning
2 T	Olive oil	1 tsp	Garlic salt
1 c	Chic-Ketts®	1/2 tsp	Celery salt
1/2 c	Mock chicken or duck	8 c	Water
1/4 c	Nutritional yeast flakes	6 oz	Linguini noodles
3 T	Chicken-Style Seasoning	1 c	Frozen peas, thawed

In a large pot, sauté vegetables and parsley in olive oil until tender. Tear the Chic-Ketts ("white meat") into large bite-size pieces and the Mock Chicken ("dark meat") into small bite size pieces and add to the pot. Add the seasonings and spices. Add water and bring to a boil. Break the noodles into 4 inch pieces, add to boiling water, cover and simmer until noodles are done. Add peas, and cook 1 minute more.

Yield 3 quarts

SEAFARER'S
NAVY BEAN SOUP

1 c	Veggie Wieners, sliced	2 cans	Navy beans, drained
1 c	Onion, chopped	1 can	Diced tomatoes (14.5 oz)
1/2 c	Celery, chopped	2 c	Water
1/2 c	Carrots, sliced	2 tsp	Chicken-style Seasoning
1/4 c	Green peppers, diced	1/2 tsp	Basil
2 med	Garlic cloves, minced	1/2 tsp	Lawry's® Seasoned Salt
1 T	Canola oil		

In a large saucepan, sauté Veggie Wieners with vegetables in oil until vegetables are crisp-tender. Add remaining ingredients and simmer about 15 minutes. Serve with crackers.

Note: For a milder flavor, replace wieners with Loma Linda® Tender Bits.

Tip: For a "quick" version, replace onions, celery, peppers and garlic with a frozen vegetable "soup starter". Steam or microwave carrots before adding to soup. Add beans, tomatoes and seasonings and simmer 5 minutes before serving.

Yield: 8 c

MINESTRONE SOUP

1 c	Onion, chopped	1 tsp	Onion powder
1/2 c	Celery, sliced	1/2 tsp	Coriander
2 med	Garlic cloves, minced	1/16 tsp	Oregano
1 T	Olive oil	1 small	Bay leaf
6 c	Water	1½ c	Kidney or red beans,
1 T	Chicken-style seasoning		canned
2 tsp	Basil, (or) 2 T fresh basil,	2 c	Diced canned tomatoes
	minced	3/4 c	Macaroni, elbow or shell
1½ tsp	Lawry's® Seasoned salt	2 c	Zucchini, sliced/quartered
1½ tsp	Sucanat	1 c	Carrots, sliced

In a large saucepan, sauté onion, celery and garlic in oil until tender. Add water, seasonings and beans. Bring to a boil. Lower heat, cover and simmer about 20 minutes. Add tomatoes and macaroni, cover and simmer about 10 minutes. Add zucchini and carrots and simmer 5 to 10 minutes more or until pasta and vegetables are tender. Remove bay leaf before serving.

Yield: 4 quarts

SAVORY SPLIT PEA SOUP

STEP ONE:

3½ c	Water	2 tsp	Bakon® Seasoning (opt)
1 c	Split peas		(or) 1/4 tsp liquid smoke
1 c	Potatoes, peeled and diced	1/2 tsp	Salt
2 tsp	Chicken-style seasoning	1 med	Bay leaf (opt)

In a large saucepan, combine above ingredients and bring to a boil. Cover and simmer about an hour until peas are soft. Set aside. When cooled, discard bay leaf. Pour remainder into a blender and process until smooth and creamy. Set aside.

STEP TWO:

1 T	Olive oil	1/4 c	Celery, sliced
1 c	Onion, chopped	1 tsp	Garlic purée

In the large saucepan, sauté above mixture in oil until onions are translucent and celery is tender.

STEP THREE:

1 c	Water	1/2 tsp	Basil
1/2 c	Carrots, diced	1/2 tsp	Parsley, dried
1 stem	Green onion, diced	1/4 tsp	Celery salt
1 T	Nutritional yeast flakes	1/4 tsp	Lawry's® Seasoned Salt

Add above ingredients to the saucepan with the onion and celery mixture, bring to a boil, cover and simmer 15 minutes or until carrots are tender. Add the blended pea mixture and stir until hot. If desired, garnish with paprika, grated carrots or croutons.

Yield: 7 c

"QUICK AS A WINK" VEGETABLE-RICE SOUP

1 qt	Water	1/4 c	Baby lima beans (frozen)
4 tsp	Chicken-style Seasoning	1/2 c	Quick-cooking brown rice
1 tsp	Beef-style Seasoning	3/4 c	Zucchini, sliced
1/4 tsp	Basil	3/4 c	Cauliflower, florets
1/8 tsp	Italian seasoning	1 can	Diced tomatoes (14.5 oz),
1 c	Italian green beans (frozen)		with Roasted Garlic
1 c	Carrots, sliced		

Combine water and seasonings and bring to a boil. Add green beans, carrots, lima beans and rice. Return to a boil, reduce heat, cover and simmer 15 minutes. Add zucchini and cauliflower and simmer 3 to 5 minutes more or until tender. Add tomatoes, stir until heated through and serve.

Note: For an even quicker and easier recipe, replace fresh vegetables with 1 package or up to 4 c of a frozen "Italian vegetable" mixture.

Variation: Add 1 c Chic-Ketts (or favorite vegetarian protein) torn into bite size pieces. Add to broth before boiling the first time.

Yield: 10 c

BROCCOLI CHEESE SOUP

1¼ c	Water	2 T	Nutritional yeast flakes
1 c	Cooked rice	2 T	Better Than Milk™ powder
1 c	Carrots, cooked	2 tsp	Chicken-style Seasoning
1/2 c	Raw cashews, rinsed	2 tsp	Onion powder
1/2 c	Tofu, firm	1½ tsp	Salt
3 oz	Pimentos	1/2 tsp	Garlic powder
2 T	Fresh lemon juice	2 c	Broccoli crowns

In a blender, combine water, rice, carrots and cashews and process until completely smooth and no longer "gritty". Add remaining ingredients, except broccoli, and blend again until creamy. Chop broccoli into bite size pieces and steam or microwave 2 to 3 minutes. Pour broccoli into a saucepan and cover with blended cheese sauce. Stir and if necessary, add additional hot water to thin sauce as desired. Heat and serve.

Variation: May use cauliflower or mixed vegetables. This cheese sauce recipe is also good over baked potatoes, rice and vegetables.

Yield: 6 1/2 c

"CREAM" OF POTATO SOUP

1 med	Onion, chopped	1 tsp	Onion salt
3/4 c	Celery, diced	1/2 tsp	Basil or herb mixture
2 lg	Garlic cloves, minced	1/2 tsp	Celery powder
1 T	Olive oil	8 c	Water (approx)
8 c	Raw red potatoes, cubed	1/2 c	Raw cashews, rinsed
2 T	Nutritional yeast flakes	1/3 c	Unbleached flour
2 tsp	Chicken-Style Seasoning	1/4 c	Fresh parsley, minced
2 tsp	Salt	1 stem	Green onion, minced

Sauté onions, celery and garlic in olive oil until tender. (May also sauté vegetables in water if preferred.) Add potatoes and spices with enough water to cover, about 8 c, and simmer until potatoes are soft. In a blender, process cashews and flour with 1c water until completely smooth and creamy. Stir cashew "cream" into soup and cook until thickened. Garnish with fresh parsley, green onion and paprika as desired.

Variation: Add 2 c frozen green peas to soup just before adding cashew cream and flour mixture. Do not over cook peas or they will lose their bright green color. Yield: 5 quarts

CREAMY VEGETABLE SOUP

1 c	Onions, diced	1/4 tsp	Basil, dried
1/4 c	Celery, sliced	1 c	Potatoes, diced
1 lg	Garlic clove, minced	1/2 c	Carrots, sliced
2 tsp	Olive oil	1 c	Water
3 c	Water	1/3 c	Raw cashews, rinsed
2 T	Chicken-style seasoning	2 T	Unbleached white flour
1/2 tsp	Salt	1 c	Cauliflower, chopped
1/2 tsp	Onion powder	1/2 c	Peas or broccoli florets
1/2 tsp	Parsley, dried		

In a 3 quart pot, sauté onions, celery and garlic in oil until tender. Pour in 3 c water, add seasonings and bring to a boil. Add potatoes and carrots, reduce heat and simmer over low heat until nearly cooked. Combine 1 c water, cashews, and flour in a blender and process on high speed until smooth and creamy. Pour cashew cream into soup stock and bring to a boil, stirring constantly until thick. Add cauliflower and peas or broccoli, reduce heat and simmer 5 minutes before serving.

Yield: 8 c

CARROT BISQUE

1 sm	Onion, chopped	2 tsp	Honey or FruitSource®
2 med	Garlic cloves, minced	1 tsp	Vege-Sal®, All Purpose
1 tsp	Olive oil		Seasoning
3 c	Water	1 c	Raw cashew pieces
1 lb	Carrots, sliced		

In a large pot, sauté onions and garlic in oil until translucent. Add water, carrots, honey and Vege-Sal and simmer until crisp-tender. Drain vegetable mixture, saving broth. In a blender, combine cashews with reserved soup broth and process until creamy. Add vegetable mixture and blend until smooth. Add additional seasoning if necessary to suit your taste. Reheat to serve. May garnish with fresh chopped chives, oyster crackers or croutons.

Variation: Replace honey with 1/2 c cooked yams.

Yield: 5 c

JIFFY MUSHROOM SOUP

1 c	Fresh mushrooms, sliced	1 T	Cornstarch
1½ c	Water	1 T	Spectrum® Spread (opt)
1/2 c	Onion, chopped	1 tsp	Chicken-Style Seasoning
4 T	Better Than Milk, powder	1/2 tsp	Salt
2 T	Unbleached all purpose flour	1/2 tsp	Basil

Sauté mushrooms in a skillet with 2 T water and 1/8 tsp salt until tender. Set aside. (May also microwave mushrooms with water and salt about 1 minute.) In a blender, combine remaining ingredients and process until smooth. Add mushrooms with liquids and flash blend a few times to break up mushrooms into pieces. Pour out into a saucepan and cook until thickened. Use this for recipes in place of canned soup. If necessary, add additional tofu milk or water to thin mixture down to desired consistency.

Variation: May substitute fresh mushrooms, 2 T water, and 1/8 tsp salt with 4 oz sliced canned mushrooms, with liquid.

Yield: 4 c

"QUICK BAKED"
GOLDEN POTATO FRIES

Slice 2 large bakers potatoes lengthwise into 1/2" wide sticks. Spray a cookie sheet with no-stick cooking spray. Spread potatoes out in a single layer. (To enhance flavor, drizzle 1 tsp olive oil over the potatoes and stir to coat evenly-only if diet permits.) Sprinkle with any combination of dried parsley, herbs, chives, onion salt, garlic salt, Spike, nutritional yeast etc. to your taste. Broil on the top oven rack at 400° F. Stir after 10 minutes and then every 5 minutes for 10 -15 minutes more or until tender, and golden brown with crispy edges. You may also want to add onion rings to the fries during the last 5 minutes of baking time. Serve hot and, if desired, with Vinegarless Ketchup (recipe on p 204) on the side.

Yield: 4 c

CHEESY DELIGHTS
(OPEN-FACED SANDWICHES)

Mix desired amount of diced green onion and/or sweet onion, sliced black and/or green olives, diced pimentos and Old El Paso chopped mild green chilies into Pimento Cheese (see page 206). Chill at least one hour or until partially set. Spread cheese mixture generously over English muffin halves, whole wheat buns, rye bread or any favorite choice of bread. If desired, place a slice of tomato on top of cheese and garnish with minced parsley, basil, onion salt and SoyCo® Lite & Less™ Parmesan Cheese Alternative. Arrange sandwiches on a cookie sheet and broil at 400 to 425° F, about 10 minutes or until cheese is bubbly and bread becomes crispy around the edges. Watch carefully to prevent burning.

Yield: Up to 28 sandwiches

GARDEN OAT BURGERS

1 c	Onions, finely diced	1/2 c	Brown rice, well cooked
1 c	Fresh mushrooms,	2 T	Vital wheat gluten
	finely chopped	4 tsp	Beef-style seasoning
1/2 c	Carrots, shredded	1 T	ENER-G® Egg Replacer
3 med	Garlic cloves, minced	2 tsp	Maggi® liquid seasoning
1 T	Olive oil	1 tsp	Garlic & Herb
1 c	Ralston® cooked cereal		("salt-free" seasoning)
1 c	Quick oats, dry	1 tsp	Onion powder
1 c	Vegan Burger crumbles	1/4 tsp	Italian seasoning (opt)
1/2 c	Black beans, mashed		

Sauté onions, mushrooms, carrots and garlic in oil until tender. Pour into a large bowl. Add cooked Ralston (cracked wheat cereal), oats, burger crumbles, beans and rice. Mix well. Add remaining ingredients and mix well. Coat a cookie sheet with no-stick cooking spray. With a measuring cup, scoop up 1/4 c to 1/3 c mixture and drop onto the cookie sheet. With hands or a canning jar lid, press and shape burger into round patties. Bake at 350° F, 25 minutes. Turn over and bake 15 to 20 minutes more or until golden brown and firm enough to hold together.

Yield: 16 burgers

Tip: Store leftover burgers in an air-tight container in the freezer. Thaw and reheat for a quick meal.

BETTER MUSTARD

3/4 c	Water	1/2 tsp	Salt
1/3 c	Fresh lemon juice	1 clove	Garlic, mashed
1/4 c	Unbleached white flour	1/2 tsp	Maggi® Seasoning
2 tsp	Turmeric	1/4 c	Canola oil

In a blender, process first 5 ingredients on high until creamy. Pour into a saucepan and cook over boiling point temperature stirring constantly until thickened. Cool. Return to blender and add garlic and Maggi Seasoning. Process on high, and slowly drizzle in oil through the lid spout. Continue to blend for one more minute. Spoon into a glass storage container. Chill before serving.

Yield: 1½ c

GARBANZO-MILLET BURGERS

1½ c	Onion, chopped	2 T	Bragg® Liquid Aminos
1 c	Cooked garbanzos, drained	1 T	Beef-Style Seasoning
2 med	Garlic cloves	1 tsp	Bernard Jensen's® -
1 c	Cooked millet or rice		Vegetable Seasoning
1 c	Pecans	1 tsp	Spike® Seasoning
1 can	Pitted olives, drained	1 tsp	Basil
2 c	Vegetarian burger	1/2 tsp	Cumin
1½ c	Quick oats	1/2 tsp	Thyme
1/3 c	Gluten flour	1 T	ENER-G®Egg Replacer
1/4 c	Nutritional yeast flakes	3 T	Water

In a food processor, combine onions, garbanzos, garlic, millet or rice, pecans, and olives. Chop mixture well. Pour out into a bowl and add burger, oats, flour, and spices and stir until well mixed. Whisk egg replacer with water until foamy. Gently fold egg substitute into the burger mixture. Form into patties and cook slowly over low to medium heat, browning both sides. For best results, use a non-stick frying pan and coat pan with a no-stick cooking spray. If diet permits, frying burgers in a small amount of olive oil speeds up process.

Variation: Omit liquid aminos, Bernard Jensen's seasoning, Spike, basil, cumin, and thyme. Replace with 1 envelope Lipton® Onion Soup.

Yield: 24 burgers

"QUICK" VINEGARLESS KETCHUP

1½ c	Tomato sauce	2 T	Fruit-Fresh®, powder
1 c	Tomato paste		(or) 1/8 tsp citric acid
1/2 c	Pineapple juice	1½ tsp	Salt
1/4 c	Fresh lemon juice	1 tsp	Onion powder
1 tsp	Lime juice	1/2 tsp	Garlic salt
3 T	Date butter (p 211)	1/2 tsp	Paprika
2 T	Pineapple/orange juice	1/4 tsp	Worcestershire sauce (opt)
	(frozen concentrate)		(Vegetarian brand)
2 T	Honey		

Combine all ingredients in a blender and process until smooth. Refrigerate. Freeze extras not used within two weeks.

Variation: For a thicker ketchup, decrease tomato sauce to 1 c and increase tomato paste to 1½ c.

Yield: 4 c

TOFU MAYONNAISE

1 c	Water	1/8 tsp	Citric acid crystals
1/2 c	Tofu milk powder	2 ½ T	Instant Clear-Jel® powder
1/2 c	Almonds (w/o skins)		(or)
1/2 c	Firm tofu	3 T	Cornstarch dissolved in
1/3 c	Canola oil		2 tablespoons water
1½ tsp	Salt	1/4 c	Pineapple juice
1/2 tsp	Onion powder	1/4 c	Fresh lemon juice
1/4 tsp	Garlic powder	1 T	Frozen O.J. concentrate

Combine water, milk powder, nuts and tofu in a blender and process on high speed until completely smooth. Reduce blender speed to lowest setting and drizzle oil in slowly. Then add salt, onion powder, garlic powder, and citric acid. Resume a high speed, remove lid spout and add Instant Clear-Jel powder one tablespoon at a time. It may be necessary to stop the blender often and stir mixture to assist the blending process. Continue blending until completely smooth. (Or, add cornstarch/water to mayonnaise mixture, blend briefly and pour out into a saucepan and simmer until thick.) Pour into a bowl and gently stir in pineapple, lemon juice and orange juice concentrate. (Do not add juices to the blender. It must be stirred in by hand .) Refrigerate 1 to 2 hours before serving to enhance flavor. Yield: 3 c

SOY MAYONNAISE

1 c	West Soy® Plus™ soy milk	1/2 tsp	Onion powder
2 T	Cornstarch or arrowroot	1/4 tsp	Garlic powder
1/2 c	Water	1/8 tsp	Citric acid
1/2 c	Better Than Milk™ powder	2 T	Instant Clear-Jel®
1/4 c	Slivered almonds, (w/o skins)	1/4 c	Pineapple juice
1/3 c	Canola oil	1/4 c	Fresh lemon juice
1¼ tsp	Salt		

Dissolve starch in soy milk. Simmer over medium heat stirring constantly until thick. Cool. In a blender, combine water, milk powder, and almonds, and process on high speed until completely smooth. Reduce blender speed and slowly dribble in oil through the lid spout. Turn the blender off, add the cooled soy milk and spices then blend again until well mixed. Keep the blender running at a high speed and add Instant Clear-Jel powder one tablespoon at a time. It may be necessary to stop often and stir mixture to assist the blending process. Continue blending until completely smooth. Pour into a bowl and gently stir in the pineapple and lemon juice. (Do not add juices to the blender.) Refrigerate 1 to 2 hours before serving. Yield: 2½ c

PIMENTO CHEESE

1 1/4 c	Water	4 oz	Pimentos, canned
1 c	Cooked rice	2 T	Lemon juice
4 T	Emes Kosher-Jel®, plain	2 tsp	Onion powder
1/2 c	Tofu, x-firm	2 tsp	Salt
1/2 c	Raw cashews, rinsed	1/2 tsp	Garlic powder
3 T	Nutritional yeast flakes		

In a blender, combine water, rice, Emes Jel, tofu and cashews. Process on high speed until completely smooth and creamy. Add remaining ingredients and blend well. Pour into a container coated with no-stick cooking spray. Refrigerate several hours until set. Gently shake out to slice cheese.

Note: To grate cheese easily, freeze mixture at least 2 hours first. For a creamy sauce to serve over vegetables or noodles, do not refrigerate mixture after blending, but heat and serve immediately. Or, if using previously "set" leftovers, heat mixture slowly until cheese melts.

Yield: 3 c

MOZZARELLA CHEESE

1 c	Water	4 tsp	Fresh lemon juice
1 c	Cooked rice, brown or white	1½ tsp	Salt
3/4 c	Tofu, x-firm	1 tsp	Onion powder
1/2 c	Raw cashews, rinsed	1/4 tsp	Garlic powder
4 T	Emes Kosher-Jel®, plain		

In a blender, combine all ingredients and process on high speed, stopping and stirring as necessary, until completely smooth and creamy (3 - 5 minutes). The sauce will heat up and appear "shiny" when completed. Pour into a container coated with no stick cooking spray. Refrigerate 2 to 4 hours until set. Gently shake out to slice cheese.

Note: To grate cheese easily, freeze mixture at least 2 hours first. For a creamy sauce to pour over vegetables or noodles; do not refrigerate mixture after blending, but heat and serve immediately. Or, if using previously "set" leftover cheese, heat mixture slowly over lo-med heat, stirring frequently until melted.

Tip: May substitute cashews with slivered blanched almonds (w/o skins).

Yield: 3 c

THREE GRAIN "NO-OIL" BREAD

2 c	Warm water	2 T	Wheat germ
2 c	Warm applesauce	1 T	Do-Pep, vital wheat gluten
3 T	Honey or brown sugar	1/2 c	Rye flour
2 T	Active dry yeast	6 c	Whole wheat flour
1 T	Salt	1 c	Unbleached flour
1/4 c	Quick oats	1 c	Unbleached flour
1/3 c	Wheat bran		(for kneading)

In a large bowl, combine water, applesauce, honey or sugar, and yeast. Set aside for 10 minutes until bubbly. Add salt, oats, wheat bran, wheat germ and Do-Pep. Allow to sit 5 minutes. Then stir in rye and wheat flour. Gradually add 1 c unbleached white flour until it becomes too difficult to stir. Oil hands or spray hands with cooking spray. Turn dough out unto a floured board or counter and knead in remaining 1 c flour. Add more flour if dough is too sticky, but take care not to add any more than is necessary. Knead well up to 10 minutes. When texture is correct, dough should spring back when pressed. Place in a clean, oiled bowl in a warm place and cover with a towel. Let rise until doubled, 25 to 30 minutes. Punch down and divide dough into 2 equal parts for large loaves or 3 parts for medium size loaves. Knead lightly, shape loaves and place in bread pans coated with cooking spray. Cover with a towel and let rise again until doubled in size. Bake in a pre-heated oven at 350° F, 40 to 45 minutes. Bread should sound hollow when tapped if it is done. Remove from pans, cover with a towel and cool on a wire rack.

Yield: 2 to 3 loaves

AUTOMATIC BREAD MACHINE
Whole Wheat Bread Recipe

1 c	Warm water	2 ½ tsp	Rapid- rise yeast
2 T	Canola oil	2 c	Whole wheat flour
2 T	Honey	2/3 c	Unbleached white flour
1¼ tsp	Salt	2 T	Vital wheat gluten

Combine water, oil, honey, salt and yeast in the bread machine bowl. Then add flours and set the machine for automatic bread according to directions.

Note: If making bread on a delayed time setting, it is important to place the yeast on top of the flour in order to keep it dry until the processing begins.

Variation: For a whole grain version with higher fiber, use 2 1/3 c whole wheat flour to 1/3 c unbleached white flour. Yield: 1 loaf

SPROUTED WHEAT BREAD

STEP ONE:

1 c	Hard winter wheat berries
2 c	Water (for soaking)

Cover berries with water and soak uncovered 24 hours. Then place berries in the refrigerator and soak 24 hours more. Drain and discard water after 48 hours is completed.

STEP TWO:

3 c	Warm water	3 c	Whole wheat flour
2 T	Active dry yeast		

In a blender, combine soaked wheat berries and half the water (1½ c) and process 2 minutes on high speed. Pour blended berries out into a large bowl. Mixture should be stringy. Add remaining water and yeast. Using a slotted spoon, stir until well mixed. Add flour to make a "sponge", hand whipping 2 or 3 minutes.

STEP THREE:

1 T	Salt	2 T	Vital wheat gluten
1/3 c	Brown sugar or honey	4 c	Whole wheat flour
1/4 c	Canola oil	1 c	Flour (for kneading)

Add each ingredient, (except kneading flour), one at a time into the center of the sponge, but don't mix until all ingredients have been added. Then mix in a folding motion. Use hands to turn dough toward the center of the bowl until stiff. When dough becomes sticky, add 1/2 c flour around the edges of the bowl. Dust hands with flour as needed. Turn dough out onto a floured counter or bread board. While kneading, handle bread as lightly as possible and dust with flour as needed. Knead about 10 minutes. To test if dough is done, gently pull a small piece apart. If it resists breaking, it is done. Place dough into an oiled bowl in a warm, draft free spot and cover with a clean cloth. Let rise until double. Punch down and knead again briefly. Divide into 2 or 3 equal portions. Shape into loaves and place into bread pans coated with no-stick cooking spray. Let rise until 1 inch above top of pan. Bake at 350° F, 40 to 45 minutes. Bread should sound hollow when tapped. Remove from pans and allow to cool on a bread rack or standing on end.

Yield: 2 large loaves (or) 3 small loaves

BOSCH BREAD MACHINE
Whole Wheat Bread

STEP ONE:

6 c	Warm water	3 T	Yeast
1/2 c - 2/3 c	Honey	3 c	Whole wheat flour
1/2 c - 2/3 c	Canola Oil		

Combine above ingredients in bread bowl with dough hooks assembled, place both lids on bowl and turn machine on to speed "2" and mix for 2 minutes.

STEP TWO:

1 T	Vital wheat gluten flour	2 T	Salt
1 tsp	Citric acid (or) 1T lemon juice		

Turn machine off. Add above ingredients. Then resume mixing, speed "2".

STEP THREE:

1 c	Quick oats	3 c	Unbleached white or bread flour
2/3 c	Rye flour	6 c	Whole wheat flour (plus or minus)
1/2 c	Wheat bran		

Remove "center" lid and add above ingredients slowly while continuing to operate on speed "2". Continue adding flour until dough pulls away from side of the bowl and is wiped clean. Then replace center lid and continue mixing for 8 minutes.

STEP FOUR:

Remove dough from bowl and place on a floured surface. Using a large knife, divide dough into 4 equal parts for large loaves, or 5 equal parts for medium size loaves. Knead briefly, flatten and roll dough up and shape into loaves. Place into bread pans and let rise to 90% of full size. Bake in a pre-heated oven at 350° F, 35 to 40 minutes or until loaf sounds hollow when tapped. Remove loaves from oven, turn out on bread racks, cover with a tea towel and let cool.

Yield: 4 to 5 loaves

GARBANZO-OLIVE
SANDWICH SPREAD

1 can	Garbanzos (chickpeas), drained	1/4 tsp	Garlic salt
1 c	Chopped olives	1/4 tsp	Basil
1/3 c	Green onion, finely diced	1/3 c	Soy Mayonnaise
1/4 tsp	Chicken-Style Seasoning		(see page 205)

Mash garbanzos until soft. Add olives and seasonings and mix well. Add Soy Mayonnaise to moisten spread. Add more or less to suit your taste. Serve as a sandwich spread or with crackers.

Variation: Substitute garbanzos with pinto beans and add 3/4 tsp McKay's® Beef-Style Seasoning. For variety, add finely chopped walnuts, or mild green chilies.

Yield: 2 ½ c

CRISPY SESAME-OAT
CRACKERS

5 c	Quick oats	1/3 c	Sesame seeds
1 ½ c	Whole wheat flour	1 ½ c	Water
1/2 c	Brown sugar or Sucanat	1/2 c	Canola oil
1/2 c	Ground almonds or pecans	2 tsp	Salt

In a large bowl, combine oats, flour, sweetener, nuts and sesame seeds. In a separate bowl, combine water, oil and salt. Combine liquid and dry ingredients and stir until well mixed. Coat a cookie sheet with no-stick cooking spray. Pour mixture onto the cookie sheet and roll out to the edges with a rolling pin. Bake 1 hour at 250° F. Take out of oven and score into 2 or 3 inch squares. Return to oven and bake 30 minutes more. Cool and break into squares.

Yield: 5 dozen crackers

OATMEAL-DATE COOKIES

1/2 c	Date butter (see below)	1/2 c	Canola oil
1 c	Old-fashioned oats	1/3 c	Honey or Sucanat®
2 c	Quick oats	1/3 c	Frozen apple juice
1 c	Whole wheat flour		(concentrate)
1/2 c	Unbleached white flour	1 tsp	Vanilla
1/2 c	Better Than Milk™ powder	1/2 tsp	Maple flavoring
1 tsp	Salt	1 T	ENER-G® Egg Replacer,
1/2 c	Walnuts, chopped		mixed in 4 T water

Prepare date butter according to directions below and set aside. Combine dry ingredients. Combine liquids and pour into the dry ingredients and mix well. Use 2/3 of cookie mixture and drop by heaping tablespoonfuls on a baking sheet and gently shape into cookies. Take care not to press mixture together too much. Press a small "well" into the center of each cookie. Spoon 1 tsp date butter into each "well" and top with enough cookie dough to just cover. Bake in a pre-heated oven at 350° F, 16-18 minutes or until lightly browned. Cool slightly then place in a covered air tight container.

Note: Make **DATE BUTTER** by combining 1 cup pitted dates with 1/2 cup water and simmering 2-3 minutes until soft. Cool. Mash dates well with a fork or pour into a blender and process until dates are smooth and creamy.   Yield: 1 c

Variation: For a delicious low-fat version, substitute half or all canola oil with equal proportions of WonderSlim® Fat & Egg Substitute.

Yield: 2 dozen

FROZEN FRUIT ICE CREAM

Freeze any combination of fruits you like. In a blender, process 4 cups fruit with 6 T Better Than Milk™ powder. Add a small amount of 100% fruit juice, only if necessary to assist the blending process. Serve at once as soft ice cream or return to freezer 1 or 2 hours for hard ice cream. Scoop up, garnish with toppings and serve immediately.

Variation: Add 1/2 c almonds or raw cashews for extra creaminess.
Toppings: Sprinkle with grated coconut, chopped nuts, carob chips, sunflower seeds, or fresh chopped fruit for added flavor.

Yield: 3 c

MOCHA - BANANA NUT
ICE CREAM

1 c	Water	2 or 3 T	Pure maple syrup
1/2 c	Raw cashews	1 T	Vanilla, natural
1/2 c	Better Than Milk™ powder	1 tsp	Maple flavoring, natural
2 T	Carob powder	5 or 6	Ripe bananas, frozen
1/8 tsp	Roma (coffee substitute)		

In a blender, combine water and cashews and process until completely liquefied. Add dry ingredients and flavorings and blend until smooth. Break bananas into chunks and add through the lid spout while blending on high speed until total volume equals 5 c. Serve immediately for soft ice cream or for firm ice cream, pour into a shallow container and freeze several hours before scooping. Serve plain or garnish with choice of sliced almonds, chopped pecans or walnuts, grated coconut, carob shavings, raspberries, strawberries, or mint leaves.

Variation: Increase cashews up to 1c if a richer, creamier taste is desired.

Yield: 5 c

A Bit of Country

Featuring

Southern specialties guaranteed to give you that good old country feeling and a taste of Southern hospitality.

MACARONI 'N "CHEESE"

NOODLES:
2 c   Macaroni, spirals or elbow

TOPPING:
1/4 c	Seasoned bread crumbs	1 T	Olive oil
3 T	SoyCo® Parmesan Cheese Alternative		

Combine ingredients in a bowl and mix with fingers to make crumbs. Pour into a pie tin or spread on a cookie sheet and bake in a pre-heated oven at 300° F, about 10 minutes or until topping is crispy. Watch carefully to avoid browning.

AMERICAN "CHEESE" SAUCE:
1½ c	Water	1½ T	Fresh lemon juice
1 c	Cooked white rice, or millet	1½ tsp	Salt
1/2 c	Firm tofu	1 tsp	Onion powder
1/2 c	Slivered almonds, (w/o skins)	1/4 tsp	Garlic powder
1/2 c	Cooked carrots, mashed		
2 T	Nutritional yeast flakes		

In a blender, combine all ingredients and process on high speed until completely smooth and creamy. Bits of almonds or carrots should not be visible. Sauce will appear "shiny" when done.

METHOD:
Cook macaroni in boiling water until tender adding 1 tsp of salt to the water. While noodles are cooking, prepare and bake "Topping". Then prepare "Cheese Sauce". Pour into a sauce pan and heat until ready to use. Drain and rinse cooked noodles well. Transfer to a bowl and pour 2 cups "cheese sauce" mixture over the hot noodles and toss lightly. Add tofu milk or water to mixture if it seems too stiff. Pour into a shallow serving dish and sprinkle the topping evenly over the Macaroni & Cheese.

Variation: Add sautéed onions and/or bell peppers. Alternative toppings include a choice of crushed Pepperidge Farm Corn Bread Stuffing, crushed croutons, toasted sesame seeds or poppy seeds.

Yield: 6 c

"CHICKEN" STYLE POTPIE

4 c	Potatoes, diced	2 T	Chicken-style seasoning
2 c	Carrots, diced		(or) 1½ tsp salt
3 c	Water	1 T	Nutritional yeast flakes
1 c	Onion, diced	1½ tsp	Onion powder
1 c	Celery, diced	1/8 tsp	Garlic powder
2 T	Canola oil	1 c	Mushrooms, sliced
3 c	Soy or tofu milk	1 c	Frozen green peas
3/4 c	Soy cream (recipe below)	6 T	Unbleached white flour
2 c	Chic-Ketts™, diced	4 T	Water

Cook potatoes and carrots in water until 3/4 done. Drain. Set aside. Sauté onion and celery in oil until transparent. In a large pot, combine potatoes, carrots, onion, and celery with soy milk, soy cream, Chic-Ketts, seasonings, mushrooms, and peas. Mix flour with water and stir until no longer lumpy. Add to the vegetable mixture and cook over medium heat to thicken. Pour mixture into a large casserole dish and cover with a whole grain pie crust (see Wheat or Oat Pie Crust recipes). Seal edges around dish. Bake at 350° F for 40 to 45 minutes or until browned and flaky. Or, make individual pot pies but you may wish to use a bottom and a top crust for this method. Bake at 350° F for about 30 minutes for small pot pies.

Yield: 18 servings (cut 6 x 3)

SOY CREAM

1/2 c	Water	1/8 tsp	Garlic powder
1/4 c	Soyagen powder	1/4 c	Canola oil
1/4 tsp	Salt	2 T	Fresh lemon juice
1/4 tsp	Onion powder		

In a blender, combine water, Soyagen, and seasonings and process until smooth. Remove lid spout and add oil slowly while blending. Pour mixture out into a bowl and fold in the lemon juice until well mixed.

Yield: 1 c (scant)

WHEAT PIE CRUST

1 c	Whole wheat pastry flour	6 T	Water
1 c	Unbleached white flour	3/4 tsp	Salt
1/2 c	Canola oil		

Mix flours. Combine oil, water and salt. Combine the flours and liquids and mix together lightly to form a ball. Place dough between two sheets of wax paper and roll out with a rolling pin.

Yield: 3 c

OAT PIE CRUST

2/3 c	Mashed potatoes, cooked	1 tsp	Salt
1½ c	Oat flour	2/3 c	Water
1/2 c	Whole wheat flour	1/3 c	Canola oil
2 T	Better Than Milk™ powder		

Peel, cube and boil 2 potatoes. Mash enough potatoes to equal 2/3 c and set aside. Combine flours, tofu milk powder and salt. Mix water and oil together and pour into the dry ingredients. Stir until just moistened. Add mashed potatoes to the dough. Knead mixture together until a soft, pliable dough is formed. Let dough rest several minutes. Roll dough out on a floured surface.

Yield: 3½ c

CASHEW-BARLEY CRUST

1 c	Barley flour	1/2 c	Raw cashew butter
1 c	Unbleached white flour	1/3 c	Canola oil
2 T	Wheat germ (opt)	1/2 c	Hot Water
1 tsp	Salt (scant)		

Combine flours, wheat germ and salt. In a separate bowl, mix the cashew butter, oil and water together. Pour into flour and stir until dough is moist. Knead into a ball. Divide into two balls, one larger than the other. Roll out each ball between 2 pieces of plastic wrap or wax paper. Press the larger crust in the bottom of a 9" pie plate. Add the filling and top crust. Bake according to directions.

Variation: May replace cashew butter with raw almond butter.

Yield: 3½ c

"CHICKEN" & RICE CASSEROLE

2 ½ c	Water	2½ tsp	Chicken-Style seasoning
2 c	Instant brown rice	1/2 tsp	Onion salt
1 c	Instant white rice		

Bring water to a boil. Add rice and seasoning. Cover and simmer 5 minutes and remove from heat. Pour rice into a large bowl and set aside.

1 c	Mock chicken	1/2 c	Jicama, julienned
1 c	Onion, chopped	1/2 c	Lightly roasted cashews
1/2 c	Celery, diced	1/4 c	Green onions, sliced
1 T	Olive oil	1/4 c	Fresh parsley, minced
1½ c	Jiffy Mushroom Soup	1 T	Sesame seeds
1/2 c	Soy Mayonnaise (p 167)		

Tear mock chicken into bite size pieces and combine with onions, celery and oil in a skillet. Sauté until vegetables are tender. Stir mixture into rice. Add soup (see below), mayonnaise, and remaining ingredients. Mix well. Coat a casserole dish with no-stick cooking spray. Spread rice mixture evenly into the casserole dish. Garnish with cashews, green onions and sesame seeds. Cover and bake at 350° F, 20 to 30 minutes until heated through and bubbly.

Yield: 9 x 13 casserole

JIFFY MUSHROOM SOUP

1 c	Fresh mushrooms, sliced	1 T	Cornstarch
1½ c	Water	1 T	Spectrum® Spread (opt)
1/2 c	Onion, chopped	1 tsp	Chicken-Style Seasoning
4 T	Better Than Milk™ powder	1/2 tsp	Salt
2 T	Unbleached all purpose flour	1/2 tsp	Basil

Sauté mushrooms in a skillet with 2 T water and 1/8 tsp salt until tender. Set aside. (May also microwave mushrooms with water and salt about 1 minute.) In a blender, combine remaining ingredients and process until smooth. Add mushrooms with liquids and flash blend a few times to break up mushrooms into pieces. Pour out into a saucepan and cook until thickened. Use this for recipes in place of canned soup. If necessary, add additional tofu milk or water to thin mixture down to desired consistency.

Variation: May substitute fresh mushrooms, 2 T water, and 1/8 tsp salt with 4 oz canned mushrooms, with liquid. Yield: 3 c

VEGETARIAN
"BEEF STEAKS" WITH GRAVY

HOMEMADE GLUTEN

1 c	Vital wheat gluten (Do Pep)	1 c	Water
1/4 c	Unbleached flour		

Combine flours and mix very well. Add water and quickly stir to make a ball of gluten. Let sit at least 20 minutes. While waiting, make the broth (see recipe below). When gluten is ready, form a long roll. Cut into 1 inch pieces. Flatten pieces out into a round shape and drop into boiling broth. Gluten will soon float if made properly. Simmer uncovered 30 to 45 minutes, stirring occasionally. When done, cut gluten "steaks" into strips and coat with Breading Meal # 1 (see recipe below). Lightly coat a large non-stick frying pan with olive oil and heat on med-lo setting. Add gluten "strips" and spray "Olive Oil Pam" over gluten evenly. Fry until golden brown. Serve with ketchup or choice of Mushroom-Onion or Country Gravy. (See gravy recipes on p 221)   Yield: 12 steaks

BROTH

2 qt	Water	2 T	Bragg liquid aminos
1/2 c	Onion rings	1½ T	Beef-style seasoning
1/2 c	Celery leaves	1 tsp	Celery salt
1 pkg	Lipton soup "onion-mushroom"	1 tsp	Garlic powder
2	Bay leaves	1/2 tsp	Cumin
4	Fresh basil leaves (or ½ tsp dried basil)		

Combine all ingredients in a large pot and bring to a boil.
Yield: 2½ qts

BREADING MEAL #1

1/2 c	Unbleached flour	1 tsp	Onion powder
1/2 c	Yellow corn meal	1/2 tsp	Garlic powder
2 T	Nutritional yeast flakes	1 T	Parsley, dried
2 tsp	Chicken-style seasoning	1/8 tsp	Salt
1 tsp	Garlic & Herb seasoning ,"salt free"		

Combine all ingredients and store in an air-tight container.
Yield: 1¼ c

MUSHROOM-ONION GRAVY

1 c	Mushrooms, sliced	2 tsp	Beef-style seasoning
1/2 c	Onion, slices	2 tsp	Chicken-style seasoning
1/4	Bell pepper, chopped (opt)	1/2 c	Hot water
1/2 tsp	Garlic, minced	2 T	Unbleached white flour
2 T	Olive oil	1 c	Water

Sauté vegetables in half the olive oil and remove from pan. Brown the beef and chicken flavored seasonings in remaining oil. When dark brown, dash in the 1/2 c water. Mix flour with the remaining water, pour into the pan and stir until thick. Add the sautéed vegetables. Pour gravy over "Beef Steaks".

Yield: 3 c

COUNTRY GRAVY

1 c	Onion, sliced	2 tsp	Beef-style seasoning
1 c	Fresh mushrooms, sliced	2 tsp	Chicken-style seasoning
1/2 c	Bell pepper, chopped	1/2 c	Hot water
1 tsp	Garlic purée	2 T	Unbleached white flour
2 T	Olive oil	1 c	Water

Sauté vegetables and garlic in 1 T oil. Remove from pan. Brown seasonings in remaining oil until dark brown. Dash in 1/2 c hot water. Mix flour with remaining water, pour into the pan and stir until thick. Stir in the sautéed vegetables. Pour over Choplets and serve.

Yield: 4 c

CHOPLETS 'N GRAVY

1 can	Choplets®	1/4 c	Breading Meal #2
	(or vegetarian gluten)	1 recipe	Country Gravy

Slice Choplets into strips or bite-size pieces. Shake Choplets with Breading Meal #2 (recipe on p 222) in a zip-lock bag to coat the pieces evenly. Brown in a small amount olive oil and cover with Country Gravy (recipe above).

Yield: 3 c

BREADING MEAL #2

1/2 c	Flour, wheat or white	1 T	Nutritional yeast flakes
1/4 c	Cracker crumbs, finely blended	1 tsp	Onion powder
1/4 c	Yellow corn meal	1/2 tsp	Salt
2 tsp	Beef or chicken-style seasoning	1/2 tsp	Garlic powder

Mix ingredients together and store in an air tight container.

Yield: 1 1/8 c

VEGETARIAN "CHICKEN" & "SAUSAGE" GUMBO

2 c	Brown rice	4 oz	Old El Paso®, mild green
3/4 c	Unbleached white flour, browned		chilies, chopped
		1½ tsp	Lawry's® Seasoned Salt
1 c	Onion, chopped	1 tsp	Salt
1 c	Red onion, chopped	2 cubes	Vegetable bouillon
1 c	Green onions, sliced		(or) 1 tsp powdered
1 c	Celery, diced		vegetable seasoning
3/4 c	Bell pepper, diced	12 oz	Vegan Sausage Crumbles
1/3 c	Fresh parsley, chopped	8 oz	Chic-Ketts™, torn
4 med	Garlic cloves, minced		into bite size pieces
1/4 c	Canola oil	1 c	Frozen sliced okra, thawed
4 c	Water		

Prepare rice according to directions on the package and set aside. Brown flour in a large frying pan over med/high heat stirring constantly until medium brown in color. Set aside. In a large pot, combine all onions, celery, pepper, parsley and garlic in oil and sauté until vegetables are tender. Add water, chilies, seasonings and browned flour and stir until well mixed. Stir in "chicken and sausage" meat substitutes and okra. Bring to a boil, then cover and reduce heat and simmer 10 minutes. Ladle gumbo into serving bowls and dollop 2 to 4 T rice into the center of the gumbo.

Yield: 14 c

222

SUCCOTASH

20 oz bag	Frozen lima beans	1 T	Flour or cornstarch
1 tsp	Salt	1 tsp	Marjoram
1 c	Frozen whole kernel corn	1/2 tsp	Chicken-style seasoning
1/4 c	Water	1/4 tsp	Onion powder
6 T	Better than Milk™ powder	(opt)	Salt to taste

In a saucepan, add lima beans and enough water to just cover beans. Add salt, cover and simmer until almost tender. Add corn, return to a boil and simmer 5 more minutes. Combine 1/4 c water with the remaining ingredients and mix until dissolved. Pour into vegetables and stir until thick. Serve hot.

Yield: 3 c

BLACK-EYED PEA STEW

2 c	Onion, chopped	2 cans	Diced tomatoes, plain
1/2 c	Bell pepper, diced		(14.5 oz size each)
2 med	Garlic cloves, minced	1 can	Diced tomatoes, Italian
2 T	Olive oil		(14.5 oz size)
2 c	Vegetarian Burger, canned	1½ c	Frozen sliced okra, thawed
4 c	Black-eyed peas, cooked		

In a large pot, sauté onions, peppers, and garlic in oil until tender. Add burger and fry until lightly browned. Add remaining ingredients and simmer 10 to 15 minutes.

Yield: 12 c

BLACK-EYED PEAS

2 c	Black eye peas, dry	(opt)	Salt to taste
2 1/4 c	Water	(opt)	Bac-Os® to garnish
1/2 c	Onion, chopped		(Imitation bacon bits)

Wash and sort peas. Cover peas with water and soak overnight or at least 4 hours. Drain. Simmer peas in water with onions and salt to taste until tender. Garnish with Bac-Os® if desired.

Yield: 3 c

SAVORY KALE
with
PEPPERS & ONIONS

1/2 lb	Kale, fresh	1 tsp	Olive oil
1 c	Onions, chopped	1/3 c	Water
1/4 c	Red Peppers, diced	1 tsp	Chicken-style Seasoning
2 lg	Garlic cloves, minced	(opt)	Salt

Soak and wash kale in water. Remove the large stems and discard any tough or discolored leaves. Stack 6 to 8 leaves at a time and cut crosswise into 1 inch strips. In a large saucepan, sauté onions, peppers and garlic in oil over medium heat until onions are translucent. Add water and kale, cover and simmer or steam 20 to 30 minutes. (Large leaves may require up to 60 minutes.) Add seasoning and salt to taste.

Variation: Replace kale with collards or other greens.

Yield: 2 c

MAZIDRA
(A Lentil and Onion Lebanese Dish)

4 c	Water	1 tsp	Garlic purée
1 c	Brown lentils, dry	1 tsp	Salt
1½ tsp	Mesquite Grill Seasoning	2 T	Canola or light olive oil
1/2 tsp	Beef-style Seasoning	1 lg	Onion, thinly sliced in rings

In a saucepan, combine water, lentils, seasonings, garlic and salt. Bring to a boil, reduce heat, cover and simmer 30 to 40 minutes or until lentils are tender. In a large non-stick frying pan, sauté onions in oil until translucent. (If crispier onions are desired, transfer sautéed onions to a cookie sheet coated with no-stick cooking spray. If needed, drizzle onions with 1 to 3 tsp additional olive oil and bake at 425° F, 5 to 10 minutes or until onions are lightly browned and edges begin to get crispy.) To serve, spoon lentils over cooked rice and cover with a generous portion of onion rings.

Yield: 6 c

MAMA'S
MASHED POTATOES

4 lg	Potatoes, peeled and cubed	2 tsp	Chicken-style seasoning
1/2 c	Mori-Nu® tofu, soft	(opt)	Salt to taste
1/4 c	"Soy Good" Sour Cream (opt)		

Boil potatoes until tender. Drain, reserving 1 c potato water. Mash potatoes in a large mixing bowl. Add tofu and Sour Cream (recipe below) and beat with an electric mixer until fluffy adding water or tofu milk if necessary. Add seasoning and/or salt to taste and continue beating until thoroughly mixed. Serve hot.

Yield: 6 c

"SOY GOOD"
TOFU SOUR CREAM

1½ c	Mori-Nu Silken Tofu, firm (12.5 oz box)	1/4 tsp	Salt
3 T	Sunflower oil	1/4 tsp	Honey
1/4 tsp	Citric acid crystals		

In a blender, combine all ingredients and process until smooth and creamy.

Variation: Add 1 tsp fresh lemon juice for a stronger sour taste.

Yield: 1½ c

SUMMER SQUASH STIR-FRY

1 sm	Onion, sliced	1/2 c	Frozen peas or pea pods
2 med	Yellow summer squash, sliced	1 tsp	Chicken-style seasoning
2 med	Zucchini, sliced	(opt)	Salt to taste
1 med	Carrot, cut diagonally		

In a large skillet, sauté onion in a small amount olive oil or water. Add squash and carrots, with just enough water for simmering. Cover and cook until tender. Add thawed peas and simmer 2 to 3 more minutes. Season with chicken-style seasoning and/or salt to taste.

Yield: 6 c

TOMATO-CUCUMBER SALAD
WITH
HERB DRESSING

3 c   Tomatoes, chopped   1/2 c   Onion, chopped
3 c   Cucumbers, chopped   1/2 c   Herb Dressing

Mix cold tomatoes, cucumbers and onions in a bowl. Pour Herb Dressing (see recipe below) over the vegetables and serve.

Yield: 7 c

HERB DRESSING

Add to one .75 oz pkg. Good Seasons® "Garlic & Herb" Dressing Mix:

3 T   Fresh Lemon juice   1/3 c   Water
3 T   Pineapple juice concentrate   1/4 c   Olive oil

Shake until well blended. Chill and shake again before serving.

Yield: 1 c

CARROT - PINEAPPLE SALAD

3 c   Carrots, shredded   1/2 c   Pineapple tidbits, drained
3/4 c   Raisins   1/2 c   Pecans, chopped

Combine above ingredients and chill. Stir in Creamy Dressing (see below) when ready to serve.

CREAMY DRESSING

1/2 c   Raw cashews, rinsed   1/2 tsp   Fresh lemon juice
1/2 c   Pineapple juice   1/4 tsp   Salt (scant)
1/4 c   Mori-Nu ® Tofu, x-firm   1 tsp   Instant Clear Jel
2 T   Apple juice concentrate   (food thickener)
2 tsp   Pineapple juice concentrate

In a blender, combine all ingredients, except food thickener, and process until completely smooth and creamy. Add Clear Jel and continue blending about 10 seconds more. Chill. Mix into salad when ready to serve.

Yield: 6 c

MACARONI SALAD

4 c	Cooked elbow macaroni	1/4 c	Sliced olives, black or green
3/4 c	Red onion, chopped	1/2 c	Soy mayonnaise, (see p 167)
3/4 c	Celery, sliced	1/2 tsp	Garlic salt
3/4 c	Dill pickles, chopped	1/8 tsp	Celery salt

Combine all ingredients and mix lightly. Chill before serving.   Yield: 7 c

CORNBREAD
(Yeast-raised)

1 c	Warm water	1½ c	Unbleached white flour
3 T	Honey	3/4 c	Yellow cornmeal
2 T	Canola oil	3 T	Tofu milk powder
2½ tsp	Yeast	1 tsp	Salt

Combine water, honey, oil and yeast. Let stand 3 minutes. Stir in remaining ingredients and mix well. Pour into an 8" square pan coated with no-stick cooking spray. Let rise 30 minutes or until double. Bake at 350° F, 25 to 30 minutes until golden brown. Cool 10 minutes before trying to remove cornbread from pan.

Variation: For "quick cornbread", replace yeast with 1 T non-aluminum baking powder. Reduce salt to 1/2 tsp. Bake at 375° F, 20 to 25 minutes.

Yield: 8 inch square pan or 12 muffins

OLD FASHIONED CORNBREAD

3 c	Yellow cornmeal	2 T	Rapid rise yeast
1 c	Soy flour	2 T	Canola oil
2 c	Unbleached white flour	1/4 c	Brown sugar or honey
2 tsp	Salt	2½ c	Warm water

Combine dry ingredients in a large bowl. In a separate bowl, mix oil, sweetener and water together and add to the dry ingredients. Mix well. Coat bakeware with no-stick cooking spray. Pour into muffin tins, mini bread pans or cake pans, 3/4 full, and let rise 10 to 15 minutes. Bake at 350° F, about 20 minutes in muffin tins, 25 minutes in mini bread pans and 30 to 35 minutes in cake pans.

Yield: 18 muffins

GRANDMA'S
HOME-STYLE BISCUITS

1 c	Warm water	2 c	Unbleached white flour
2½ tsp	Rapid-rise yeast	1 c	Whole wheat flour
1 tsp	Honey	1/4 c	Canola oil
3/4 tsp	Salt	1 T	Wheat germ or oat bran

Dissolve yeast in warm water. Add honey, salt and unbleached white flour and mix well. Let rise until light and fluffy. Stir in remaining ingredients. Turn out on a floured surface and knead lightly until smooth (about 30 seconds). Roll out 3/4 inches thick and cut with a 2 inch biscuit cutter. Place on an oiled cookie sheet and let rise in a draft free area 15 minutes. Bake at 350° F, about 20 minutes or until light brown.

Yield: 18 biscuits

HEARTY SOUTHERN BISCUITS

1 c	All purpose flour	1/2 c	Water
3/4 c	Barley flour	1/4 c	Oil
1/4 c	Whole wheat flour	1 T	Honey
1 T	Baking powder	1/2 c	Soft tofu
1/2 tsp	Salt		

Mix flours, baking powder and salt in a medium bowl. In a blender, combine water, oil, honey, and tofu and blend until smooth and creamy. Pour blender ingredients into dry ingredients. Stir quickly and briefly. Knead lightly on a floured surface. Roll dough out to 1 inch thickness. Cut with a biscuit cutter into 2 inch circles. Place side by side on a cookie sheet. Bake at 425°F, 13 to 15 minutes.

Yield: 1 dozen

"HEART SMART"
CORN BUTTER

1 c	Cold water	2 T	Canola oil
1/4 c	Yellow corn meal	1 T	Emes Kosher-Jel®, plain
1/2 c	Mori-Nu Silken tofu, x-firm	1 T	Cooked carrot (opt for color)
1/2 c	Warm water	1 tsp	Honey
1/4 c	Almonds	1 tsp	Imitation butter flavored salt
3 T	Spicery Shoppe® Natural -	½ tsp	Salt
	Butter Flavor (vegan)	Pinch	Citric acid

Combine cold water and corn meal in a small saucepan and bring to a boil stirring constantly. Reduce heat to low, cover and simmer 10 minutes. Refrigerate until completely cool and "set". In a blender, combine water, almonds, butter flavoring, oil and Emes. Process on high speed until no longer "gritty". Spoon chilled corn meal mush into the blender mixture and all remaining ingredients and process until smooth and creamy. Bits of carrot should not be visible. Refrigerate several hours before serving until "butter" thickens to a spreadable consistency.

Yield: 3 c

ORANGE HONEY BUTTER

Add the following ingredients to 1 cup of cold, pre-set Corn Butter:

1/2 tsp	Grated orange peel
1 T	Frozen orange juice concentrate
2 T	Creamy "spun" honey (SueBee® or similar brand)

Whip at high speed until fluffy. Refrigerate before serving.

Yield: 1 1/8 c

APRICOT JAM

2 c	Dried sulfured apricots, quartered	1 tsp	Fresh lemon juice
1 ½ c	Pineapple juice, unsweetened		

Combine all ingredients in a saucepan and bring to a boil. Reduce heat and simmer 5 minutes. Cool. Pour into a blender and process on high speed until smooth. Chill.

Yield: 3 c

PINEAPPLE-DATE JAM

| 1 c | Pitted dates | 1/2 c | Crushed pineapple |
| 3/4 c | Water | 1 tsp | Lemon juice |

Combine dates and water in a saucepan and bring to a boil. Reduce heat and simmer 3 minutes. Cool. Pour into a blender and process on high speed until smooth. Pour out into a bowl and add pineapple and lemon juice. Stir until well mixed. Chill.

Yield: 2 c

APPLE SPICE JAM

| 2 c | Dried apples, packed | 1/2 c | Pineapple juice |
| 2 c | Hot water or apple juice | 1/2 tsp | Cinnamon |

Soak apples in water or juice 15 minutes. Pour into a blender and add remaining ingredients. Process on high speed until smooth. Chill.

Yield: 3 c

SOUTHERN PEACH PRESERVES

12 oz	White grape juice (frozen) concentrate	4 c	Fresh peaches, mashed (drain and reserve juice)
1 c	Water	1/2 tsp	Fresh lemon juice
4 T	Minute tapioca or cornstarch		

In a saucepan, combine white grape juice, water and thickener of choice. Stir until dissolved. Add reserved peach juice and lemon juice. Bring to a boil and simmer (about 15 minutes if using tapioca or 5 minutes for cornstarch) until juice is clear. Add mashed peaches and continue cooking a few more minutes. Cool and refrigerate.

Note: Purée peaches if you prefer a "jam" consistency.

Yield: 7 c

GRAPE JAM

1 c	Golden raisins	1½ c	Water
7 oz	100% purple grape juice	1/4 c	Minute tapioca
	(frozen) concentrate	2 T	Fructose
1/2 c	Blueberries, frozen		

Combine raisins, grape juice, and blueberries in a saucepan. Bring to a boil. Reduce heat, cover and simmer about 5 minutes until raisins are tender. Cool. Pour mixture into a blender and process until raisins are completely puréed. Return to the saucepan and add water, tapioca, and fructose. Cover and simmer, stirring frequently, until mixture clears and thickens or about 10 minutes. Refrigerate. Serve cold.

Yield: 3 c

BLACKBERRY JAM

4 c	Blackberries	12 oz	Water (or less for sweeter jam)
12 oz	White grape juice	4 T	Cornstarch, or tapioca powder
	(frozen) concentrate	1/2 tsp	Fresh lemon juice

Purée blackberries in a blender. If desired, may strain puréed blackberries to remove seeds. In a saucepan, combine juice concentrate, water and thickener of choice and stir until dissolved. Bring to a boil and simmer until mixture clears. Add blackberry purée and lemon juice to the saucepan with the thickened juice and continue to cook stirring constantly until jam is thick. Cool and refrigerate.

Yield: 5 c

STRAWBERRY TROPIC JAM

| 1/2 c | Dried papaya or mango, diced | 3 c | Strawberries, fresh |
| 1/4 c | Pineapple juice, unsweetened | | (or frozen - thawed) |

Combine dried fruit and pineapple juice in a saucepan, cover and simmer 5 to 10 minutes or until softened. Cool. Pour into a blender, add strawberries and process on high speed 3 to 5 minutes until smooth. Chill.

Yield: 4 c

AUNT BEA'S
OLD-FASHIONED APPLE PIE

8 c	Tart apples, thinly sliced	3 T	Minute® Tapioca
6 oz	Dole® "Orchard Peach"	1 tsp	Cinnamon
	(frozen juice concentrate)	1/4 tsp	Salt
1 c	Date sugar or Sucanat®	1 tsp	Vanilla

Slice "Granny Smith" or "York" apples for a tart pie or use "Golden Delicious" apples if you prefer a sweeter and softer filling. Place apples in a bowl with the juice concentrate and coat the apples to prevent them from turning brown. Stir in remaining ingredients until well mixed. If using Granny Smith apples and you prefer a softer cooked apple, just microwave the apples with the juice for 2 to 3 minutes before adding the remaining ingredients. Pour into a 9" pie crust. (See selections of whole grain pie crusts on p 218) Place top crust over filling, flute edges and slit crust. Bake at 350°F, about 1 hour. Serve with "Instant" Whipped Topping (recipe below).

Yield: 9" pie

"INSTANT"
WHIPPED TOPPING

1½ c	Water	1/3 c	Canned coconut milk
2/3 c	Better than Milk™ powder		"Lite" (unsweetened)
1/2 c	Blanched almonds (w/o skins)	2 tsp	Vanilla, (natural)
3½ T	Emes Kosher-Jel®, plain	1/4 tsp	Salt
3 T	Honey or powdered sugar		Ice

In a blender, combine the water, milk powder, almonds and Emes Jel and process until the almonds are liquefied completely. Add remaining ingredients and process briefly. Finally, begin adding ice slowly through the lid spout and continue processing on high speed to make a total volume equal to 5 cups. Turn blender off and wait briefly. Mixture should now be light and fluffy. Best served immediately. If stored, and mixture becomes too firm, hand whip or beat gently with an electric beater before serving.

Yield: 5 c

"LAZY DAISY"
OATMEAL CAKE

2 c	Quick oats	2 tsp	Salt
2 c	Date sugar	1½ tsp	Cinnamon
1½ c	Whole wheat flour	1/2 tsp	Nutmeg
1½ c	All purpose flour	3 c	Water
2 T	Baking powder	2/3 c	Honey
2 T	ENER-G® Egg Replacer	4 tsp	Vanilla

Combine dry ingredients and spices. Combine water, honey and vanilla and pour into the dry ingredients. Stir until well mixed. Pour into two 9" round cake pans or one 9 x 13 baking dish. Bake at 350° F, for 55 to 60 minutes.

Note: Spread Date-Nut Frosting (recipe below) on warm cake.

Yield: 9 inch layered cake or 9 x 13 sheet cake

DATE-NUT FROSTING

1 c	Dates, pitted	1/2 tsp	Salt
2 c	Water	2 c	Pecans, chopped
1/2 c	Better Than Milk™ powder	2 c	Grated coconut
2 tsp	Vanilla, natural	1/4 c	Vital wheat gluten (opt)

Simmer dates in water until soft. Cool slightly. Transfer dates to a blender. Add milk powder, vanilla and salt and process until smooth. Return mixture to saucepan and fold in the nuts and coconut. If using frosting on a layered cake, it is necessary to add vital wheat gluten in order for the frosting to stick to the sides of the cake. If using frosting on a sheet cake, this step is not necessary. Spread frosting on cake while still warm. Sprinkle cake with additional grated coconut for garnish and to improve appearance.

Yield: 5 c

Holiday Burger Loaf
Yams with Orange Glaze
Non-Dairy Pumpkin Pie
Crescent Rolls

A
Thanksgiving
Tradition

Featuring

A vegetarian Thanksgiving dinner complete with "Turkey" and all the trimmings. A feast that's sure to please.

HOLIDAY TURKEY

GLUTEN BASE:

4 c	Do-Pep gluten flour	2 T	Nutritional yeast flakes
1 c	All purpose flour	4 T	Soy sauce
2 pkg	George Washington Broth®	4 c	Water

Combine ingredients and knead gluten into a ball. Take off a piece of the gluten about the size of your fist and set aside to be used later for the turkey skin.

FILLING:

3 lg	Onions, quartered	1½ c	Walnuts or pecans
4 stalks	Celery	1 c	Pepperidge Farm®
6 cloves	Garlic		Cornbread Stuffing

Take the big lump of gluten and push it through a meat grinder a little at a time with the above seasonings. Use half the stuffing mix to work the gluten through the grinder and then use the last half at the end to clean any remaining gluten out of the grinder. Pour mixture into a bowl.

SPICES:

3 T   McKay's® Chicken-Style Seasoning   2 tsp   Sage (opt)

Stir spices into the above gluten mixture.

PROCEDURE:
Take the gluten you saved for the skin and spread it out as thin as possible into a large rectangle. Put the ground turkey mixture in the center and wrap the skin around it making an oblong shape like a turkey breast. Now wrap turkey in several layers of cheesecloth. See that the cheesecloth is wrapped quite firmly around the turkey and sew securely with a needle and thread across the top seam and on both ends.

Continued on next page

BROTH:

2 med	Onions, chopped	3 c	Tomato juice or tomato sauce
6 cloves	Garlic, minced	1/2 c	Soy sauce
2 stalks	Celery, chopped	2 env	Lipton® Mushroom-Onion Soup
2 sm	Bell peppers, chopped (optional)	1 T	Chicken or Beef-Style Seasoning

Sauté onions, garlic, celery and peppers in a small amount of oil or water until half tender. Add remaining ingredients. Place turkey and broth in a roaster and cover. Set oven on 250° F, and simmer turkey 3 to 4 hours. Baste turkey every 30 minutes with the broth and turn turkey over half way through cooking time. Then turn heat off and leave turkey in the oven to soak 6 to 8 hours. Remove the turkey from the oven and cut off the cheesecloth wrapper. Serve on an oval platter and garnish with dressing or rice and vegetables. If not eaten the same day, just freeze leftover turkey until needed and thaw in the refrigerator before re-heating.

Yield: 15 to 20 servings

VEGETARIAN MEATLOAF

3/4 lb	Fresh tofu, x-firm, mashed	6 oz	Italian tomato paste
1½ c	GranBurger®	1/4 c	Fresh parsley, chopped
1½ c	Pepperidge Farm® Stuffing	1/4 c	Nutritional yeast flakes
1 c	Quick oats	1/4 c	Gluten flour
1 can	Mock duck, finely chopped	2 T	ENER-G® Egg Replacer,
1 env	Lipton® Onion Soup Mix		(mixed in 1/4 c water)
1/2 c	Pecans, chopped	1 tsp	Beef-Style Seasoning
1 med	Onion, chopped	1 tsp	Sage
1 stalk	Celery, diced	1/2 c	Vinegarless ketchup *
2 large	Garlic cloves, minced	1/3 c	Crushed pineapple
1/3 c	Bell pepper, chopped	2 or 3 T	Brown sugar or Sucanat®
1/4 c	Vinegarless ketchup (see p 239)		

Coat a large loaf pan with no-stick cooking spray. Mix all ingredients together except 1/2 c ketchup, pineapple and brown sugar. Squeeze the pineapple dry and add the ketchup and brown sugar. Pour the pineapple mixture into the bottom of the pan. Press loaf mixture into the pan over the pineapple mixture. Bake at 350° F, 1 hour and 5 minutes. Let cool at least 15 minutes before removing loaf. Invert loaf onto an oval platter dressed with a lettuce bed. Garnish with carrot curls, crushed pineapple, and fresh parsley on top. Border loaf with potatoes, broccoli, cherry tomatoes and orange twists.

Yield: 1 (oversized) loaf pan

HOLIDAY BURGER LOAF
with
SWEET 'N SOUR GLAZE

3 T	Extra virgin olive oil		1 T	Beef-Style Seasoning
2 c	Onion, diced		1 tsp	McCormick® Garlic & Herb
1 c	Carrots, grated			("Salt-free" Seasoning)
1/2 c	Fresh mushrooms, chopped		1 tsp	Sage
1/3 c	Red and/or green		1 tsp	Maggi® Seasoning
	bell peppers, diced		3/4 tsp	Kitchen Bouquet®
3 med	Garlic cloves, minced		1/2 tsp	Onion salt
4 c	Fresh bread crumbs, wheat		3 T	Water
1 can	Worthington® brand		2 T	ENER-G Egg Replacer
	Vegetarian Burger (20 oz)		1/2 c	Vital wheat gluten (Do-Pep)

In a large skillet, add oil, onion, carrots, mushrooms, peppers and garlic. Sauté over med heat until vegetables are tender. Pour mixture out into a large bowl. Break up about 2 slices of bread at a time, add to a blender and process until crumbly. Pour into a measuring cup and continue procedure to equal 4 c. Add bread crumbs and burger to the vegetable mixture and mix well. In a small bowl, combine all seasonings with the water and egg replacer and whisk until well mixed. Add to the burger mixture and stir until evenly moistened. Last, add gluten flour and mix well. Set aside.

GLAZE:

1/2 c	Ketchup, "Quick" Vinegarless (p 239)	3 T	Water
3 T	Brown sugar		

Combine all ingredients and stir to dissolve sugar. Coat a loaf pan with no-stick cooking spray. Pour about 2/3 of glaze mixture into the bottom of the pan. Pack the burger mixture into the loaf pan and smooth out until level. Pour remaining glaze over burger. Bake at 350°F, 60 to 65 minutes or until sides begin to pull away from the pan and the glaze has darkened to a deep red color. Cool about 10 minutes before attempting to turn out of pan. If desired, garnish loaf with additional ketchup, and a border of parsley or other greenery, cherry tomatoes and cooked vegetables.

Note: If unable to use Vegetarian Burger, replace it with 2 c Mock Duck or beef flavored gluten finely ground and 3/4 c TVP rehydrated in 3/4 c hot water.

Tip: Leftover Burger Loaf makes a great sandwich filling!

Yield: 1 (9x5) loaf

"QUICK" VINEGARLESS KETCHUP

1½ c	Tomato sauce	2 T	Fruit-Fresh®, powder
1 c	Tomato paste		(or) 1/8 tsp citric acid
1/2 c	Pineapple juice	1½ tsp	Salt
1/4 c	Fresh lemon juice	1 tsp	Onion powder
1 tsp	Lime juice	1/2 tsp	Garlic salt
3 T	Date butter (p 211)	1/2 tsp	Paprika
2 T	Pineapple/orange juice	1/4 tsp	Worcestershire sauce (opt)
	(frozen concentrate)		(Vegetarian brand)
2 T	Honey		

Combine all ingredients in a blender and process until smooth. Refrigerate.
Freeze extras not used within two weeks.

Variation: For a thicker ketchup, decrease tomato sauce to 1 c and increase
tomato paste to 1½ c.

Yield: 4 c

MOZZARELLA CHEESE

1c	Cooked rice, brown or white	4 tsp	Fresh lemon juice
1 c	Water	1½ tsp	Salt
3/4 c	Tofu, x-firm	1 tsp	Onion powder
1/2 c	Raw cashews, rinsed	1/4 tsp	Garlic powder
4 T	Emes Kosher-Jel, plain		

In a blender, combine all ingredients and process on high speed, stopping and
stirring as necessary, until completely smooth and creamy (3 - 5 minutes). The
sauce will heat up and appear "shiny" when completed.   Pour into a container
coated with no stick cooking spray. Refrigerate 2 to 4 hours until set. Gently
shake out to slice cheese.

Note: To grate cheese easily, freeze mixture at least 2 hours first. For a
creamy sauce to pour over vegetables or noodles; do not refrigerate
mixture after blending, but heat and serve immediately. Or, if using
previously "set" leftover cheese, heat mixture slowly over lo-med
heat, stirring frequently until melted.

Tip: May substitute cashews with slivered blanched almonds (w/o skins).

Yield: 3 c

DINNER ROAST

1 lb	Fresh tofu, "extra firm",	2 T	Extra virgin olive oil
1 c	Vegan Burger Crumbles	1 tsp	McCormick® Garlic & Herb
3/4 c	Mozzarella Cheese Sauce		(Salt-free Seasoning)
	(see p 127)	1/2 tsp	Beef-Style Seasoning
1 env	Lipton®Mushroom Soup mix	2 T	ENER-G® Egg Replacer
1/2 c	Pecans, chopped	4 T	Water
1/2 c	Onions, chopped	4 c	"Product 19" Dry Cereal
1/2 c	Olives, chopped		(or similar cereal)

Squeeze as much excess water out of tofu as possible. Or, freeze tofu and thaw to creates a bean curd which allows you to squeeze most of the water out. (Some tofu brands are not suitable for this method. If tofu becomes like a dry tough sponge, avoid this step.) In a large bowl, crumble tofu and burger. Add cheese sauce (this should be made ahead or use leftovers), soup mix, pecans, onions, olives and oil. Add seasonings and stir evenly through the tofu-burger mixture. Whip Egg Replacer in water until foamy and fold gently into mixture. Last, add cereal and stir lightly until well mixed. Pour into a casserole baking dish coated with no-stick cooking spray. Spread mixture out evenly but lightly. (Do not pack down.) Bake at 350° F, 40 minutes. Serve with Country Gravy, Cashew Gravy or Brown Gravy. (p 241)

Variation: May add 1 cup cooked rice. Yield: 9 c

"GIBLET" DRESSING

1 c	Onions, chopped	1/2 tsp	Sage
1 c	Celery with tops, finely diced	1/4 tsp	Marjoram
1/3 c	Olive oil	1/8 tsp	Coriander
1 can	Mock Duck, shredded	1/8 tsp	Thyme
4 c	Pepperidge Farm® Stuffing	1/8 tsp	Savory
4 c	Whole wheat bread cubes, dry	1/4 c	Fresh parsley, snipped
1 can	Black olives, sliced	2 1/3 c	Better Than Milk™
4 tsp	Chicken-Style Seasoning		

Sauté onions and celery in oil. Add the shredded mock duck. Combine the stuffing mix, bread, olives and seasonings. Add mixture to the sautéed vegetables and duck. Heat milk and pour over the dressing mixture and stir lightly but thoroughly. Spoon dressing into a large baking dish coated with no-stick cooking spray. Bake at 350° F, 45 minutes to 1 hour.

Yield: 10 c

CASHEW GRAVY

1/2 c	Raw cashews, rinsed	1 T	Nutritional yeast flakes
2 c	Hot water	2 tsp	Chicken-Style Seasoning
2 T	Cornstarch	2 tsp	Onion powder
2 T	Liquid aminos or "lite" soy sauce		

Rinse cashews well. In a blender, process cashews with half the hot water until very smooth. Add remaining water and ingredients and continue blending until thoroughly mixed. Pour out into a saucepan and bring to a boil stirring constantly until thick.

Variation: Add fresh mushrooms and green onions before boiling.

Yield: 2 ½ c

BROWN GRAVY

3 c	Water (potato water if available)	1½ T	Dried onion flakes
2 T	Maggi® Seasoning	3/4 c	Unbleached flour
1½ T	McKay's® Beef-Style Seasoning	1/2 c	Water

Combine 3 c water, Maggi seasoning, beef-style seasoning and onion flakes in a saucepan and simmer 5 minutes. Mix flour and 1/2 c water together in a small bowl and stir until completely smooth and pour into saucepan. Stir constantly and continue cooking until gravy thickens. Serve hot.

Yield: 4 c

COUNTRY GRAVY

1 c	Onion, sliced	2 tsp	Beef-style seasoning
1 c	Fresh mushrooms, sliced	2 tsp	Chicken-style seasoning
1/2 c	Bell pepper, chopped	1/2 c	Hot water
1 tsp	Garlic purée	2 T	Unbleached white flour
2 T	Olive oil	1 c	Water

Sauté vegetables and garlic in 1 T oil. Remove from pan. Brown seasonings in remaining oil until dark brown. Dash in 1/2 c hot water. Mix flour with remaining water, pour into the pan and stir until thick. Stir in the sautéed vegetables. Pour over Choplets and serve.

Yield: 4 c

CRANBERRY SAUCE

1/2 c	Pineapple juice concentrate	1 T	Brown sugar (opt)
1/2 c	Chiquita® "Raspberry Passion"	12 oz	Fresh cranberries
	(frozen juice concentrate)	1 tsp	Grated orange peel
1/4 c	Honey		

Bring juices and sweeteners to a boil. Add cranberries, reduce heat and boil gently 5 to 10 minutes until all the skins pop. Remove from heat when sauce is thick. Let cool slightly before adding orange peel. Cool completely and refrigerate until needed.

Yield: 2 ¼ c

YAMS WITH ORANGE GLAZE

4	Yams or sweet potatoes	1 tsp	Grated orange rind
1 c	Orange juice	1/2 tsp	Grated lemon rind
1½ T	Cornstarch	1/4 tsp	Salt
1/4 c	Pure maple syrup		

Cook yams, peel and slice into a baking dish. Combine half the orange juice with cornstarch in a saucepan and stir to dissolve starch. Add remaining orange juice and other ingredients and bring to a boil, stirring constantly. Simmer mixture until thick and clear. Pour glaze over yams and serve.

Yield: 6 c

GREEN "PETITE" PEAS
with
PEARL ONIONS

16 oz	"Petite" green peas, frozen	1/2 tsp	Onion salt
1 c	Pearl onions, frozen		(or)
1/4 c	Water	1 tsp	Chicken-style seasoning
1 T	Spectrum® Spread		

In a saucepan, combine all ingredients. Bring to a boil, cover and reduce heat. Simmer 1 or 2 minutes. Turn off heat. Wait 2 minutes and remove from heat.

Yield: 4 c

MANDARIN ALMOND
HOLIDAY SALAD

CARAMELIZED ALMONDS:
1/2 c   Sliced almonds
1/4 c   Fructose, granulated

Caramelize by cooking over medium heat, stirring occasionally until fructose melts, and sticks to nuts. Remove immediately from heat, cool in a pan and break into small pieces. This step can be done ahead.

ITALIAN DRESSING:
Add to one .7 oz package of Good Seasons® "Italian" Dressing mix:

3 T   Fresh lemon juice
3 T   Pineapple juice concentrate
2 T   Fresh parsley, minced

1/3 c   Water
1/4 c   Light olive oil
3 T   Honey

Mix together in a jar or an air-tight container. Shake well and refrigerate. Shake again before serving.

SALAD:
1 head   Romaine lettuce
2 c   Celery, chopped

20 oz   Mandarin oranges, drained
4 stems   Green onions, finely diced

Just before serving, assemble salad. Toss with dressing. Sprinkle 1/2 cup almonds over top.

Variation: Sprinkle salad with crispy Ramen noodles just before serving.

Yield: 12 c

CRESCENT ROLLS

1½ tsp	Active dry yeast	1 c	Whole wheat flour
3/4 c	Warm water	1 c	All purpose flour
1 T	Oil	4 T	Quick oats
2 T	Brown sugar	1 T	Wheat germ
1 T	Better Than Milk™ powder	1 tsp	Salt

Combine the yeast, warm water, oil and brown sugar in a measuring cup and set aside. Combine remaining dry ingredients in a mixing bowl. Pour yeast mixture into dry ingredients and mix together to form a ball. Turn the dough out onto a floured surface and knead 5 to 8 minutes until the dough becomes like elastic. Return dough to an oiled bowl and turn to coat lightly. Cover with a clean, dry towel and place in a warm draft-free spot to rise until doubled. Roll out dough into a 12 inch circular shape, 1/4 inch thick. Cut into 12 wedges. Start with the wider side and roll wedges inward. Place each crescent-shaped roll on a cookie sheet coated with no-stick cooking spray. Allow rolls to rise until double. Bake at 375° F, 15 to 18 minutes.   Yield: 12 rolls

BASIC WHOLE WHEAT ROLLS

SPONGE:

2 ¾ c	Warm water	3 c	Whole wheat flour
1/2 c	Warm applesauce	1/4 c	Vital wheat gluten
	(or) 1/4 c oil	1½ T	Active dry yeast

In a mixing bowl, combine the above ingredients and beat well with a wooden spoon to make a sponge. Let stand 10 minutes.

ADD:

2 tsp	Salt	1 T	Lemon juice
3 to 4 c	Whole wheat flour		

Stir enough flour into the sponge to form a ball, but avoid getting too stiff. Turn out onto a lightly floured surface and knead at least 10 minutes until smooth and elastic. To reduce sticking, oil or coat your hands with a no-stick cooking spray. Pinch off pieces of dough and shape dough into rolls and place side by side on a 11" x 15" pan. Or shape into 2 loaves and place in loaf pans coated with no-stick cooking spray. Let rise in a warm oven 25 to 30 minutes or until doubled. Set oven to 350° F. Bake rolls 35 minutes, or bake loaves 45 minutes until golden brown. Remove from pans and cool on a wire rack. May brush tops lightly with oil while still warm.   Yield: 2 dozen rolls or 2 loaves

"HEART SMART" CORN BUTTER

1 c	Cold water	2 T	Canola oil
1/4 c	Yellow corn meal	1 T	Emes Kosher-Jel, plain
1/2 c	Mori-Nu Silken tofu, x-firm	1 T	Cooked carrot (opt for color)
1/2 c	Warm water	1 tsp	Honey
1/4 c	Almonds	1 tsp	Imitation butter flavored salt
3 T	Spicery Shoppe® Natural -	½ tsp	Salt
	Butter Flavor (vegan)	Pinch	Citric acid

Combine cold water and corn meal in a small saucepan and bring to a boil stirring constantly. Reduce heat to low, cover and simmer 10 minutes. Refrigerate mixture until completely cool and "set". In a blender, combine water, almonds, butter flavoring, oil and Emes. Process on high speed until no longer "gritty". Spoon chilled corn meal mush into the blender mixture and all remaining ingredients and process until smooth and creamy. Bits of carrot should not be visible. Refrigerate several hours before serving until "butter" thickens to a spreadable consistency.

Yield: 3 c

ORANGE HONEY BUTTER

Add the following to 1 cup of cold, pre-set Corn Butter (see above):

1/2 tsp	Grated orange peal
1 T	Frozen orange juice concentrate
2 T	Creamy "spun" honey (SueBee® or similar brand)

Whip at high speed until fluffy. Refrigerate before serving.

Yield: 1¼ c

RASPBERRY BUTTER

1 c	Corn Butter (recipe above)	1/4 c	Raspberry Jam, seedless

Gently swirl jam into cold, pre-set and pre-whipped "Corn Butter". Place in freezer 30 minutes. Scoop mixture out with a melon ball spoon and arrange butter on a small plate. Return to freezer until 5 minutes before serving.

Variation: Add cranberry sauce instead of the raspberry jam.

Yield: 1¼ c

NON-DAIRY PUMPKIN PIE

2 ½ c	Mori-Nu®, x-firm tofu	15 oz	Libby's® Pumpkin
1/2 c	Honey	1/3 c	Brown sugar (opt)
1 T	Frontier® Pumpkin Pie Spice	1/4 tsp	Salt

Process tofu and honey in a blender until smooth and creamy. Add remaining ingredients and blend well. Pour into a 9 inch unbaked whole grain pie shell. Bake at 400° F, 1 hour or until toothpick comes out clean. For better results, cover edges of crust with foil or pie edge guards to prevent over-browning. Cool completely before slicing.   Yield: 10 inch pie

Variation # 1: Substitute pumpkin pie spice with 2 tsp cinnamon, 1/2 tsp nutmeg, 1/4 tsp allspice, 1/4 tsp ginger and 1/8 tsp cloves.
Variation # 2: Decrease pumpkin pie spice to 1 tsp. Add 2 tsp cinnamon.

9" CASHEW-BARLEY CRUST

1/2 c	Barley flour	1/4 c	Raw cashew butter
1/2 c	All purpose flour	1/4 c	Hot water
1 T	Wheat germ (opt)	2 ½ T	Canola oil
1/2 tsp	Salt		

Combine flours, wheat germ and salt. In a separate bowl, mix the cashew butter, water and oil together. Pour into flour and stir until dough is moist. Knead into a ball. Roll dough out into a large circle between 2 pieces of wax paper. Press into a 9" pie plate. Trim and flute edges.   Yield: Single crust

"INSTANT" WHIPPED TOPPING

1½ c	Water	1/3 c	Canned coconut milk
2/3 c	Better than Milk™ powder		"lite" (unsweetened)
1/2 c	Blanched almonds (w/o skins)	2 tsp	Vanilla, (natural)
3½ T	Emes Kosher-Jel®, plain	1/4 tsp	Salt
3 T	Honey or powdered sugar		Ice

In a blender, combine the water, milk powder, almonds and Emes Jel and process until the almonds are liquefied completely. Add remaining ingredients and process briefly. Finally, begin adding ice slowly through the lid spout and continue processing on high speed to make a total volume equal to 5 cups. Turn blender off and wait briefly. Mixture should now be light and fluffy. Best served immediately. If stored, and mixture becomes too firm, hand whip or beat gently with an electric beater before serving.   Yield: 5 c

"DATE" PECAN PIE

CRUST:

1 c	Rolled oats	1/3 c	Canola oil
1 c	Unbleached white or whole wheat flour	1/3 c	Pure maple syrup (or) use 1/3 c water with
1/2 tsp	Salt		1/2 tsp maple flavoring
1/4 tsp	Ground nutmeg	1 tsp	Vanilla
1/4 tsp	Ground cardamom	1/2 tsp	Grated lemon rind

Grind rolled oats in a blender or food processor to make a coarse flour. Place ground oats in a mixing bowl, add flour, salt and spices. (If using a food processor, add these ingredients to ground oats; crust can be made in the processor). Add oil and remaining ingredients. Mix until dry ingredients are well coated. Place dough between two pieces of waxed paper and roll out into an 11 inch circle, Chill for at least two hours. Spray a 9" pie plate with no-stick cooking spray. Place dough in center of pan and press to cover bottom and sides of pan. Flute edges. Prick crust several times with a fork. Bake crust in a pre-heated oven at 350 °F, 20 minutes or longer until completely baked.

FILLING:

2 c	Pecan halves	2 T	Frozen orange juice (concentrate)
1 c	Pitted dates		
1/2 c	Raisins or currants	2 tsp	Vanilla
2 c	Apple, orange or pear juice	1½ tsp	Fresh lemon juice
		1/4 tsp	Each of ground allspice,
2 T	Emes Kosher-Jel®, plain		nutmeg, cardamom, & ginger
1/4 c	Cold water	Pinch	Salt

Spread pecans over a large baking tray or cookie sheet. Roast in a 350° F oven for 7 minutes or until pecans turn slightly darker and taste lightly roasted. Remove from the oven and set aside.

Place dates and raisins or currants in a saucepan. Add juice, bring to a boil, cover, lower heat and simmer for 10 to 15 minutes, until dried fruit is very soft. Soften Emes gelatin in cold water, add to hot fruit mixture. Remove from heat and stir in frozen orange juice, vanilla, lemon juice, spices and salt. Purée mixture in a blender or food processor until very smooth. Pour out into a bowl. Add only 1½ c pecan halves to the date mixture. Stir and pour into pie crust. Garnish the top of the pie with the remaining 1/2 c of pecans. Refrigerate until set. Serve with "Instant Whipped Topping" (see p 246) if desired.

Yield: 9 inch pie

MIXED BERRY PIE

1/4 c	Chiquita® "Caribbean Splash" (frozen juice concentrate)	3 T	Minute® Tapioca
		1/8 tsp	Salt
1/4 c	Honey	5 c	Berries Supreme®
2 tsp	Fresh lemon juice		(frozen berry mixture)

Stir juice and honey together until dissolved. Add lemon juice, tapioca and salt. Gently fold into berries. Pour into a 9" unbaked crust. Arrange top crust & flute edges. Bake at 425° F, 10 minutes. Slit top crust. Lower heat to 350° F, and bake for an additional 35 minutes.

Yield: 9 inch pie

ALMOND-BARLEY CRUST

1 c	Barley flour	1/2 c	Raw almond butter
1 c	All purpose flour	1/2 c	Hot Water
2 T	Wheat germ (opt)	5 T	Canola oil
1 tsp	Salt		

Combine flours, wheat germ and salt. In a separate bowl, mix the almond butter, water and oil together. Pour into flour and stir until dough is moist. Knead into a ball. Divide into two balls, one larger than the other. Roll out each ball between 2 pieces of plastic wrap or wax paper. Press the larger crust in the bottom of a 9" pie plate. Add the filling and top crust. Bake according to directions.

Yield: Double crust

PEACHES and "CREAM" PUNCH

2 c	Orange juice, unsweetened	2 T	Honey or fructose
2 c	Frozen peach slices	1 tsp	Cook's® Vanilla Powder
1 c	Better Than Milk™		(or use clear vanilla)
1/2 c	Peach nectar	1/4 tsp	Nutmeg (opt)

Combine all ingredients except nutmeg in a blender and process until smooth. Chill. Pour into glasses over crushed ice and sprinkle nutmeg on top, if desired. May also serve from a punch bowl with a peach ice ring.

Variation: Make an ice ring by pouring additional punch into a mold and freeze. Before serving, turn the ring out into a punch bowl. Garnish with orange peel "roses", mint leaves and cranberries.

Yield: 5 1/2 c

Jingle Bells Buffet

Featuring

An assortment of appetizers, breads, salads and Christmas "goodies" perfect for your holiday drop-in parties. When entertaining family and friends, give them the special gift of deliciously healthy treats.

SPINACH-POTATO PUFFS

10 oz	Fresh spinach, chopped	2 T	Nutritional yeast flakes
1/2 c	Onion, chopped	1 T	ENER-G® Egg Replacer
1 c	Fresh tofu, firm-mashed	2 tsp	Chicken-style Seasoning
1/2 c	Raw potatoes, finely shredded	1 tsp	Salt
1 c	Mozzarella cheese, grated (opt)	1/2 tsp	Savory
	(see p 127)	1/2 tsp	Onion powder
1/2 c	Pepperidge Farm®	1/4 tsp	Garlic powder
	Corn Bread Stuffing mix	1/8 tsp	Rosemary
6 T	Vital wheat gluten		

Steam or cook spinach until blanched and squeeze out excess liquid or may also use 10 oz frozen spinach, thawed and squeezed dry. Combine spinach with onion, tofu and potatoes. (If optional Mozzarella Cheese is desired, stir into mixture next and reduce salt listed above to 1/2 tsp.) In a separate bowl, mix all seasonings and dry ingredients together and pour evenly over the spinach mixture. Stir or use hands if necessary to work mixture together well. Form into 1½ inch balls and arrange on a cookie sheet coated with no-stick cooking spray. Cover with another cookie sheet (up side down) or a foil "tent" and bake at 400° F, 20 to 30 minutes. Uncover and bake 10 more minutes until slightly browned. Serve plain or cover with Fresh Tomato Sauce (see recipe below).

Yield: 16 balls

FRESH TOMATO SAUCE

1/2 c	Onion, chopped	1/2 tsp	Oregano
1 T	Olive oil	1/2 tsp	Basil
14.5 oz	Hunt's® Diced Tomatoes	1/4 tsp	Thyme (opt)
1/2 tsp	Garlic powder	1/8 tsp	Salt

In a saucepan, sauté onion in oil until translucent. Add tomatoes and spices. Bring to a boil. Cook about 10 minutes, stirring frequently. Pour sauce over the cooked Spinach-Potato Puffs (see recipe above) and serve.

Yield: 2 c

NUT RISSOLES

BREAD:
1 recipe "Crescent Rolls" (see recipe below)

FILLING:

1 c	Worthington® Vegetarian Burger	1 tsp	Beef-Style Seasoning
1/2 c	Onion, chopped	1/2 tsp	Garlic powder
1/4 c	Celery, diced	1/8 tsp	Sage
1/4 c	Fresh mushrooms, chopped	3/4 c	Olives, chopped
2 tsp	Olive oil	1/4 c	Pecans, finely chopped
1 T	Nutritional yeast flakes	1 T	Fresh parsley, minced

Sauté burger, onion, celery, and mushrooms in oil until vegetables are tender and burger is browned. Add seasonings, olives, pecans and parsley and mix together well. Spoon 1 T of burger mixture onto the wide end of each crescent roll wedge, roll up and fold ends under and place on a cookie sheet. Allow rolls to rise until doubled. Bake at 375° F, 18 minutes or until golden brown.

Variation: Place a Loma Linda® "Little Link" inside each crescent roll and bake as directed above for a quick appetizer.

Yield: 12 rissoles

CRESCENT ROLLS

3/4 c	Warm water	1 c	Whole wheat flour
1½ tsp	Active dry yeast	4 T	Quick oats
2 T	Brown sugar	1 T	Better Than Milk™ powder
1 T	Canola oil	1 T	Wheat germ
1 c	All purpose flour	1 tsp	Salt

Combine the warm water, yeast, brown sugar and oil in a measuring cup and set aside. Combine remaining dry ingredients in a mixing bowl. Pour yeast mixture into remaining dry ingredients and mix together to form a ball. Turn the dough out onto a floured surface and knead 5 to 8 minutes until the dough becomes like elastic. Return dough to an oiled bowl and turn to coat lightly. Cover with a clean, dry towel and place in a warm draft-free spot to rise until doubled. Roll out dough into a 12 inch circular shape, 1/4 inch thick. Cut into 12 wedges. Start with the wider side and roll wedges inward. Place each crescent-shaped roll on a cookie sheet sprayed with no-stick cooking spray. Allow rolls to rise until double. Bake at 350° F, 15 to 18 minutes.

Yield: 12 rolls

RATATOUILLE

1 med	Onion, chopped	1 sm	Zucchini, diced
2 cloves	Garlic, minced	1 tsp	Salt
1 med	Green pepper, chopped	1/2 tsp	Oregano
2 T	Olive oil	1/4 tsp	Basil
1 med	Eggplant, peeled and diced	1/8 tsp	Thyme (opt)
4 oz	Mushrooms, sliced and undrained	1/8 tsp	Onion salt
14.5 oz	Hunt's® "Ready" Special Sauce		

In a large saucepan, sauté onion, garlic and green pepper in olive oil until tender. Add remaining ingredients and simmer about 45 minutes or until vegetables are tender. Spoon into baked Pastry Cups, baked wonton wrappers, (see below) or over a brown and wild rice mixture and serve immediately.

Note: To prepare wonton wrappers, press 1 wrapper into a muffin tin coated with no-stick cooking spray. Spray wrappers with Pam® and bake at 350° F, 5 minutes. Remove from heat and place wrappers on a cookie sheet. Fill each wrapper with the Ratatouille mixture and return to the oven and bake an additional 5 minutes. Sprinkle with SoyCo® Parmesan Cheese Substitute before serving if desired. Serve hot.

Yield: 6 c

STUFFED SHELLS

1½ c	Water	1/4 c	Green pepper, chopped
1/2 c	Lentils	1	Green onion, diced
1/4 tsp	Salt	2 T	Fresh parsley, minced
1 med	Tomato, diced	1/2 c	Sour Cream Supreme (p 258)
3/4 c	Broccoli, finely chopped	12	Jumbo shells, cooked

Rinse and drain lentils. In a small saucepan combine water, lentils and salt. Bring to a boil, cover saucepan, reduce heat and simmer 20 to 25 minutes or until the lentils are tender. Drain. Cover and chill until ready to serve. Prepare vegetables. In a large bowl, toss the chilled lentils with all the vegetables except parsley. Combine the parsley and sour cream. Stir half the sour cream mixture into the lentil mixture. If necessary, season with additional salt to taste. Stuff each shell with 2 to 3 T of the lentil mixture. Garnish each shell with a spoonful of the remaining sour cream over the lentil mixture. Serve shells "open side up" on a lettuce bed with a border of sliced tomatoes.

Yield: 12 shells

HUMMUS
(A Middle Eastern Chickpea Puree)

2½ c	Cooked garbanzos, drained, (reserve broth)	4 cloves	Garlic
		1½ tsp	Onion powder
1/2 c	Tahini (sesame seed butter)	1 tsp	Salt
7 T	Garbanzo broth or water	4 oz	Green chilies, chopped
6 T	Fresh lemon juice		(Old El Paso® preferred)

Combine all ingredients, except chilies, in a blender and process on high speed 1 to 2 minutes until smooth and creamy. Pour out into a bowl and stir in chilies.

Tip: Delicious as a spread on bread and crackers, or as a dip with chips and raw vegetables. Also great in pocket bread stuffed with falafels.

Yield: 3 cups

STUFFED MUSHROOMS

1/2 lb	Large fresh mushrooms	1/2 tsp	Onion salt
1/4 c	Onion, finely chopped	2 T	Fresh parsley, chopped
2 cloves	Garlic, minced	1/4 c	Dry bread crumbs, fine
1 T	Olive oil		

Clean mushrooms well. Remove stems and hollow out each mushroom. Mince stems and sauté with onions and garlic in oil until mushrooms are tender and onion is translucent. Sprinkle mixture evenly with the onion salt. Add parsley, stir briefly and remove from heat. Stir in bread crumbs. Mound each mushroom cap with stuffing mixture and arrange in a shallow baking dish or on a cookie sheet coated with no-stick cooking spray. Bake at 425° F, 5 to 10 minutes or until thoroughly heated..

Variation: Stuff at least 1 lb mushrooms, (24 or more) with the "Dinner Roast" recipe (page 240) and bake at 400° F, 20 minutes or until well done.

Yield: 12 lg mushrooms

"CHEESY" ARTICHOKE DIP

2/3 c	Cheese Sauce (see recipe below)	1/4 c	Pepperidge Farm® - Cornbread Stuffing
1 c	Onion, chopped	2 T	Fresh parsley, minced
2 med	Garlic cloves, minced	1/2 tsp	Lawry's® Seasoned Salt
2 T	Olive oil	1/8 tsp	Salt
1/2 c	Tofu, firm	1/8 tsp	Oregano powder
2 T	Fresh lemon juice	8 oz can	Artichoke hearts, chopped

Make the Cheese Sauce recipe first and set aside 2/3 c. Sauté onion and garlic in oil until onion is translucent. In a blender, process tofu and lemon juice until smooth and creamy. Pour out into a bowl. Add stuffing mix, parsley and spices and mix well. Add artichokes, onion-garlic mixture and cheese sauce to the tofu-stuffing mixture and mix thoroughly. Pour into a 8 x 8 pan and bake at 350° F, 30 minutes. Cool.

Tip: For a dip, scoop mixture out and mound it into the hollowed out center of a round loaf of sour dough or pumpernickel bread. Place loaf in the center of a large round platter and surround loaf with chunks of bread or crackers.

Yield: 3 c

CHEESE SAUCE

1 c	Hot water	1 T	Fresh lemon juice
1 c	Cooked brown rice	1½ tsp	Salt
3/4 c	Raw cashews, rinsed	1 tsp	Onion powder
1/4 c	Sliced carrots	1/4 tsp	Garlic powder
2 T	Nutritional yeast flakes		

In a blender, combine water, rice, cashews and carrots and process until smooth and creamy. Add remaining seasonings and blend well.

Yield: 3 c

PEANUT BUTTER PÂTÉ

2 c	Tomato juice, canned	2 stalks	Celery, diced
1 c	Peanut butter, creamy	1/2 c	Cornstarch
1 sm	Onion, diced	1/4 tsp	Salt
4 oz	Pimento, finely diced		

Combine all ingredients. Pour into a double boiler, coated with no-stick cooking spray. Steam 4 hours. Invert on a platter covered with lettuce. Garnish with cherry tomatoes and parsley. Serve with crackers or as a sandwich spread.

Yield: 4 c

CHRISTMAS ORANGE SALAD

6	Valencia "juice" oranges	2 med	Bananas, sliced
1/2 c	Pecans, chopped	1 sm	Red apple, cubed
1/2 c	Frozen fresh coconut, grated		

Cut chilled oranges into slices. Remove seeds and cut orange sections away from peelings over a bowl in order to save juice. Add remaining ingredients and toss lightly. Serve immediately.

Yield: 8 c

STRAWBERRY SURPRISE SALAD

1¼ c	Hot water	2	Ripe bananas, mashed
3/4 c	Chiquita® "Calypso Breeze"	1 c	Walnuts, chopped
	(frozen juice concentrate)	1 c	Sour Cream Supreme
3 T	Emes Kosher-Jel®, plain		
16 oz	Birds Eye® Strawberries in "lite" syrup		

In a large bowl, mix water with juice concentrate and set aside. Pour 1/2 c of the Calypso Breeze mixture into a small sauccpan, add Emes Jel and heat stirring constantly until dissolved. Pour back into bowl of juice. Thaw strawberries and chop into smaller pieces. Add strawberries with juice, bananas and walnuts to the juice mixture. Divide mixture in half. Pour half into a large jello mold coated with no-stick cooking spray. Chill until set. Meanwhile, prepare Sour Cream recipe of choice (see p 258) and chill. Pour 1 cup sour cream over set layer of jello. Pour remaining jello mixture over sour cream and chill until set.

Yield: 7 c

SOUR CREAM SUPREME

1¼ c	Mori-Nu® Tofu, firm (10.5 oz box)	1 tsp	Honey
1/4 c	Sunflower oil	1/2 tsp	Salt
2 ½ T	Fresh lemon juice		

In a blender, combine all ingredients and process until smooth and creamy.

Yield: 1½ c

"SOY GOOD" TOFU SOUR CREAM

1½ c	Mori-Nu™ Tofu, firm (12.5 oz box)	1/4 tsp	Salt
3 T	Sunflower oil	1/4 tsp	Honey
1/4 tsp	Citric acid crystals		

In a blender, combine all ingredients and process until smooth and creamy.

Variation: Add 1 tsp fresh lemon juice for a stronger sour taste.

Yield: 1½ c

RASPBERRY JELLO FLUFF

16 oz	Frozen raspberries	3½ T	Emes Kosher-Jel®, plain
12 oz	Chiquita® "Raspberry Passion" (frozen juice concentrate)	1½ c	Instant Whipped Topping (recipe on page 259)

Thaw raspberries and reserve juice. Stir Emes Jel into reserved juice. Heat mixture up slightly to dissolve the gelatin. Add to raspberries. Combine raspberry mixture, frozen juice concentrate and water if necessary to equal 3½ cups. Add 1/4 c of the pre-set whipped topping to the jello mixture and hand whip until well blended. Pour half of the raspberry mixture into a jello mold coated with no-stick cooking spray. Chill until set. Pour enough of the remaining whipped topping over jello to measure about 1/2 inch thick, and return to refrigerator until set. Top with remaining raspberry mixture and chill several hours until set.

Yield: 5 c

"INSTANT" WHIPPED TOPPING

1½ c	Water	1/3 c	Canned coconut milk
2/3 c	Better than Milk™ powder		"lite" (unsweetened)
1/2 c	Blanched almonds (w/o skins)	2 tsp	Vanilla, (natural)
3½ T	Emes Kosher-Jel®, plain	1/4 tsp	Salt
3 T	Honey or powdered sugar		Ice

In a blender, combine the water, milk powder, almonds and Emes Jel and process until the almonds are liquefied completely. Add remaining ingredients and process briefly. Finally, begin adding ice slowly through the lid spout and continue processing on high speed to make a total volume equal to 5 cups. Turn blender off and wait briefly. Mixture should now be light and fluffy. Best served immediately. If stored, and mixture becomes too firm, hand whip or beat gently with an electric beater before serving.

Yield: 5 c

VEGETABLE DIP

10 oz	Frozen spinach, chopped	2 c	Sour Cream Supreme(p 258)
1 pkg	Knorr's® Vegetable Soup mix	1/2 c	Tofu Mayonnaise (p 167)
8 oz	Water chestnuts, chopped	1/2 c	Red bell pepper,
3 stems	Green onions, chopped		finely chopped (opt)

Thaw spinach and squeeze dry. Stir spinach together with remaining ingredients. Add salt to taste if needed. Cover and refrigerate 2 hours before serving. Stir again just before serving.

Variation: Replace water chestnuts with jicama.

Yield: 5 c

CHRISTMAS PUNCH

40 oz	Welch's® "White Grape Juice"
12 oz	Welch's® "Cran-Apple", frozen juice concentrate, diluted
12 oz	Chiquita® "Raspberry-Passion", frozen juice concentrate, diluted

Dilute frozen juices according to directions. Mix and serve from punch bowl. Garnish with a "fresh grape" ice ring mold.

Yield: 17 c

TOFU - BANANA BREAD #2

BLENDER INGREDIENTS:

1/2 c	Firm tofu	1/4 c	Canola oil
1/2 c	Brown sugar	1/4 c	Honey
1/3 c	Better Than Milk™	2 tsp	Vanilla
2 large	Ripe bananas	2 tsp	ENER-G® Egg Replacer

DRY INGREDIENTS:

1 c	Whole wheat flour	2 T	Wheat germ
1 c	All purpose flour	2 tsp	Baking powder
1 c	Pecans or walnuts, chopped	3/4 tsp	Salt
1/2 c	Grape Nuts® cereal	1/2 tsp	Soda

Combine blender ingredients and process until smooth. In a large bowl, combine all dry ingredients. Pour blender ingredients into the dry mixture and stir gently until well blended. Pour into a loaf pan coated with no-stick cooking spray. Bake at 350° F, approximately 55 minutes.

Variation: For Banana-Nut Muffins; increase baking powder to 1 T, fill muffin cups 3/4 full, sprinkle additional finely chopped nuts on top and bake at 375° F, 25 minutes.

Yield: 1 loaf or 12 muffins

CRANBERRY BREAD

1½ c	All purpose flour	1/2 c	Walnuts
1 c	Whole wheat pastry flour	1/2 c	Apple juice concentrate
2 tsp	Baking powder	1/2 c	Honey
1/2 tsp	Soda	1/4 c	Canola oil
1/2 tsp	Salt	1/2 c	Firm tofu
1½ c	Fresh cranberries	1 T	ENER-G® Egg Replacer

Combine dry ingredients. Chop walnuts and cranberries in a food processor and add to the dry mixture. Combine liquid ingredients, tofu and egg replacer in a blender and process until smooth. Pour into dry ingredients. Stir gently until well mixed. Pour into a loaf pan coated with no-stick cooking spray. Bake at 350° F, 55 minutes.

Yield: 1 loaf

CAROB FUDGE

2 c	Carob chips, date or malt sweetened	1 tsp	Vanilla, natural
1/3 c	Tofu, soy or almond milk	1/2 c	Dry coconut,
1 c	Walnuts or pecans, chopped		finely grated and
1/2 c	Almond, cashew or peanut butter		unsweetened, (opt)

Combine carob chips and milk in a saucepan. Cook over lo-med heat stirring constantly until chips are melted. (A double boiler also works well for this.) Stir in walnuts and nut butter until well mixed. Stir in vanilla last. Pour into an oblong pan, score into squares and sprinkle with coconut if desired. Chill. When firm, break into pieces and store in an airtight container.

Yield: 3½ c

FRUIT "NUTTY" BALLS

2 c	Pitted dates	4 c	Nuts, (walnuts,
1 c	Raisins		almonds or pecans)
1 c	Dried apricots	4 c	Shredded coconut

Chop or grind dried fruits through a food processor or a grinder. Place mixture in a bowl and set aside. Then process nuts until finely chopped. Add nuts to the dried fruit mixture. Stir in 2 cups of coconut and mix well. With hands, form 1 inch balls and roll them in remaining 2 c of coconut. Place in an air tight container and refrigerate until ready to serve.

Variation: Add 1½ T carob powder to mixture.

Yield: 60

OATMEAL-DATE COOKIES

1/2 c	Date butter (see below)	1/2 c	Canola oil
1 c	Old-fashioned oats	1/3 c	Honey or Sucanat®
2 c	Quick oats	1/3 c	Frozen apple juice
1 c	Whole wheat flour		(concentrate)
1/2 c	Unbleached white flour	1 tsp	Vanilla
1/2 c	Better Than Milk™ powder	1/2 tsp	Maple flavoring
1 tsp	Salt	1 T	ENER-G® Egg Replacer,
1/2 c	Walnuts, chopped		mixed in 4 T water

Prepare date butter according to directions below and set aside. Combine dry ingredients. Combine liquids and pour into the dry ingredients and mix well. Use 2/3 of cookie mixture and drop by heaping tablespoonfuls on a baking sheet and gently shape into cookies. Take care not to press mixture together too much. Press a small "well" into the center of each cookie. Spoon 1 tsp date butter into each "well" and top with enough cookie dough to just cover. Bake in a pre-heated oven at 350° F, 16-18 minutes or until lightly browned. Cool slightly then place in a covered air tight container.

Note: Make **DATE BUTTER** by combining 1 cup pitted dates with 1/2 cup water and simmering 2-3 minutes until soft. Cool. Mash dates well with a fork or pour into a blender and process until dates are smooth and creamy.   Yield: 1 c

Variation: For a delicious low-fat version, substitute half or all canola oil with equal proportions of WonderSlim® Fat & Egg Substitute.

Yield: 2 dozen

CAROB CHIP COOKIES

1 c	Whole wheat flour		1/4 c	Spectrum Spread®
1/2 c	Unbleached white flour		1/4 c	Wonderslim® or
1/2 c	Walnuts, chopped			Lighter Bake®
1/3 c	Carob chips			(Fat and Egg Substitute)
1/4 tsp	Salt		2 tsp	Vanilla
1/3 c	Honey		1/2 tsp	Walnut flavoring

Combine flour, walnuts, carob chips and salt. In a separate bowl, combine remaining ingredients. Pour liquids into dry ingredients and stir until well mixed. Cookie dough will seem sticky. Drop by spoonfuls onto a cookie sheet sprayed with no-stick cooking spray. Oil fingers and lightly spread dough out into round shapes. Avoid mashing. Bake at 350°F, 18 to 20 minutes. Cookies will become crispier as they cool.

Variation: Replace half (2 T) of Spectrum Spread with equal amounts raw natural nut butter (cashew, almond or peanut). Cookies will be crunchier with this method.

Yield: 18 cookies

PUMPKIN MOUSSE DESSERT

1 T	Emes Kosher-Jel®, plain		1 tsp	Pumpkin pie spice
1/3 c	Cold water		1 T	ENER-G® Egg Replacer
3/4 c	Canned pumpkin			dissolved in 4 T water
1/2 c	Honey		2 c	"Instant" Whipped Topping
1/2 c	Firm tofu, blended smooth			(see recipe on page 259)
1/2 tsp	Salt		1/3 c	Pecans, chopped

In a saucepan, soften gelatin in water. Stir over low heat until dissolved. Add pumpkin, honey, tofu, salt and pie spice. Cook over med. heat, stirring constantly until thoroughly heated. Cool. Whisk Egg Replacer with water until foamy. Fold into pumpkin mixture. Alternate layers of pumpkin mixture, pecans and pre-set whipped topping in parfait glasses. Chill before serving.

Yield: 6 to 8 parfaits

CAROB-BANANA CAKE

2 c	Whole wheat flour		2 c	Water
1 c	All purpose flour		1 c	Ripe banana, mashed
2 c	Date sugar		1/2 c	Canola oil
1/2 c	Carob powder		1/2 c	Honey
2 tsp	Roma®, coffee substitute		2 T	Lemon juice
2 tsp	Baking powder		1 T	Vanilla
2 tsp	Soda		1 T	ENER-G® Egg Replacer
1 tsp	Salt			

Combine flours, date sugar, carob powder, Roma, leavening agents and salt. In a blender, process water with banana, oil, honey, lemon juice, vanilla and egg replacer until smooth. Combine wet and dry ingredients, stir just until moistened. Pour into two 8" or 9" cake pans. Bake at 350° F, 30 to 35 minutes or until toothpick comes out clean and cake springs back after touch. Spread icing of choice (see below or page 265) on the completely cooled cake.

Note: For 9" x 13" cake: Bake at 350° F, 50 minutes.
For brownies: eliminate soda and add 1 c chopped walnuts. Bake at 350° F, 45 minutes.

Yield: 9 x 13 or 2 layer cake

NON-DAIRY COCONUT ICING

2 c	Better Than Milk™		1/3 c	Honey or fructose
1 box	Mori-Nu® Tofu, x-firm		4 T	Instant Clear Jel® powder
2 tsp	Cook's® Vanilla, powder (or use clear vanilla)		2 c	Shredded coconut
			2	Bananas, sliced lengthwise

Combine first 4 ingredients in a blender and process until smooth. Add the Instant Clear Jel through the lid spout while blender is on high speed, 1 T at a time until mixture is thick. Pour icing into a bowl and stir in 1½ cups coconut. Chill. When completely cooled, slice cakes in half horizontally. Layer in order: Cake, sliced banana, (may dip bananas in pineapple juice to preserve color) icing, cake, etc. Cover outside of cake with icing. Garnish top and sides of cake with remaining coconut. Chill until ready to serve.

Note: Substitute part of tofu milk with coconut milk "lite" for a richer taste.

Yield: 6 c

DATE-NUT FROSTING

1 c	Dates, pitted		1/2 tsp	Salt
2 c	Water		2 c	Pecans, chopped
1/2 c	Better Than Milk™ powder		2 c	Grated coconut
2 tsp	Vanilla, natural		1/4 c	Vital wheat gluten (opt)

Simmer dates in water until soft. Cool slightly. Transfer dates to a blender. Add milk powder, vanilla and salt and process until smooth. Return mixture to saucepan and fold in the nuts and coconut. If using frosting on a layered cake, it is necessary to add vital wheat gluten in order for the frosting to stick to the sides of the cake. If using frosting on a sheet cake, this step is not necessary. Spread frosting on cake while still warm. Sprinkle cake with additional grated coconut for garnish and to improve appearance. Yield: 5 c

RICH 'N CREAMY
CAROB ICING

2/3 c	Raw almond butter		2 T	Carob powder
1/2 c	Sucanat®		1/2 tsp	Vanilla
1/3 c	Mori-Nu® Tofu, x-firm		1/8 tsp	Roma®, coffee substitute
2 T	Almond, tofu or soy milk			

Combine all ingredients in a small mixing bowl and beat with an electric mixer until creamy. May refrigerate unused portion up to 2 weeks.

Note: For a layered cake or for a 9" x 13" cake - double recipe.
Tip: Spread icing between 2 graham cracker for a quick and delicious treat kids love!

Yield: 2 c

LITE 'N LUSCIOUS
CAROB ICING

1 box	Mori-Nu® Tofu, x-firm (10.5 oz)		3 T	Carob powder
1/2 c	Almond Mylk™, vanilla flavor		3 T	Cornstarch
1/2 c	Sucanat®		1 tsp	Vanilla

In a blender, combine all ingredients and process until smooth and creamy. Pour into a saucepan and cook over medium heat stirring constantly until thick. Refrigerate until cold. Cake should be cooled before spreading icing.

Note: For a layered cake or for a 9" x 13" cake - double recipe.

Yield: 2½ c

Glossary of Ingredients

Almonds, blanched: Drop whole almonds into boiling water for not more than one minute or they will discolor. Pour into a colander and rinse under cold water. Drain. Skins will now pop off easily. Slivered almonds have already had the skins removed and usually are already blanched when purchased.

Almond butter: Almonds ground to the same consistency as peanut butter. This can be purchased at most natural food stores. You can also do this at home with a Champion Juicer. Be sure almonds are lightly roasted and you may prefer to remove the skins before grinding if almond butter is used in a pie crust recipe.

Almond Mylk™: Manufactured by Wholesome and Hearty Foods, Inc. A rich creamy dairy milk alternative made from almonds in regular or vanilla flavor. Available at most natural food stores.

Arrowroot: Starchy flour from a tropical tuber used for thickening. Usually less processed than cornstarch. Can be substituted in equal proportions for cornstarch.

Bakon Seasoning: Turula yeast with a natural "hickory smoke" flavor. Delicious on Scrambled Tofu or as a flavor enhancer in sandwich spreads.

Barley Flour: A white, mild-flavored whole grain flour that performs well as a substitute for all purpose white flour in recipes such as pie crust, cakes, muffins and cookies. The gluten content is lower than wheat flour.

Better Than Milk™: Manufactured by Sovex Natural Foods, Inc. A dairy milk substitute made from tofu in powdered or ready to drink form. Available in most natural food stores. The "European" formula contains the milk protein "casein".

Bernard Jensen's Seasoning®: ("Natural Vegetable Seasoning and Instant Gravy"). A delicious seasoning made from soybeans, alfalfa, corn and whole wheat. It adds a savory taste to gravy, soups, patties, casseroles, etc. Available at many natural food stores.

Bragg® Liquid Aminos: An unfermented soy sauce substitute made from soybeans. It is high in amino acids and minerals, but a little lower in sodium than regular soy sauce. Look for it in natural food stores and most Adventist health food stores.

Brown rice syrup: A thick, sweet syrup used interchangeably with honey or other liquid sweeteners. Available in most natural food stores.

Canola oil: A light-colored flavorless oil which is high in mono-unsaturated fat and a good source of Omega-3 fatty acids.

Cardamom: A relative of ginger and native to India, this aromatic spice is used widely in Scandinavian and Indian cooking. The small black seeds have a spicy-sweet flavor. Available ground or in whole seed form.

Carob powder: A dark brown cocoa-like powder made from the highly nutritious locust bean pod, also called St. John's Bread. It is naturally sweet and high in calcium, phosphorus, potassium, iron, and magnesium. Carob is reminiscent of chocolate; however it contains no caffeine and has half the fat of chocolate.

Chic-Ketts®: Chicken flavored vegetable protein made by Worthington Foods, Inc. Does not contain egg whites. Look for it in the freezer section of Adventist health food stores.

Choplets®: Beef flavored vegetable protein, canned. Does not contain egg whites. Available at Adventist health food stores and some supermarkets.

Cilantro: Bright green lacy leaves and stems of the coriander plant. Used in Asian , Italian and Mexican cuisine. It is also called Chinese parsley.

Citric acid crystals: An extremely tart flavoring derived from citrons, lemons, oranges, or similar fruits. Available at some supermarkets, pharmacies and most health food stores.

Cook's® Vanilla Powder: Real vanilla in a white powder form. Available at some supermarkets and bakery supply stores. If you are unable to find this, substitute with clear vanilla found in supermarkets.

Date butter: Made from dates that have been simmered in water until soft and then blended until smooth. Used as a natural sweetener in several recipes. Also a delicious spread on bread, or muffins.

Date sugar: This whole food sweetener is made from ground dried dates and is used as an excellent substitute for brown sugar. Because it is less refined, it provides less sugar grams per tsp when compared to refined sweeteners. Delicious in most cake and pie recipes.

Do-Pep: Also referred to as "vital wheat gluten", this flour has the highest gluten content available. Used in bread recipes to restore elasticity when the gluten content of the ingredients is low. Also works as a binder in recipes that call for eggs.

Emes Kosher-Jel®: An all-vegetable gelatin containing carrageenan, locust bean gum, and cottonseed gum. Available in several flavored and sweetened varieties but all recipes in this cookbook call for the unsweetened and unflavored form. Dissolves in liquids when heated and will gel as it cools.

ENER-G® Egg Replacer: A non-dairy powdered leavening and binding agent used as a substitute for eggs in baked goods. It is made from tapioca flour, potato starch and leavening and is available at natural food stores.

FruitSource®: A substitute for honey. It is a natural sweetener made from grapes and grains in both liquid and granulated form. Available in most natural food stores.

Garbanzos: Also called chickpeas. In the legume family easily recognized by their pea shape with a protruding shoot, beige color and nutty flavor. Available dried or canned. Traditionally used in hummus, falafel and salads.

Garbanzo flour: Made from dry garbanzos which have been ground into flour. Available at some natural food stores or can be made at home with a Magic Mill II flour mill.

GranBurger®: Dehydrated vegetable protein granules with an artificial beef flavor by Worthington Foods, Inc. Used as a substitute for ground beef. Available at natural food stores and Adventist health food stores.

Instant Clear Jel®: A pre-cooked Amioca starch derived from waxy corn. It thickens almost immediately upon contact with liquids and therefore does not require cooking. To prevent lumping, it is necessary to mix it with liquids in an electric blender. Made by National Starch and Chemical Corporation and available at a bakery supply house. You may also call the Product Orders/Shipping Dept. at (916) 637-4111, Ext. 7410.

Isolated Soy Protein Powder: A supersource of soy protein and isoflavones, used in research and now sold in some health food stores. Dissolves in fluids and can be sprinkled on foods.

Jicama: A beet shaped root vegetable with thin brown skin and crisp, white flesh. Usually eaten raw in salads but is also delicious in stir-fry vegetables or

Oriental cooking. The texture is between an apple and a pear but not as sweet. Can replace water chestnuts in most recipes. When purchasing jicama, look for firm small tubers free from scrapes. Once peeled, best if eaten within 3 days.

Liquid smoke: Bottled hickory smoke flavoring. Available in supermarkets.

Maple syrup: A popular substitute for honey. Always use 100% pure maple syrup from supermarkets and natural food stores.

McKay's® "Chicken-Style or Beef-Style" Instant Broth and Seasoning: An excellent all-vegetarian seasoning widely used to give chicken or beef flavorings to recipes. The "No-MSG" type is recommended.

Millet: Small golden whole grain kernels with a sweet nutty flavor. Rich in minerals and can be used like rice.

Mock Abalone: Also called "Cha'i-Pow-Yü" braised canned gluten. Available in most oriental food stores and Adventist health food stores. Most common brand is Companion®.

Mock Duck: Also called "Mun-Cha'i-Ya" braised canned gluten. Available in most oriental food stores and Adventist health food stores. Most common brand is Companion®.

Mori Nu® Silken Tofu: A smooth textured, custard-like tofu made from the soybean. It is sold in aseptic packages as a non-perishable which gives it the advantage over fresh tofu. It is available in soft, firm and x-firm consistencies. Available at natural food stores and most supermarkets.

Mori Nu® "Lite" Silken Tofu: The low-fat version to the above.

Nutritional yeast flakes: An edible brewer's yeast (dead yeast) in flake form high in B vitamins. Good tasting brewer's yeast flakes are yellow in color and have a cheese-like flavor. Common brands are KAL® (my first choice but a bit more expensive) and Red Star®.

Oat Bran: A fiber-rich bran derived from the outer shell of the oat grain. Adds moisture and a hearty flavor to baked goods. Known for its distinct benefits of improving health.

Olive oil: The oil highest in mono-unsaturated fat. Delicious in Italian cooking, salads, sautéed vegetables where its distinctive flavor enhances the other ingredients.

Pam: A vegetable non-stick spray which can be applied to frying pans and baking dishes. Also used to lightly coat some foods before cooking.

Rice Dream®: A non-dairy milk substitute made from brown rice. Available in a variety of formulas and ready to drink. The calcium-added formula is recommended, especially for children.

SoyCo® "Lite & Less" Grated Parmesan Cheese Alternative: A delicious substitute for parmesan cheese. Available soy or rice based. Contains the milk protein casein.

Sucanat®: Made from organic sugar cane juice in granulated form. Unrefined and retains all of the vitamins and minerals provided by nature. An excellent substitute for brown sugar and can be used interchangeably in baked goods or for any recipe which calls for sugar sweetening.

Tahini: A thick, smooth paste made from ground sesame seeds. A staple of Middle Eastern cuisine.

Tofu: Fresh soybean curd. White easily digestible curd made from cooked soybeans. High in protein. Available in Japanese-style silken (softest) tofu in shelf-stable aseptic packages, often referred to as "boxed tofu". Most common name brand is Mori-Nu®. Also available in Chinese-style water-packed tubs in the refrigerated section of supermarkets. Often referred to as "fresh tofu" and available in 12, 14 or 16 oz sizes. Both types come in soft, firm and extra-firm styles. The "boxed" styles are also available as fat-reduced.

Textured Vegetable Protein or TVP: Very low fat meat substitute made from defatted soy flour that is compressed until the protein fibers change in structure. Sold in dehydrated granular or chunk form. Available in beef, chicken or unflavored varieties. Must be rehydrated before use. Popular in recipes requiring burger, like chili, spaghetti sauce or sloppy joes, or in chunk form for stews. Available in most health food stores and food cooperatives.

Vegetarian Burger™: Beef flavored vegetable protein hamburger substitute. Does not contain egg whites. Available canned or frozen at Adventist health food stores and some supermarkets.

Vegetarian Oyster Sauce: A delicious vegetarian mushroom sauce which replaces oyster sauce in oriental recipes. Unfortunately, this may be very difficult to find in America. Try looking for it in oriental food stores.

West-Soy® "Plus" Soy Milk: A delicious non-dairy beverage made from soybeans. Available in most natural food stores.

Wheat Bran: Derived from the outer shell of the wheat kernel. A good source of protein, B vitamins, iron and phosphorus. Adds fiber content and bulk into our diets.

Wheat Germ: The most vital part of the wheat kernel - the heart. It is rich in protein, iron, vitamin B1 and vitamin E. Available raw or toasted.

Whole Wheat Flour: Flour containing all of the wheat including the bran and the germ. Contains high amounts of fiber and nutrients.

Whole Wheat Pastry Flour: The best flour to use for most baked goods (excluding yeast bread) such as muffins, cookies, cakes and pie crust.

WonderSlim® Fat & Egg Substitute: Replaces high-fat shortenings or oil in the recipe. It is made from plums and is becoming widely available in natural food stores. Other similar brands are Lighter Bake® or Just Like Shortnin'™

Recommended Reading List

1. Anderson, James, W., MD, **Diabetes**, Warner Books, 1981.

2. Barnard, Neal, MD,**Food for Life,** Crown Trade, 1993

3. Craig, Winston, J., PhD, RD, **Nutrition for the Nineties,** Golden Harvest Books, 1992.

4. Erasmus, Udo, PhD, **Fats That Heal, Fats That Kill,** Alive Books, 1994.

5. Foster, Vernon, W., MD, **Newstart**, Woodbridge Press, 1988.

6. Hansen, Richard, A., MD, **Get Well at Home,** 1994.

7. McDougall, John, A., MD, **The McDougall Program**, Plume/ Penguin Books, 1990.

8. Messina, Mark, PhD, Virginia Messina, RD and Kenneth Setchell, PhD, **The Simple Soybean and Your Health,** Avery Publishing Group, 1994.

9. Nedley, Neil, MD, **Proof Positive: How to Reliably Combat Disease and Achieve Optimal Health Through Nutrition and Lifestyle",** written by Neil Nedley, MD and edited by David DeRose, MD, 1998.

10. Ornish, Dean, MD, **Eat More Weigh Less**, Harper Perennial, 1993.

11. Rhodes, Richard, **Deadly Feasts, Tracking the Secrets of a Terrifying New Plague,** Simon & Schuster, 1997.

12. Whitaker, Julian, M., MD, **Reversing Diabetes**, Warner Books, 1987.

13. Whitaker, Julian, M., MD, **Reversing Heart Disease**, Warner Books, 1985.

14. White, Ellen, G., **Counsels on Diet and Foods**, Pacific Press, 1938 and 1976.

Recommended
Newsletters & Journals

1.   **The American Institute for Cancer Research Newsletter,** 1759 R Street NW, Washington, DC, 20009. Free.

2.   **Clinical Pearls News, A Health Letter on Current Research in Nutrition and Preventive Medicine,** ITServices, 3301 Alta Arden #3, Sacramento, CA 95825.

3.   **Current Issues in Vegetarian Nutrition: Proceedings of an International Conference, 1996,** Edited by Winston Craig, PhD, RD, Department of   Nutrition, Andrews University, Berrien Springs, MI 49104-0210.

4.   **Harvard Health Letter**, Subscription Department, PO Box 420299, Palm Coast, FL, 32142-9858. $24.00.

5.   **Harvard Heart Letter**, P.O. Box 420235, Palm Coast, FL 32142-0235. $20.00.

6.   **Journal of Health & Healing**, P. O. Box l09, Wildwood, GA, 30757. $10.00.

7.   **Mayo Clinic Nutrition Letter**, Rochester, Minnesota, USA, 55905. $39.00.

8.   **Nutrition Action Health Letter**, Center For Science in the Public Interest, 1875 Connecticut Ave NW, Suite 300,   Washington DC USA, 20009-5728. $24.00.

9.   **Nutrition 2000, Proceedings of an International Vegetarian Conference, 1994,** edited by Winston Craig, PhD, RD, Department of Nutrition, Andrews University, Berrien Springs, MI 49104-0210.

10.   **Tufts University Diet and Nutrition Letter**, P.O. Box 57857, Boulder, CO 80322-7857, $20.00.

11.   **Vegetarian Nutrition and Health Letter,** 1707 Nichol Hall, School of Public Health, Loma Linda University, Loma Linda, CA 92350, $24.00.

Nutritional Analysis[1]

Recipe	Serv Size	Cal	Prot gm	Carb gm	Fiber Total gm	Fat Total gm	Fat Sat gm	Fat Mono gm	Fat Poly gm	Vit B12 mcg	Vit D mcg	Ca mg	Fe mg	Na mg	Zn mg
Almond Apple Bar	1	131	2.9	17.8	1.6	5.7	0.5	3.3	1.5	0.7	0.0	68	0.8	84	0.2
Almond Barley Crust	1/12	179	3.8	16.1	1.9	12.3	1.0	7.6	2.9	0.0	0.0	31	0.8	179	0.3
Almond Broccoli Stir-Fry	1 c	152	10	15	5.0	7.7	1.0	3.8	2.2	0.0	.08	153	4.1	146	0.8
Almond Cheesecake Delight	1/4 c	172	5.4	19.1	.95	8.8	.9	4.9	2.4	.08	0.0	110	2.4	99	.82
Almond Cream	1/3 c	50	1.7	1.5	1.05	4.0	0.0	0.0	0.0	0.0	0.0	20.6	0.3	44	.026
Almond Pie Crust	1/12	88	1.8	7.8	.93	6.1	.5	3.81	1.43	0.0	0.0	15.4	.41	89	.16
Alpine Cheese	1 T	19	0.48	2.41	0.21	0.84	0.17	0.48	0.15	0.0	0.0	8.17	0.17	93	0.15
American Cheese Sauce	2 T	28.6	1.33	2.87	0.31	1.47	0.16	0.80	0.43	0.0	0.0	16.3	0.62	103	0.16
Apple Butter	2 t	14.6	.09	3.7	.15	.02	.01	0.0	.01	0.0	0.0	1.83	.07	1.07	.01
Apple Spice Butter	2 t	5.1	.02	1.34	.15	.01	0.0	0.0	0.0	0.0	0.0	.7	.03	1.4	.01
Apple Spice Jam	1 T	11.4	0.04	3.0	0.2	0.02	0.0	0.0	0.01	0.0	0.0	1.6	0.07	2.6	0.01
Apricot Jam	1 T	27	0.35	7.0	0.7	0.05	0.01	0.02	0.01	0.0	0.0	5.6	0.45	1.0	0.1
Arroz Mexicano	1/2 c	111	2.0	18.6	1.7	2.09	3.36	.49	2.2	.46	0.0	22	.66	211	.49
Asparagus Almond Crepes	1	109	5.2	12.1	3.3	4.8	0.06	0.01	0.09	0.0	0.0	50.4	1.19	384	0.78
Aunt Bea's Apple Pie	1/12	227	2.02	43.4	2.5	6.4	0.54	3.82	1.51	0.0	0.0	24.2	0.71	138	0.22
Auto Bread Machine Bread	1 sl	99	3.6	16.4	2.1	2.2	0.2	1.1	0.5	0.0	0.0	7.0	1.0	167	0.07
Baked Corn Fritters	1	128	2.8	23	1.5	2.8	0.2	1.5	0.8	.08	0.0	57	1.2	206	0.3
Baked Egg Rolls	2	111	5.7	15.7	1.9	3.0	0.4	1.3	0.7	0.0	0.0	33	0.9	396	0.3
Baked Eggplant Parmesan	2	157	3.8	21.3	2.8	7.2	1.3	2.7	2.8	0.0	.08	46.3	1.9	761	.59
Banana Cake	1/48	48	1.3	7.5	0.5	1.6	0.2	0.8	0.5	0.0	0.0	19	0.7	44	0.1
Barbecue Sauce	1 T	16	0.4	4.0	0.3	0.02	0.0	0.0	0.01	0.0	0.0	13	0.4	151	0.03
Barley Nut Waffles	1	273	8.5	45.3	9.6	7.9	0.9	4.2	2.2	0.04	0.0	74	2.7	284	2.4
Basic Nut Milk	1 c	117	3.6	6.6	1.7	9.3	0.9	6.0	2.0	0.0	0.0	4.8	0.7	91	0.5

Recipe	Serv Size	Cal	Prot gm	Carb gm	Fiber Total gm	Fat Total gm	Fat Sat gm	Fat Mono gm	Fat Poly gm	Vit B12 mcg	Vit D mcg	Ca mg	Fe mg	Na mg	Zn mg
Bean Thread Salad	1/2 c	67	3.2	8.6	1.1	2.5	.35	1.2	.8	0.0	0.0	12.1	.54	116	.32
Better Mustard	1 t	8.6	0.06	0.44	0.03	0.77	0.05	0.47	0.21	0.0	0.0	0.36	0.04	17.7	0.0
Better Than Milk Combo	1 c	112	2.0	22	0.0	0.8	0.0	0.0	0.0	0.4	0.4	427	0.05	152	0.0
Black Eyed Pea Stew	1 c	159	11	22	6.3	3.6	0.7	2.1	0.7	0.6	0.0	111	1.9	252	1.1
Black Eyed Peas	1/2 c	58.4	1.9	12.3	2.97	0.23	0.06	0.02	0.1	0.0	0.0	73.1	0.65	2.6	0.6
Blackberry Jam	2 t	10	0.06	2.5	0.22	0.03	0.01	0.0	0.01	0.0	0.0	2.01	0.04	0.28	0.02
Blue Ribbon Baked Beans	1/2 c	39.3	.84	7.3	.92	.92	.13	.63	.1	0.0	0.0	13.4	.41	42	.19
Blueberry Oat Bran Muffins	1	180	2.6	28.2	1.7	7.2	.64	3.97	2.07	0.0	.18	101	1.2	320	.34
Blueberry Preserves	2 t	10.6	.05	2.6	.15	.04	.01	.01	.02	0.0	0.0	.89	.02	.34	.01
Blueberry Topping	2 T	24.7	.17	6.4	.5	.08	.01	.02	.05	0.0	0.0	2.1	.06	2.3	.02
Blueberry Yum Yum	1/12	287	6.6	47	2.4	8.6	1.2	3.9	1.6	0.1	0.0	127	1.8	185	0.6
Bosch Whole Wheat Bread	1 sl	114	3.6	21	2.9	2.2	0.2	1.1	0.7	0.0	0.0	9.3	1.2	205	0.7
Breading Meal #1	1 T	26	0.86	5.4	0.61	0.13	0.02	0.02	0.05	0.0	0.0	3.03	0.34	73.2	0.12
Breading Meal #2	1 T	25	.71	4.9	.25	.27	.05	.0	.06	0.0	0.0	3.7	.31	134	.05
Breakfast Banana Crisp	1/2 c	254	7.0	42.5	4.4	6.8	2.6	1.6	2.0	0.04	0.0	57	2.0	214	1.7
Breakfast Scones	1	102	2.6	16.8	1.6	2.8	0.2	1.5	0.8	0.05	0.0	41	1.0	100	0.1
Broccoli Cheese Rice Ring	1/2 c	93	3.5	16	2.3	2.0	0.4	0.9	0.5	0.0	0.0	41	1.2	232	0.6
Broccoli Cheese Soup	1 c	77	2.7	10.9	1.15	2.74	0.51	1.46	0.47	0.05	0.0	49.6	0.96	355	0.48
Broccoli in Lemon Sauce	1/2 c	40.2	1.3	3.3	1.2	2.8	0.19	1.65	.79	.03	0.0	35.2	.37	60	.15
Brown Gravy	2 T	13	0.3	2.5	0.1	0.03	0.0	0.0	0.01	0.0	0.0	0.8	0.1	160	0.02
Cabbage & Walnut Stir-Fry	1/2 c	30	1.0	3.3	1.3	1.7	0.2	0.6	0.85	0.0	0.0	16	0.2	60	0.1
Carob Banana Cake	1/24	88	1.22	16.5	1.75	2.45	0.19	1.4	0.68	0.0	0.0	24.9	0.49	113	0.21
Carob Chip Cookies	1	123	2.3	16.1	1.3	5.9	0.7	2.6	2.2	0.04	0.0	47.5	0.6	49	0.2
Carob Fudge	1 T	72	1.7	5.0	0.8	5.4	0.9	2.7	1.5	0.08	0.0	46	0.3	13	0.25
Carob Pecan Milk	1 c	159	3.6	18.4	0.9	8.2	1.6	4.7	1.4	0.3	0.0	196	1.2	158	1.0
Carob Pudding Parfait	1	179	5.9	18.4	2.8	9.9	0.09	6.2	2.0	0.01	0.0	61	0.78	124	0.57
Carrot Bisque	1 c	222	5.4	22.8	3.4	13.8	2.67	8.16	2.32	0.0	0.0	45.6	2.28	356	1.86
Carrot Cake with Frosting	1/36	159	2.2	20.8	1.6	7.9	1.7	3.6	2.3	0.0	0.0	32	0.8	200	0.4

Recipe	Serv Size	Cal	Prot gm	Carb gm	Fiber Total gm	Fat Total gm	Fat Sat gm	Fat Mono gm	Fat Poly gm	Vit B12 mcg	Vit D mcg	Ca mg	Fe mg	Na mg	Zn mg
Carrot Pineapple Salad	1/2 c	135	2.8	18	1.6	6.6	0.9	3.8	1.6	0.0	0.0	34	1.4	58	0.8
Carrot Raisin Cookie	1	105	1.2	18	1.2	3.5	.52	1.3	1.5	0.0	0.0	17	.73	68	.3
Carrots & Orange Sauce	1/3 c	42.4	.55	10.5	1.04	.09	.01	.01	.03	0.0	0.0	13.7	.25	58.1	.01
Cashew Apple French Toast	1	165	4.1	24	1.8	6.4	1.4	3.5	1.1	0.0	0.1	24	1.7	233	0.9
Cashew Banana French Toast	1	185	5.7	28	2.9	6.8	1.4	3.7	1.2	0.0	0.07	34	2.1	391	1.4
Cashew Barley Crust	1/12	179	4.2	17.8	1.8	11.3	1.4	6.7	2.5	0.0	0.0	6.8	1.09	0.35	0.75
Cashew Gravy	1/4 c	53	1.6	4.7	0.25	3.2	0.6	1.9	0.5	0.0	0.0	6.0	0.5	194	0.4
Cashew Jack Cheese	2 T	45	1.19	5.62	.53	2.1	.42	1.2	.38	0.0	0.0	25.2	.4	232	.37
Champagne Chicken	1 c	183	10	14	1.6	9.6	1.0	3.6	0.9	0.0	0.4	143	1.0	604	0.7
Cheese Enchiladas	1	186	13	13.6	2.0	10.2	1.6	4.0	4.0	0.0	0.0	174	8.4	775	1.4
Cheese Sauce	1 T	24	.84	2.2	.44	1.4	.11	.85	.34	0.0	0.0	1.4	.08	73	.06
Cheesy Artichoke Dip	1 T	11	0.36	1	0.29	0.67	0.08	0.42	0.11	0.0	0.0	1.97	0.05	31.1	0.02
Cheesy Delights	1/2	82	3.5	14.2	3.4	1.9	0.3	0.87	0.53	0.0	0.0	92	1.4	282	0.63
Cheesy Hashbrown Casserol	1/2 c	102	2.2	19.4	1.1	1.4	.14	.43	.30	0.0	0.0	24	.48	187	.07
Chicken & Rice Casserole	1/24	98	3.5	12.9	0.9	3.6	0.5	1.3	0.4	0.02	0.02	21.6	0.6	174	0.3
Chicken & Sausage Gumbo	1/2 c	171	8.9	21.6	3.13	5.5	0.54	2.57	2.02	0.32	0.0	62.5	2.24	509	0.73
Chicken Enchiladas	1	98	4.5	12.3	.93	3.5	.19	.92	.17	.01	.01	58	.38	152	.07
Chicken Kelaguen	1/2 c	130	9.4	4.3	2.4	8.8	4.1	1.6	2.8	0.82	0.0	17	1.5	412	0.51
Chicken Mushroom Crepes	1	202	9.95	16.7	2.2	10.7	1.5	4.8	3.6	0.81	0.38	134	1.7	721	0.51
Chicken Noodle Soup	1 c	144	9	15.3	2.48	5.39	0.47	1.69	0.3	0.0	0.0	22.3	0.95	626	0.38
Chicken Style Pot Pie	1/30	190	6.9	21.3	2.8	9.0	0.6	4.2	1.8	0.0	0.04	22	1.0	380	0.4
Chili Beans	1/2 c	91	5.5	15.4	4.9	1.05	.12	.45	.22	0.0	0.0	46	2.2	268	.48
Chili Powder Substitute	1/4 t	1.05	.05	.22	.06	.03	.03	0.0	.01	0.0	0.0	2.4	.09	.18	.01
Choice Coleslaw	1/2 c	26	.93	5.7	1.2	.18	.03	.01	.08	0.0	0.0	20.5	.36	12.2	.12
Christmas Orange Salad	1/2 c	94	4.28	14.8	2.45	4.28	1.65	1.66	0.69	0.0	0.0	31.4	0.30	1.08	0.33
Christmas Punch	1 c	67	0.34	16.5	0.12	0.13	0.08	0.01	0.03	0.0	0.0	13.9	0.21	5.3	0.02
Classic Potato Salad	1/2 c	51	1.15	10.8	1.3	.54	.08	.34	.08	0.0	0.0	14.6	.4	242	.19
Coleslaw Dressing	2 T	46.2	.42	7.5	.22	1.8	.12	1.05	.46	.05	.06	45.8	.09	76.9	.04

Recipe	Serv Size	Cal	Prot gm	Carb gm	Fiber Total gm	Fat Total gm	Fat Sat gm	Fat Mono gm	Fat Poly gm	Vit B12 mcg	Vit D mcg	Ca mg	Fe mg	Na mg	Zn mg
Cookie Haystacks	1	102	1.5	15.5	2.07	4.7	2.2	.66	1.5	0.0	0.0	11.5	.58	25	.29
Cornbread with Yeast	1	134	3.9	22.3	1.7	3.4	.33	1.62	1.14	0.0	0.0	12.7	1.4	179	.11
Country Biscuits with yeast	1	113	2.7	17	1.3	3.9	0.3	2.2	1.1	0.13	0.0	93	0.8	205	0.32
Country Gravy	2 T	18	0.24	1.6	0.2	1.2	0.16	0.83	0.11	0.0	0.05	2.2	0.09	75	0.04
Cranberry Bread	1 sl	221	4	35.6	1.79	8.13	0.63	3.53	3.21	0.0	0.0	78	1.02	214	0.20
Cranberry Sauce	1 T	26	0.2	6.7	0.35	0.03	0.0	0.01	0.01	0.0	0.0	4.0	0.1	0.4	0.05
Cream Cheesy Spread	1 T	40	0.5	0.5	0.0	4.0	1.5	1.5	1.0	0.0	0.0	0.0	0.0	100	0.0
Cream of Potato Soup	1 c	95	2.2	16.9	1.32	2.4	0.43	1.44	0.37	0.0	0.0	17.2	0.69	276	0.45
Creamed Tofu Eggs	1/2 c	83	6.0	7.C	0.4	4.0	0.6	1.4	1.7	0.09	0.14	129	307	239	0.6
Creamy Dressing	1/2 c	48	1.3	5.13	0.21	2.73	0.53	1.56	0.45	0.0	0.0	7.58	0.41	87	0.34
Creamy Mushroom Sauce	1/4 c	54.3	1.3	7.C	0.48	1.9	0.25	1.25	0.17	0.1	0.16	72.1	0.4	274	0.09
Creamy Vegetable Soup	1 c	106	3.0	15	1.8	4.8	0.7	2.4	0.6	0.0	0.0	22.7	0.9	458	0.6
Crescent Rolls	1	97	3.0	17.5	1.7	1.7	0.2	0.8	0.4	0.03	0.0	25	1.1	184	0.09
Crispy Corn Chips	4	24	.5	4.75	0.0	.25	0.0	0.0	0.0	0.0	0.0	20	.1	1.25	0.0
Date & Walnut Bread	1 sl	167	3.4	31	3.4	4.6	.44	1.5	2.4	0.0	0.0	84	1.2	303	.71
Date Nut Frosting	2 T	86.1	1.02	6.82	1.3	6.61	2.56	2.62	1.02	0.06	0.0	45	0.31	40.3	0.42
Date Pecan Pie	1/12	345	4.7	43	3.2	18.9	1.5	11.5	4.9	0.0	0.0	33	1.7	118	1.6
Dinner Roast	1/24	98	5.0	8.0	0.5	5.6	0.7	2.7	1.6	1.3	0.2	61	5.4	220	3.0
Enchilada Sauce	1	23	.84	4.4	.94	.63	.08	.3	.12	0.0	0.0	20	.83	305	.18
English Trifle	1/2 c	189	7.0	39	3.5	1.8	0.3	0.4	1.9	0.04	0.0	106	2.8	78	0.3
Fat-Free Italian Dressing	2 T	22.9	.08	6.3	.05	.03	.01	0.0	.01	0.0	0.0	3.03	.06	259	.02
French Dressing	2 T	21	0.22	5.25	0.2	0.06	0.01	0.0	0.03	0.0	0.0	4.2	0.16	151	0.04
French Onion Soup	1 c	109	1.87	12.5	1.75	5.5	0.75	3.86	0.52	0.0	0.0	25.1	0.37	692	0.27
French Tarts	1	144	2.8	21	1.23	6.3	1.02	3.5	1.3	0.04	0.0	65.2	0.77	122	0.47
Fresh Fruit Pudding Compote	1 c	161	4.2	32	2.5	3.1	1.04	.38	.94	0.0	0.0	43	2.3	6.4	.48
Fresh Spring Rolls	1	69	3.9	11	1.2	1.5	0.2	0.3	0.7	0.0	0.0	54	2.3	116	0.36
Fresh Tomato Sauce	1 T	7.6	0.15	0.8	0.15	0.43	0.06	0.31	0.04	0.0	0.0	3.5	0.14	38.7	0.01
Frozen Fruit Ice Cream	1/2 c	105	1.7	23.8	1.7	.62	.07	.05	.12	.3	0.0	209	.37	61.4	.14

Recipe	Serv Size	Cal	Prot gm	Carb gm	Fiber Total gm	Fat Total gm	Fat Sat gm	Fat Mono gm	Fat Poly gm	Vit B12 mcg	Vit D mcg	Ca mg	Fe mg	Na mg	Zn mg
Fruit Filled Sweet Rolls	1	173	4.2	31.8	3.4	4.1	0.4	1.3	1.9	0.0	0.0	18	1.5	135	0.2
Fruit Nutty Balls	1	98	2.5	9.5	1.51	6.6	1.9	1.15	3.15	0.0	0.0	9.5	0.57	203	0.38
Fruit Sweetened Granola	1/2 c	220	5.7	26.3	3.7	6.4	0.9	2.8	2.1	0.0	0.0	30	10.2	92	1.0
Fumi Salad	1/2 c	92	2.5	9.0	1.7	6.0	0.6	3.1	1.6	0.1	0.0	54	1.0	275	0.5
Garbanzo Millet Burger	1	133	7.6	13.1	2.12	5.9	0.51	3.01	1.17	1.24	0.0	34.2	1.25	332	0.78
Garbanzo Olive Sand. Spread	2 T	40	1.5	5.05	1.0	1.7	0.14	0.62	0.24	0.0	0.0	15.1	0.70	89	0.26
Garden Oat Burger	1	82	4.7	12.5	2.6	1.5	0.21	0.76	0.27	0.01	0.08	33	1.08	267	0.56
Garlic Butter	1 T	21.6	.37	1.0	.11	1.83	0.2	.54	.22	0.0	0.	3.2	.05	57	.03
German Potato Casserole	1 c	173	7.0	23	3.3	6.5	0.3	2.0	1.3	0.0	0.0	31	1.4	303	.05
Giblet Dressing	1/2 c	164	5.4	22	1.84	6.3	1.0	3.8	0.6	0.07	0.02	80	1.5	611	0.12
Golden Potato Fries	1/2 c	51	1.1	11.7	1.1	.05	0.01	0.0	.02	0.0	0.0	5.2	.64	52	.15
Golden Sauce	1T	32	.75	.84	.15	2.9	.18	1.7	.74	0.0	0.0	4.3	.03	65	.02
Grandmas Homestyle Biscuit	1	104	3.0	16	1.4	3.3	0.3	1.9	1.0	0.0	0.0	5.2	1.0	90	0.4
Granola Pie Crust	2 T	101	2.6	11.7	2.2	5.5	.98	1.56	2.9	0.0	0.0	12.7	.84	2.04	.75
Grape Jam	2 t	16	0.1	4.1	0.11	0.02	0.01	0.0	0.01	0.0	0.0	1.61	0.07	0.56	0.01
Green Beans Almondine	1/2 c	57	1.82	4.6	1.95	2.8	0.22	1.68	1.65	0.0	0.0	38.1	2.04	66.4	0.17
Guacamole	2 T	32	.53	2.05	.78	2.7	.4	1.66	.4	0.0	0.0	5.4	.3	94	.08
Hashbrowns	1/2 c	104	1.8	16.8	1.6	3.5	0.5	2.5	0.3	0.0	0.0	13.8	0.7	231	0.27
Hawaiian Banana Nut Bread	1 sl	246	5.2	33	3.0	11.3	.94	4.3	5.3	0.0	0.0	82	1.6	331	.77
Heart Smart Corn Butter	1 T	21.2	.35	.92	.11	1.83	.20	.54	.22	.36	.24	3.14	.05	57	.02
Heart Smart Granola	1/2 c	193	6.4	36	3.6	3.9	0.6	1.5	1.0	0.0	0.0	210	1.8	55	0.3
Heart Southern Biscuits	1	121	3.8	15.7	1.28	5.75	0.46	3.02	1.8	0.27	0.0	109	1.75	181	0.24
Hearty Multigrain Waffle	1	267	8.3	45.5	6.2	6.5	0.7	2.0	3.2	0.0	0.0	180	2.2	268	1.7
Herb Dressing	2 T	73	0.11	3.5	0.04	6.76	0.91	4.98	0.57	0.24	0.0	3.04	0.09	0.26	0.03
Holiday Burger Loaf	1/12	221	17	27	4.6	6.6	0.9	2.5	2.1	0.0	0.0	123	5.0	457	1.2
Holiday Turkey	1/20	234	19	25	4.5	7.5	0.7	1.6	3.7	0.0	0.0	32	1.1	774	0.4
Homemade Muesli	1/2 c	158	14.3	23.5	3.3	6.5	1.6	2.5	2.0	0.28	0.3	22	1.4	49	1.4
Honey Granola	1/2 c	349	8.4	50.4	4.7	13.5	1.3	7.3	4.0	0.24	0.0	221	2.4	51	1.3

278

Recipe	Serv Size	Cal	Prot gm	Carb gm	Fiber Total gm	Fat Total gm	Fat Sat gm	Fat Mono gm	Fat Poly gm	Vit B12 mcg	Vit D mcg	Ca mg	Fe mg	Na mg	Zn mg
Hot Herbed Garlic Br Spread	1 t	6.5	0.02	0.06	0.02	0373	0.16	0.0	0.0	0.0	0.0	.55	0.01	19.2	0.0
Huevos Rancheros Salsa	1 T	3.2	.11	.66	.16	.01	0.0	0.0	0.0	0.0	0.0	3.7	.0	24	.01
Hummus	2 T	61	2.5	6.3	1.5	3.3	0.4	1.2	1.4	0.0	0.0	24	0.8	109	0.8
Instant Whipped Topping	1/4 c	63	3.4	7.2	0.3	2.3	0.8	0.9	0.3	0.2	0.0	114	0.3	64	0.1
Italian Bread Sticks	1	136	4.0	18.7	1.9	5.4	0.9	2.9	1.1	0.0	0.0	16.8	1.6	91	0.6
Italian Style Meatless Balls	2	111	5.4	8.6	1.6	6.7	.77	3.6	1.9	.56	0.0	45	2.2	253	1.03
Italian Style Pizza	1/12	97	2.92	16.5	1.4	2.4	.36	1.46	.34	0.0	.05	16.1	1.4	242	.22
Jack Cheese Sauce	2 t	40.4	1.2	4.6	0.53	2.11	.42	1.21	0.38	0.0	0.0	5.3	0.4	229	0.37
Jiffy Mushroom Soup	1 c	77	2.0	15.3	0.7	0.4	0.03	0.02	0.06	0.3	0.3	210	0.5	403	0.2
Kabob Sauce	1 T	7.6	.26	1.74	.13	.02	0.0	0.0	.01	0.0	0.0	1.5	.08	105	.03
La Fiesta Splash	1 c	98	.9	24.3	2.42	.34	.08	.08	.06	0.0	0.0	20	.34	3.65	.12
Lazy Daisy Oatmeal Cake	1/24	151	3.22	34.7	2.9	0.75	0.16	0.17	0.22	0.0	0.0	107	1.28	270	0.50
Lemon Chiffon Pie	1/12	143	4.6	26	0.4	2.8	0.5	1.6	0.5	0.1	0.0	81	0.7	52	0.4
Lemon Chiffon Topping	1 T	12.3	.68	2.1	.05	.12	0.0	0.0	0.0	0.0	0.0	1.9	.03	11.9	.01
Lemon Custard Pie	1/12	130	1.5	26	0.4	2.8	0.5	1.6	0.5	0.10	0.0	79	0.6	44	0.4
Lemon Pudding	1 T	24	1.5	3.0	0.1	0.8	0.1	0.2	0.4	0.0	0.0	20	1.0	8.0	0.2
Lemon Wonton Soup	1 c	114	3.3	21	1.3	1.7	0.2	0.7	0.6	0.0	0.1	31	1.3	635	0.4
Lentil Vegetable Soup	1 c	86	2.5	15.2	2.21	2.01	0.28	1.36	0.23	0.0	0.0	26.5	1.15	348	0.38
Lite & Luscious Carob Icing	1/24	34.4	1.0	7.59	0.09	0.2	0.0	0.0	0.0	0.0	0.06	5.6	0.06	14.5	0.02
Lite Italian Dressing	2 T	78.2	.11	4.5	.04	6.8	.91	4.9	.57	0.0	0.0	3.04	.09	320	.03
Macaroni & Cheese	1/2 c	152	5.7	21.6	1.2	4.98	0.59	2.8	1.3	0.0	0.0	45.6	2.2	304	0.62
Macaroni Salad	1/2 c	80	2.2	13.3	1.0	2.0	0.08	0.23	0.15	0.0	0.0	16.6	0.7	233	0.3
Maja Blanka	1/4 c	96	354	16.6	.31	3.4	2.1	.03	.02	0.0	0.0	1.3	.14	69	.09
Mama's Mashed Potatoes	1/2 c	102	2.6	21.3	1.4	0.78	0.09	0.08	0.37	0.0	0.0	11	0.32	73	0.28
Mandarin Salad	1 c	139	1.9	20	1.3	6.7	0.8	4.7	0.9	0.0	0.0	39	0.9	237	0.5
Marinated Bean Salad	1/2 c	56	2.9	9.5	2.8	.9	.12	.4	.24	0.0	0.0	26	1.3	86.5	.46
Mazidra	1/2 c	80	5.0	10.0	2.2	2.5	0.2	1.4	0.7	0.0	0.0	10	1.5	291	0.6
Mexican Enchiladas	1	149	4.9	22.8	2.15	5.2	.65	2.5	.75	0.0	0.0	99	2.22	424	.58

Recipe	Serv Size	Cal	Prot gm	Carb gm	Fiber Total gm	Fat Total gm	Fat Sat gm	Fat Mono gm	Fat Poly gm	Vit B12 mcg	Vit D mcg	Ca mg	Fe mg	Na mg	Zn mg
Millet Porridge	1/2 c	193	4.5	36	2.8	3.4	2.1	0.3	0.7	0.0	0.0	8.7	1.0	184	1.3
Minestrone Soup	1 c	70	2.8	12	2.4	1.1	0.15	0.7	0.2	0.0	0.0	26	1.2	264	0.4
Mixed Berry Pie	1/12	220	3.3	32	5.3	10.0	0.8	5.9	2.8	0.0	0.0	28	1.3	203	0.7
Mixed Vegetable Quiche	1/16	113	6.3	11.8	2.1	4.9	.35	2.6	1.01	0.0	0.0	31	.42	410	.21
Mocha Banana-nut Ice cream	1/2 c	140	2.5	25	1.5	3.7	0.7	1.9	0.6	0.24	0.0	170	0.7	2.4	0.6
Mock Duck Blk Bean Sauce	1/2 c	72	5.8	7.2	1.75	2.4	0.5	1.0	0.14	0.0	0.0	14.5	0.39	257	0.10
Mock Egg Salad	1/4 c	70	4.8	3.0	0.3	4.9	0.5	1.4	1.5	0.0	0.0	67	3.2	229	0.5
Mock Egg Salad	1/4 c	70	4.8	3	0.3	4.9	0.5	1.4	1.5	0.0	0.0	67	3.2	229	0.5
Mozzarella Cheese	2 T	39	1.8	3.8	0.3	2.0	0.4	0.9	0.6	0.0	0.0	31	1.0	149	0.3
Mushroom Gravy	2 T	5.8	0.3	1.13	0.03	0.01	0.0	0.0	0.0	0.0	0.03	0.69	0.03	92	0.01
Mushroom Onion Gravy	2 T	16.3	0.19	1.2	0.13	1.2	0.16	0.83	0.1	0.0	0.05	1.25	0.08	74.4	0.03
Navy Bean Soup	1 c	252	16.4	34	11.7	5.9	0.8	2.1	2.6	0.0	0.0	104	3.5	571	1.6
Non-Dairy Coconut Icing	1/24	77	1.7	9.9	1.22	3.9	3.2	0.16	0.05	0.05	0.0	49.3	0.32	28	0.15
Non-Dairy Oat crepes	1	73	2.2	12.3	1.4	1.7	0.15	0.82	0.48	0.1	0.0	80	0.51	109	0.38
Non-Dairy Parmesan Cheese	1 t	16.3	.65	1.2	.19	1.05	.1	.66	.22	.02	0.0	18.6	.17	20.3	.06
Non-Dairy Pumpkin Pie	1/12	229	9.9	30.0	1.7	9.7	0.6	1.0	2.5	0.0	0.0	121	5.7	234	0.8
Nut Rissoles	1	64	3.5	5.03	1.63	3.6	0.37	2.33	0.6	0.0	0.03	33.6	1.18	225	0.39
Oat Crust	2 T	55	1.2	6.6	.91	2.7	.19	1.6	.75	.02	0.0	15.4	.57	71	.23
Oat Pie Crust	1/12	110	2.4	13.2	1.82	5.4	0.38	3.2	1.5	0.04	0.0	30.8	1.14	142	0.46
Oat Waffles	1	157	5.0	24	3.2	5.6	0.8	2.8	1.6	0.0	0.0	21	1.5	208	0.7
Oatmeal Cookie	1	135	4.9	19.1	2.6	5.1	.89	1.1	2.9	0.0	0.0	31.5	1.3	32.5	.47
Oatmeal Date Cookie	1	222	4.9	31.5	2.8	9.18	0.71	4.49	3.33	0.13	0.0	109	1.23	148	0.79
Old Fashioned Cornbread	1	175	5.2	32	2.3	3.4	0.3	1.4	1.4	0.0	0.0	14	1.2	245	0.7
Orange Honey Butter	1 t	11	.28	1.3	.07	.57	.04	.34	.14	0.0	0.0	2.11	.04	23	.02
Orange Tofu Topping	1 T	11	0.5	2.0	0.02	0.1	0.0	0.0	0.0	0.0	0.0	6.8	0.01	22	0.01
Oriental Dressing	1 T	26	.04	2.23	.03	2.01	.15	1.2	.59	.02	0.0	1.73	.4	.01	.01
Pao	1	107	5.6	17	1.8	2.1	0.36	0.7	0.4	0.0	0.0	7.03	0.9	240	0.29
Pasta Primavera	1 c	242	6.8	30	4.2	8.68	1.69	3.64	2.71	.2	0.0	167	6.03	401	.96

Recipe	Serv Size	Cal	Prot gm	Carb gm	Fiber Total gm	Fat Total gm	Fat Sat gm	Fat Mono gm	Fat Poly gm	Vit B12 mcg	Vit D mcg	Ca mg	Fe mg	Na mg	Zn mg
Peach Nut Bread	1 sl	330	7.3	52	3.3	12.0	.07	4.4	5.9	0.0	0.0	116	2.7	236	2.13
Peach Raspberry Crisp	1/20	151	2.5	25.8	2.3	4.9	.88	1.8	1.9	0.0	0.0	16.4	.94	88	.41
Peaches & Cream Punch	1 c	121	1.5	30	1.5	0.2	.01	0.3	.04	0.1	0.0	86	0.2	25	0.2
Peanut Butter Pate	1 T	92	3.3	7.5	1.3	6.1	0.85	3.02	1.9	0.0	0.0	12.9	0.56	116	0.47
Peas & Peanuts Salad	1/2 c	116	5.2	9.8	4.2	6.9	.88	2.1	3.4	0.0	0.0	19.6	.95	200	.95
Peking Noodle Stir-Fry	1 c	282	16.0	31.1	3.7	11.5	1.5	4.8	4.3	0.0	0.08	169	8.1	250	2.0
Picnic Potato Salad	1/2 c	78	1.6	15.2	1.6	1.4	.11	.77	.38	0.0	.07	19.7	.35	189	.24
Pimento Cheese Sauce	2 T	20	0.9	2.4	0.6	0.9	0.2	0.5	0.2	0.0	0.0	4.9	0.4	148	0.2
Pinakbet	1/2 c	51	2.7	6.2	2.02	2.2	0.31	1.05	0.66	0.0	0.0	41	1.5	224	0.31
Pineapple Date Jam	1 T	17	0.14	4.5	0.5	0.03	0.01	0.01	0.0	0.0	0.0	2.4	0.09	0.2	0.02
Pistachio Ice Cream	1/2 c	244	9.7	27.2	4.4	11.1	1.5	6.0	3.2	0.0	0.0	214	2.5	81	0.3
Posole	1 c	168	4.9	27	4.8	5.4	0.7	3.0	0.0	0.0	0.0	87	1.8	413	0.4
Potato Crust	2 T	58	.92	7.1	.3	2.65	.18	1.6	.73	.02	0.0	14	.64	71	.06
Potato Salad Dressing	1 T	26	.19	1.1	.03	2.4	.15	1.41	.62	0.0	.13	17.5	.02	49	.01
Pumpkin Mousse Dessert	1	177	1.68	25.3	1.27	7.5	0.27	2.08	0.82	0.0	0.0	37.5	0.35	148	0.32
Purple Passion Fruit Salad	1/2 c	58	.34	14.3	.92	.17	.04	.02	.06	0.0	0.0	5.4	.19	1.4	.06
Quesadillas	1	135	3.27	22.6	.86	3.5	.39	1.5	.49	0.0	0.0	123	1.43	248	.24
Quick 3 Bean Chili	1 c	152	10	26	9.0	0.8	0.3	0.2	0.12	0.0	0.0	60	3.3	512	0.55
Quick Artichoke Pasta Toss	1/2 c	46	1.4	6.7	1.4	1.8	.3	1.2	.21	0.0	0.0	20	.9	124	.2
Quick Vinegarless Ketchup	1 T	11	0.2	2.7	0.2	0.05	0.01	0.01	0.02	0.0	.06	2.5	0.2	91	0.04
Raisin Bran Muffins	1	224	5.8	36.4	6.9	9.2	.81	3.8	3.8	0.0	0.0	114	2.4	241	1.4
Ranch Dressing Quick/Easy	2 T	43	0.9	1.2	0.01	3.8	0.5	2.6	0.3	0.0	0.0	3.2	0.02	125	0.01
Ranch Style Dressing	1 T	27	1.51	.76	.04	2.19	.29	.41	1.38	0.0	0.0	21	1.02	95	.15
Raspberry Bran Muffin	1	124	2.07	20.5	2.75	5.0	.36	2.85	1.38	.04	0.0	105	1.2	219	.43
Raspberry Butter	2 t	1.4	0.03	1.6	0.08	0.04	0.0	0.02	0.01	0.0	0.0	1.3	0.02	1.3	0.01
Raspberry Jam	2 t	9.7	.06	2.4	.18	.03	0.0	0.0	.02	0.0	0.0	1.4	.04	.28	.02
Raspberry Jello Fluff	1/3 c	77	0.39	15.7	1.07	1.55	0.03	0.02	0.1	0.0	0.0	24.4	0.23	3.62	0.15
Raspberry Vinaigrette	2 T	28	0.09	7.6	0.06	0.04	0.01	0.0	0.01	0.0	0.0	1.7	0.03	291	0.02

Recipe	Serv Size	Cal	Prot gm	Carb gm	Fiber Total gm	Fat Total gm	Fat Sat gm	Fat Mono gm	Fat Poly gm	Vit B12 mcg	Vit D mcg	Ca mg	Fe mg	Na mg	Zn mg
Ratatouille	1/2 c	54	1.4	8.1	2.6	2.45	0.34	1.68	0.27	0.0	0.09	13.1	0.67	400	0.23
Rice Barley Pilaf	1/2 c	147	3.6	20	2.75	4.92	0.62	3.0	1.02	0.0	0.0	26	2.95	229	1.03
Rice Pudding with Mango	1/2 c	165	3.04	34.2	2.1	2.01	0.79	0.32	0.32	0.09	0.0	74.2	0.66	22.3	0.64
Rice Vermicelli	1 c	191	13.9	23.4	3.5	4.9	0.84	1.1	2.2	0.32	0.0	148	6.5	587	0.67
Rich & Creamy Carob Icing	1/24	69.5	1.4	7.8	0.48	4.22	0.39	2.7	0.87	0.0	.02	20.8	0.31	5.3	0.23
Sausage Style Gravy	1/4 c	36	2.0	3.5	0.6	1.7	0.3	0.9	0.3	0.0	.16	12	0.5	207	0.3
Sausage/Mush Onion Quiche	1/16	79	7.1	1.04	.62	2.5	.24	1.3	.2	0.0	.16	22	.34	375	.12
Savory Kale	1/2 c	60	2.5	10.6	2.5	1.6	0.2	0.9	0.3	0.0	0.0	88	1.1	101	0.4
Savory Lentils	1/2 c	35	1.5	3.9	.78	1.8	.24	1.3	.18	0.0	0.0	13.2	.84	342	.2
Savory Split Pea Soup	1 c	150	8.0	25	3.4	2.4	0.3	1.5	0.3	0.0	0.0	33	1.8	314	1.0
Scrambled Tofu Eggs	1/2 c	107	9.4	4.5	0.4	6.7	1.0	2.4	3.0	0.0	0.08	122	6.2	217	1.0
Scrambled Tofu Eggs Curry	1 c	231	12	21	2.0	12	1.9	5.9	3.5	0.2	1.1	256	6.8	484	1.8
Seafarer's Navy Bean Soup	1 c	231	14.6	32.6	10.6	5.2	0.7	1.79	2.2	0.68	0.0	96.1	3.48	405	1.41
Seasoned Brown Rice	1/2 c	29.6	.61	6.3	.46	.21	.04	.07	.07	0.0	0.0	3.7	.14	152	.16
Sesame Oat Crackers	1	65	1.5	7.8	1.1	3.3	0.3	1.8	1.0	0.0	0.0	14	0.6	72	0.1
Siew Mai	2	87	3.0	12	0.5	1.9	0.35	0.6	0.7	0.0	0.0	12	0.6	232	0.15
Simply Smash. Stuff. Potatoe	1	93	3.4	17.3	1.6	1.2	.12	.5	.13	0.0	0.0	18.6	0.97	164	.23
Smoothies	1 c	107	1.6	24.3	1.5	0.6	0.05	0.05	0.12	0.32	0.0	221	0.39	66.2	0.11
Sour Cream Supreme	1 T	68.9	0.01	10.4	0.01	2.3	0.3	0.4	1.5	0.0	0.0	0.16	0.0	57	0.0
Southern Peach Preserves	2 t	18	0.23	4.43	0.25	0.5	0.01	0.01	0.01	0.0	0.0	2.62	0.05	0.27	0.03
Soy Cream	1 T	42	0.42	1.2	0.01	1.04	0.24	2.25	0.99	0.0	0.0	8.3	0.1	49.6	0.0
Soy Good Tofu Sour Cream	1 T	38	2.5	0.8	0.02	3.0	0.4	0.6	1.9	0.0	0.0	32	1.7	24	0.3
Soy Mayonnaise	2 t	22.4	.3	1.9	.05	1.5	.1	.89	.37	.04	.05	35	.03	54	.02
Soy Oat Waffles	1	196	7.6	31.4	4.6	5.5	0.7	2.3	1.8	0.0	0.0	46	3.3	411	0.7
Spaghetti Florentine	1 c	111	9.9	12.4	4.8	3.0	0.4	1.0	1.2	0.0	0.0	99	3.6	713	0.9
Spicy Vinegarless Ketchup	1 T	10.5	0.3	2.53	.32	.07	.01	.01	.02	0.0	0.0	3.3	.21	54	.06
Spinach & Pasta Salad	1 c	52	2.71	10.5	2.47	.34	.05	.02	.14	0.0	0.0	53	1.68	62.9	.40
Spinach Potato Crepe	1	528	1.25	5.8	0.88	3.01	0.46	2.0	.036	0.0	0.0	26.7	0.87	207	0.27

Recipe	Serv Size	Cal	Prot gm	Carb gm	Fiber Total gm	Fat Total gm	Fat Sat gm	Fat Mono gm	Fat Poly gm	Vit B12 mcg	Vit D mcg	Ca mg	Fe mg	Na mg	Zn mg
Spinach Potato Puffs	2	33	2.93	3.85	0.56	0.89	0.12	0.18	0.45	0.0	0.0	40.23	1.23	117	0.27
Spinach Potato Quiche	1/16	123	6.4	13.1	2.4	5.5	.43	3.04	1.09	0.0	.08	50	.93	460	.37
Sprouted Wheat Bread	1 sl	107	3.67	20.4	2.9	1.99	0.18	1.0	0.60	0.0	0.0	8.9	1.02	179	0.74
Strawberry Raspber. Topping	2 T	25.9	.18	6.5	.64	.08	.01	.01	.04	0.0	0.0	3.9	.13	.54	.04
Strawberry Surprise Salad	1/3 c	102	2.86	10.4	0.89	6.17	0.61	2.42	2.79	0.0	0.0	36.3	1.24	36.7	0.38
Strawberry Tropic Drink	1 c	63	.6	15.3	.48	.15	.02	.02	.05	0.0	0.0	12	.32	3.5	.1
Strawberry Tropic Jam	1 T	20	0.14	5.3	0.12	0.08	0.0	0.0	0.01	0.0	0.0	2.7	0.06	0.09	0.01
Stuffed Mushrooms	1	25	0.75	2.8	0.4	1.3	0.2	0.9	0.2	0.0	0.4	8.1	0.4	108	0.2
Stuffed Prunes	2	104	1.9	12	2.0	6.3	0.6	1.5	3.9	0.0	0.0	18	0.7	1.7	0.4
Stuffed Shells	1	79	4.1	12.5	1.7	1.6	0.19	0.24	0.96	0.0	0.0	12.8	1.2	787	0.46
Succotash	1/3 c	112	5.52	21.8	4.7	0.39	0.05	0.01	0.1	0.2	0.0	153	1.38	313	0.41
Summer Squash Stir-Fry	1/2 c	26.2	1.3	5.6	1.8	0.18	0.03	0.01	0.07	0.0	0.0	18.3	0.48	41.2	0.26
Sweet & Sour Chicken	1 c	173	9.2	22	3.9	6.2	0.35	1.7	0.32	0.0	0.0	45	0.88	431	1.17
Sweet & Sour Dip	1 T	14	.1	3.2	0.3	0.2	0.03	0.1	0.02	0.0	0.0	2.9	0.09	24	0.01
Sweet & Sour Fresh Fruit Dr.	2 T	43.3	0.65	6.7	0.15	1.6	0.29	0.21	0.87	0.04	0.0	31	0.05	39	0.02
Sweet & Sour Sauce	1/3 c	91	1.1	19.3	1.2	1.8	0.24	1.3	0.18	0.0	0.0	17.0	0.43	27	0.14
Sweet Reflections Banana	1 c	152	1.8	34.9	3.9	1.8	0.25	0.78	0.5	0.0	0.0	26.4	0.71	2.9	0.47
Raspberry Dessert															
Tabouli Salad	1/2 c	109	2.4	13.7	3.5	5.8	0.8	4.0	0.6	0.0	0.0	22	1.0	224	0.4
Tamale Pie	1/12	185	7.5	28	6.0	5.0	0.5	2.0	0.5	0.0	0.0	113	2.2	645	0.4
Tangy Mayo Kabob Dressing	1 T	26.3	.24	1.07	.12	2.4	.16	1.4	.64	0.0	.12	17	.17	37	.02
Tarter Sauce	1 T	16	0.2	1.0	0.1	1.3	0.0	0.0	0.1	0.0	0.0	4.2	0.03	92	0.01
Teriyaki Sauce	1 t	18	.14	4.7	.02	0.0	0.0	0.0	0.0	0.0	0.0	2.4	.05	38	.02
Tex Mex Enchiladas	1	238	14.4	23.8	1.6	11.3	1.52	3.9	4.1	0.0	0.0	229	8.7	633	1.5
Thick & Zesty Ketchup	1 T	14.2	0.35	3.4	.33	.1	.01	.01	.03	0.0	0.0	3.4	.21	52	.06
Thousand Island Dressing	2 T	36	0.4	3.4	0.2	2.4	0.01	0.01	0.02	0.0	0.0	6.5	0.1	136	0.04
Three Grain No Oil Bread	1 sl	105	3.8	22.9	3.22	0.57	0.10	0.08	0.22	0.0	0.0	10.3	1.17	179	0.78
Tofu Banana Bread #1	1 sl	222	5.0	31	2.23	9.9	.82	3.9	4.3	0.0	0.0	54	1.3	194	.56

Recipe	Serv Size	Cal	Prot gm	Carb gm	Fiber Total gm	Fat Total gm	Fat Sat gm	Fat Mono gm	Fat Poly gm	Vit B12 mcg	Vit D mcg	Ca mg	Fe mg	Na mg	Zn mg
Tofu Banana Bread #2	1 sl	271	5.9	38.9	2.98	11.5	0.98	4.3	5.3	0.26	0.16	98.3	1.66	297	0.93
Tofu Fish Sticks	2	192	14.4	20.5	1.3	7.12	1.03	1.57	3.93	0.0	0.0	165	9.1	179	1.47
Tofu Foo Yung	1	129	10.8	10.8	1.6	5.8	0.83	1.7	2.9	0.0	0.07	135	6.6	148	1.06
Tofu Greek Salad	1/2 c	67	4.2	4.6	.79	4.2	.6	2	1.4	0.0	0.0	60	2.8	116	.49
Tofu Lasagna	1 c	224	13.4	30.1	3.2	7.4	.95	2.43	2.5	.4	0.0	128	6.2	587	1.01
Tofu Marinade	1 t	56	.61	.79	.05	5.7	.8	3.77	.86	0.0	0.0	3.2	.08	220	.02
Tofu Mayonnaise	1 T	28	.72	1.3	.15	2.3	.19	1.4	.68	0.0	0.0	9.0	.34	68	.08
Tomato Cucumber Salad with Herb Dressing	1 c	99.6	1.6	11.2	1.6	6.2	0.85	4.26	0.69	0.0	0.0	17.3	0.79	12.8	0.25
Tropical Fruit Soup	1/2 c	82	0.6	20	0.95	0.2	0.04	0.02	0.3	0.0	0.0	16	0.3	5.7	0.09
Veg Meatballs in BBQ Sauce	3	258	40	26	13	4.5	0.4	2.4	0.6	0.0	0.0	214	6.9	187	3.6
Veg. Rice- Mushroom Soup	1 c	85	3.0	14	1.7	2.0	0.3	1.3	0.3	0.0	0.16	19	0.8	473	0.7
Vegetable Bouquet Salad	1 c	32	1.7	6.8	2.1	0.4	0.07	0.3	0.18	0.0	0.0	56.3	1.16	32	0.38
Vegetable Dip	1 T	16.5	0.53	1.1	0.31	1.19	0.13	0.34	0.62	0.0	0.0	7.1	0.92	47	0.03
Vegetable Fajitas	1	133	4.0	19	1.4	5.2	0.4	2.0	0.4	0.0	0.05	42	1.6	274	0.2
Vegetable Fried Rice	1/2 c	183	10.2	24.3	3.3	5.1	1.01	2.05	0.86	0.0	0.0	42	1.09	371	0.77
Vegetable Rice Soup	1 c	54	2.0	11.4	2.5	0.3	0.02	0.01	0.04	0.0	0.0	24	0.6	255	0.1
Vegetarian Beef Steaks	1	25	1.9	3.9	0.53	0.17	0.01	0.01	0.01	0.0	0.0	4.1	0.2	245	0.03
Vegetarian Goulash	1 c	163	7.4	26	3.0	3.0	0.5	1.5	0.8	1.2	0.0	52	2.2	356	0.5
Very Berry Cream Cheese	1 T	39	0.4	3.3	0.2	2.7	1.0	1.0	0.7	0.0	0.0	0.4	0.08	68	0.02
Very Berry Fruit Soup	1/2 c	73	0.5	18	1.5	0.2	0.04	0.03	0.06	0.0	0.0	9.8	0.3	1.7	0.1
Virgin Pina Colada	1 c	131	1.09	21.8	.94	5.2	3.8	.12	.06	0.0	0.0	19.3	.55	4.6	.21
Virgin Strawberry Daiquiri	1 c	163	.69	42.4	2.09	.26	.02	.02	.01	0.0	0.0	23	1.3	4.9	.20
Wheat Pie Crust	1/12	138	2.04	12.4	0.98	9.3	0.62	5.6	2.5	0.0	0.0	1.97	.042	0.33	0.0
Whole Wheat Rolls	1	109	4.8	20.8	3.6	0.8	0.2	0.01	0.0	0.0	0.0	13	1.5	178	0.03
Yams with Orange Glaze	1/3 c	47	0.5	11.4	0.8	0.05	0.01	0.0	0.01	0.0	0.0	12	0.2	34	0.3
Zesty Italian Dressing	2 T	79	0.11	4.6	.04	6.8	.9	4.9	.57	0.0	0.0	3.2	.09	234	.04

Sample
Lunch Box Menu

Main Dish	*Side Dish*	*Dessert*
Monday		
Vegetarian Meatloaf or	Pasta Salad	Blueberry Muffin
Dinner Roast	or	Fruit (melon)
Sandwich	Potato Salad	
Tuesday		
Vegetable-fried Rice	Dinner Roll	Oatmeal-date Cookie
		Fruit (apple)
Wednesday		
"Eggless" Egg Salad	Raw Veggies	"Fruit-Nutty" Balls
Sandwich		Fruit (peach or pear)
Thursday		
Lentil or	Crackers	Banana Bread
Vegetable Soup		Fruit (grapes)
Friday		
Bean or Hummus	Raw Nut and	Fruit Salad with
Sandwich (or)	Seed Mix	Summer Fruit Cream
Bean Burrito		

Index Of Recipes

Breakfast Dishes

Cheese Substitutes

Dressings

Entrees & Main Dishes

Salads

Sauces & Gravies

Notes

Notes

Notes

Notes

Notes

Notes

Notes

Notes